Birth's Hidden Leg

Volume 1

How Surprising Beliefs from Infancy Limit Successful Child and Adult Behavior

A Manual for Therapists, Parents, and Couples

Based on principles of: Early Attachment Dynamics, Applied Neuroplasticity®, Pre- and Perinatal Psychology, and Body-Mind Centering®

by Annie Brook, Ph.D, LPC

Published by Smart Body Books
Boulder, Colorado, USA

Cover and book design by Chelsea Iacovetto

Smart Body Books:
5412 Idylwild Trail,
Boulder, Colorado, 80301

Brook, Annie
Birth's hidden legacy: How surprising beliefs from infancy limit successful child and adult behavior / Annie Brook. – Volume 1.
p. cm.
Includes bibliographical references and index
ISBN 978-0-9760449-5-6

1. Psychology. 2. Behaviorial psychotherapy. 3. Infant Mental Health 4. Child Development
5. Somatic Psychology 6. Existential Psychology

About Annie Brook

"Deep gratitude to my mother, Florence, who taught me to never give up. Her ability to combine hard work with humor, big heartedness, and a good sense of morals has been a foundation for my continued personal and professional development. Her support allowed me to continue always to put one toot in front of the other and find the humor in experiences." Annie Brook

Annie's professional career spans over 3 decades. She has taught at universities, public schools, and mental health centers, and been in private clinical practice for over 35 years. Annie's work is broad-based, and engages the realms of movement education, psychotherapy, group dynamics, conflict resolution and communication skills, and meditation. She combines teaching methods that address body, mind, and spirit and teaches her students through a two-year training program (BodyMind Somanautics) and a sundry of classes in order to give back and share the gifts she has received.

Annie has had a consistent career in somatic psychology and the movement arts. She owned Studio Moves, was the Director of Body Psychotherapy for Naropa University Somatic Masters program, and now co-owns Colorado Therapies, where she trains interns and supports children, couples, and families to unravel difficulties and learn to thrive.

Annie's scholarship has included study with amazing teachers who guided her insight, inquiry, and practice. Movement, art, practices in nature, and in deep listening have been parts of this path. Events and difficult experiences of her life demanded she not only deal with current events, but unravel her earliest perinatal shock, which included premature birth, NICU care, and interrupted bonding. Learning to re-pattern early impressions in the nervous sytem has given Annie the "inside-out" wisdom which she shares in this book.

Listening to the bodystory, regulation of arousal states, repair of attachment issues, and offering movement re-patterning support has formed the foundation of her work that is shared in these 2 volumes.

*"You need only claim the events of your life to make yourself yours.
When you truly possess all you have been and done, which may take some time,
you are fierce with reality ... "*

– Florida Scott Maxwell

This book is dedicated to:

All those courageous souls who hold the long questions and believe in the instinct of health. Those willing to work "outside the box" in order to find answers to questions beyond the mundane.

Blessings on you!

To clinicians and parents who spend the long hard hours working for results, and finally, to my siblings Lynda, Nancy, Dave, and Rick, who put up with my perinatal imprints long enough for me to unravel them.

Thanks for your continuing love!

Table of Contents

Acknowledgments

Adults and children have "hidden stories" longing to be told. People tell these stories through behavior, through play, and in art and dreams. I personally thank all of you who work in the healing professions, and love and care for our young ones. May your efforts be rewarded with laughter, love, and mystery.

I especially wish to thank Dr. William Emerson, Dr. Ray Castellino, Myrna Martin, (MSW), and David Sawyer (LPC). They are all clinicians in Perinatal Psychotherapy methods, and have contributed long hours educating and informing people about how the earliest of experiences influence behavior and health. Each has also been instrumental in helping me to identify and heal my "hidden stories."

Susan Aposhyan's guidance in Body Psychotherapy methods helped me to move toward satisfaction, and John and Anna Chitty, (founders of Colorado School of Energy Studies) helped integrate and educate me on how cranial dynamics express as early experience. Ron Short, OD consultant and former educator with LIOS Institute, has guided my sense of group process and how to bring the personal into the organizational in a safe and clear manner.

Bonnie Bainbridge Cohen, (founder of the School for *Body-Mind Centering®) was my first mentor and is my long-standing guide in how to work with the bodymind. Bonnie has supported her students to look for the strengths within difficulties, and re-pattern obstacles through movement, presence, and hands-on-touch integration. Bonnie's mentoring in Developmental Movement and brain physiology gave me the foundation for my work in neuro-science and embodiment understandings so that I can truly help clients and children with difficulties. Body-Mind Centering® colleagues worldwide are sharing their work; and it is always a learning pleasure to participate in their offerings. Such compassionate and skilled work has given me hope for our world.

Movement Studies helped me to develop the artistry of communication through my body. This delight in improvisation and deep listening has been a tremendous gift. Thanks to: Emily Conrad and Susan Harper (Continuum), Suprapto Suryadamo (Amerta Movement), master improvisor Ruth Zapora (Action Theater), Aerial Arts instructor Terry Sendgraff (Motivity), Jonathan Fox (Playback Theater), and Clyde Rae, of Gyrotonics Boulder. Working with these masters of movement has reshaped my thinking-response patterns. Deep gratitude as well to Steve Paxton, Nancy Stark Smith, and the numerous teachers and explorers of Contact Improvisation. CI continues to give me the joy of renewal, spontaneity, deep embodied learning, and joyful play.

Finally, and always, I wish to thank my four siblings and my parents. My family nourishes my heart. I am blessed to have sisters and brothers who love me and accept my wild diversity of expression. They help me to reflect on life, and help anchor my curiosity and life-long dreams.

*Body-Mind Centering® is the brilliant hands-on and movement education modality developed by Occupational Therapist and Master Educator, Bonnie Bainbridge Cohen.

Forward

This book was created to help you, the reader, to listen for the earliest stories of life and learn how to meet the emotions and expressions of earliest memories. Also, to give hope to those instances where behavior seems unfathomable and challenging. Meeting early imprints demands a blend of knowledge, presence, skilled listening, compassion, and vulnerability. I hope this book opens your eyes and heart to understand this level of pre-cognitive experience and makes clear to you how early life events influence behavior and identity.

Perinatal* memories influence adults, children, and infants. Providing relief at this early level repairs the baseline of trust/mistrust issues. Much heartache and parenting difficulties are lessened when birth or prenatal imprints are resolved. "Good enough" parents often don't realize that their infant can be at risk for attachment difficulties due to a difficult birth or prenatal experience. Addressing perinatal experience helps children reduce anxiety and improve behavior. They re-orient internally and are willing to feel safe, protected, and understood. This is especially true if a child has "nameless" fears. When parents and clinicians understand how early terrors shape behavior, they can provide better support. Treatment can address healing shock and trauma, rather than behavior corrections. Behaviors change most effectively when the root experiences that caused difficulties with self-regulation are addressed.

This work is best learned from the "inside out." Both skills and adaptations develop during early imprints. My earliest experiences were of premature birth, and interrupted bonding due to incubator care in the NICU. I survived through behavior compensations based on those experiences. As a child I had impossible temper tantrums because I couldn't self-regulate, and my mother was at her wits' end of what to do. Later I was a quite shy teen, yet had a charismatic risk taking attitude. I didn't have a felt-sense of how to stay connected with others, and traveled abroad without even telling my mother where I was.

Skilled inner work helped me identify my strengths and tease apart those compensations. With the support of family and skilled teachers I learned to self-regulate and develop methods that dismantled compensations. This helped me understand the hidden stories children express through play therapy, and how essential body re-patterning is for self-regulation. I am thankful for this journey, as it provided the foundation to develop the clinical methods that support self-regulation and learning to thrive.

My clinical work supports clients to befriend their youngest neurological patterns of defense, find relief, and move on to enjoy life. Re-patterning movement and hands-on educative touch helps the vulnerable early body-self to repair difficult attachment, interrupt self-abandonment, and build the inner resiliency and strength necessary for successful relationship. This is the goal of this book and of clinical work.

*The word "perinatal" includes events before, after, and during the time of birth, and "prenatal" means during pregnancy. European clinicians are likely to use "perinatal" to describe both pregnancy and birth events, while in the US both the words pre- and peri-natal are used. "Perinatal" is often used in this text for simplicity.

Introduction

"Helping parents process the birth and reconnect to each other is as important as helping the child..."

– Annie Brook

"Listen, listen, listen, to my heart's song

Listen, listen, listen to my heart's song

I will never forget you, I will never forsake you

I will never forget you, I will never forsake you... .

Listen, listen, listen to my heart's song"... from the Sufi tradition

The heartsong is the song of the infant. Infants want to have a place in your heart, they want to be felt and guided and cared for, and never to be forsaken. It is a simple request and it's primal to the sense of safety and love. Feeling safe and cared for ultimately develops the ability to care about others. Perinatal psychotherapy sessions re-pattern primitive fears stored deeply in the brain, and re-establish the safety necessary in order to love. This love is the best of what Moms and Dads want to provide, and what couples want to give to each other. Repair and integration of early pre-cognitive body-based impressions re-opens the necessary ease for love, and the capacity to listen well for the heart's song in yourself and others.

When we look at birth from the perspective of the infant, we gain a new understanding of how early events shape behavior. Under stress, and at any age, the primitive brain reverts to its earliest survival strategies lodged in infant experience, and utilizes inappropriate and out of context behavior responses. Deep healing occurs when we understand how susceptible the infant nervous system is, and listen, without guilt or self-blame, to the heartsong of these earliest of stories. I find that children, couples, and adults are able to integrate memory at a brain state level; doing so allows for lasting change. Clients integrate and heal behavioral challenges that have baffled psychotherapists, parents, and psychologists.

Enjoy this book! It's not just for infants, but also for children and adults. Psychotherapists working with adult clients and parents trying to understand their children will be amazed at the level of discovery available in understanding early stories. This book invites you to explore how the bodymind records experience and makes meaning in the timeframe before one could think, talk, or walk. Knowing the importance of that early heartsong of the infant can guide treatment; so that the "infant self" in all of us relaxes and opens the heart. Then we can help remember, and help children to remember; not to abandon, self-abandon, nor forsake each other. We never forget the task of life is to love and thrive regardless of early or current difficulties. We can help those we love and our clients to mature into healthy functioning people who are able to thrive, and to love and care for themselves and each other.

Behavior Struggles as Hidden Stories

Why do some children and adults struggle more than others? They seem more frustrated in social settings; less able to handle stress. Issues of control surface as children try to control their parents, and intimate partners to control their spouse, or return again and again to drama. The inability to relax into the safety of relationship, and receive love and nourishment can be related to early fears held deep within the nervous system.

These behaviors might be related to un-named events that are traumatic "stories" rather than personality issues. Telling the stories of one's life is a normal and natural way to process difficult experience. People are trying to digest the impact of events and find meaning. Storytelling is essential, and we have both verbal and body stories. When we have told our stories enough, and to someone who has really listened, we can put them to rest. Experiences lose their traumatic hold, and become part of life experience. In therapy, this is known as having an integrated "personal narrative." This simply means people become comfortable in their own skin, and can relate to others and life with a sense of confidence and ability.

Pre-cognitive stories occur because parts of the brain register events that happen before one can think or talk. Adults often don't realize how scared, excited, or angry infants are from events at or before birth. Infant bodies have to react and respond in order to survive, and clinical work has shown that the body and primitive brain can govern child and adult behavior responses under stress.

Through years of clinical practice I have discovered that infants through adults can access perinatal memory and learn to integrate early experience in order to relax and enjoy life. It takes practice as a clinician to recognize birth stories. A young child's frequent need to spin out of control can express disorientation due to a birth with chemicals, or c-section. An adult's chronic hyper-vigilance can relate to the primitive fear of being invaded with forceps. It may seem incredulous; however the lasting results I have seen clinically speak for the effectiveness of perinatal treatment. When clinicians listen to the bodymind and nervous system at this earliest story level, the nervous system settles and behaviors change for the better.

It is an exciting time to work with behavior and the body. I have been combining neuro-science, early attachment, and BMC re-patterning methods for many years. This method is working for children, their families, and for adults and couples. Clients seem both able and willing to enter into early memory states and enjoy the relief of long-standing anxiety, inability to sleep, or reactivity. I have been impressed by their courage and success related to long-standing difficulties. *Birth's Hidden Legacy: Volume One,* will give the reader a perspective on how one's sense of safety and capability in life can be influenced by incidents related to perinatal times. *Birth's Hidden Legacy: Volume Two* offers further methods, theory, interventions, movement tools and useful props.

Compassionately identifying and treating early overwheming experiences grounds a person into their body and leads to a sense of connection and belonging. Fears become integrated and issues resolve.

There are 2 Volumes to this book

Volume One introduces the themes of Perinatal Psychology, and how such early events impact the lives of infants, children, and adults. Perinatal themes are described based on prenatal, birth, and post-birth events. Themes are organized in a developmental time-line for ease of treatment and application.

Application of themes is made explicit in the Case Studies chapter. Ten clients are followed through the healing of behaviors shaped by perinatal events. Sessions include work with children, couples, and adults. Case studies show perinatal themes in daily life and give a context for theory. Treatment methods address ineffective behavior, cyclic patterns of despair or addiction, emotional melt-downs, internalized beliefs, and recurring accidents that have a template traceable to pre-cognitive somatic experience. Volume One helps the reader begin to locate the "Hidden Stories beneath Difficult Behaviors."

Volume Two shares intervention theory, and treatment methods that release perinatal and attachment difficulty. Included are practice explorations and theory to cultivate 'inside out' learning so essential for re-patterning shocking events. Interventions include key awareness practices to build the in-depth skills necessary for working with others at the perinatal level.

Volume Two is tailored for therapists, professional clinicians, movement educators, and parents interested in a deeper understanding of theory and intervention. Advanced neuro-science, kinesthetic science, and re-patterning through the body are shared, plus treatment maps for how the body stores and processes pre-cognitive experience and memory. A helpful guide for treatment progression and useful "office tools" and "props" are shared.

Volume Two address psychological theory of attachment dynamics, and character styles, including a Jungian perspective on origins of self. A treatment map from perinatal educator and clinician David Sawyer explores Object Relations and the body. An entire chapter is devoted to body repatterning interventions, and includes the somatic understanding of Body-Mind Centering, as well as other modalities to heal shock and trauma.

The Resource Section is reprinted in both Volumes to help the reader to find practitioners and training programs in this work, as well as references for reading.

Note on language and grammar choices found in this text

I use both anatomical language and human terms when speaking about perinatal imprints. Human terms help one develop a "felt-sense" of early experiences as relational, and show the impact of encoded body fears and responses. This felt-sense is essential in providing the understanding and empathy required for clinical treatment.

You will see in this text phrases such as "the prenate feels ..." These phrases are not this author's assumptions, but based on actual statements made by adults and children in treatment. These statements point to prenatal and newborn experiences as a useful component of clinical healing. Session interviews and observations are a part of clinical research, and provide a window into the world of reported life events. Information expressed was assessed for consistency through a number of clients and multiple treatments. Such research is used to develop critical assessment theory and treatment protocol.

In Support of Bonding and Reducing Perinatal Shock

Difficult birth or post-birth events can interrupt the ability to bond. Healthy bonding is an important component of social safety, and the ability to handle stimulus on a body/brain-processing level. Repair of bonding that includes the body is essential. Sensory regulation difficulties are often not recognized until a child is faced with the added stimulation and social pressures of school. Difficulties for Couples usually appear once there is enough trust (or stress) to surface imprints of early attachment or birth. Such difficulties oten center around power struggles over early un-met needs and internalized fears of invasion or abandoment. Informed parents, teachers, and birth providers who understand perinatal imprints and their consequences can provide greater ease and support.

Bonding and attachment repair following a difficult birth is the work of trained Perinatal Therapists. Obstetricians who know how a difficult labor and birth interrupts bonding can recommend post-birth treatment that releases shock for baby and parents. Physicians who recommend post-birth treatments are providing an essential service for parents. Mothers who complete their "birth-push" post c-section recovery have a better chance to meet the demands of their newborn. Infants bond better who discharge birth pain, rotational torquing, and anesthesia through hands-on work via Body-Mind Centering® or cranial sacral sessions. When this is coupled with the psychological/emotional work of perinatal therapy sessions, birth shock resolves. Early intervention reduces defensive body and relational responses imprinted during a difficult or medicated birth. Re-establising the easeful body supports successful crawling and brain development so necessary for reading and learning skills.

Aware health care professionals and parents can help obstetricians understand the impacts of managed labor. Aware obstetricians may influence post-birth treatment protocol, as well as the training methods of obstetrics. The 2008 choice of the American Obstetrics Society to allow non-necessary C-sections shows that ignorance still abounds. When one understands the effects of prenatal, birth, and post-birth interventions they can better assess and weigh the risks involved in intervention choices related to perinatal care.

Chapter 1

Perinatal Psychology Overview

Theory and Treatment Methods

This chapter introduces the reader to the field of perinatal psychology and how early experience records in the body to shape identity beliefs and behaviors.

"We can understand the anxiety mechanism, which is repeated almost unaltered in cases of phobia (claustrophobia, fear of railways, tunnels, traveling, etc) as the unconscious reproduction of the anxiety of birth..."

— Otto Rank, The Trauma of Birth, 1924

"I was assured by neurologists that the nervous system of the baby was such that it was out of the question that any memory to do with birth could be reliably recorded as fact. I relayed my incredulity to my patients, and, as always happens in such cases, they tended thereafter to express what I was evidently unprepared, for so-called scientific reasons, to believe; that then a number of cases emerged in which the reliving of specific birth injuries, of forceps delivery, of the cord round the neck, of the stretched brachial plexus, and various other dramatic episodes were so vivid, so unmistakable in their origin, and afterwards confirmed by the mother or other reliable informants, that my suspicion was shaken."

— Dr. Frank Lake. Clinical Theology

Birth as Impacting Sense of Self... at the time of Freud and to present day

Western Psychologists have considered that birth impacts behavior since the time of Freud, and parents have observed their child's struggles and wondered if that "difficult birth" has something to do with their childs' behavior. Through interactive experience and scientific study we see that babies are in fact aware and sensitive, even in the womb. Non-Western cultures speak to the spirit of the baby, and mothers create a "welcome song" that is sung during pregnancy and by the villagers to welcome the newborn into community. Attuned pregnant mothers around the world listen and dialog with their unborn in prepartion for the relationship to come.

Otto Rank, colleague of Sigmund Freud, believed that birth had a significant and lasting impact on later development. Rank contributed to Western psychological thought through his book, *The Trauma of Birth* wherein he advised therapists to pay attention and look for early stories. Psychologists Frank Lake and Stanley Groff offered sessions and training to help clients explore birth imprints and events.

The research and writings of John Bowlby and Margaret Mahler explored formation of self based on post-birth interactions between mother and infant. Early attachment became a relational theory which is in wide use today. Mahler wrote an excellent book, *The Psychological Birth of the Infant.* Later researchers and authors contributed immensely: Edward Tronic, of Harvard, Daniel Stern, Thomas Verny, and Bertrand and Cramar supported the understanding of the importance of early experience. (see resources section). Jacqueline H. Wolf, in *Deliver Me From Pain*, documents the progression of birth medications, and how birth practice became focused on pain management rather than supporting an aware and awake birthing relationship between mother and infant.

Theorists from the Occupational Therapy disciplines were simultaneously developing keen insight and treatment methods for children struggling with developmental skills. Jean Ayers' sensory regulation and motor planning sequences were highlighted in *The Out-Of-Sync Child* by Carol Kranowitz. Clinicians from the behavioral, medical, psychological, and body-based research fields were joining to bring developmental questions to the foreground in examining child behavior.

Members in the pre- and perinatal field include MDs, psychotherapists, doulas, midwives, educators, and parents. They are sharing knowledge that experiences encoded during pregnancy, birth, and early post-birth shape behavior, in hopes to influence protocol. Perinatal experiences shape infant threat response, influence the body, engage the mind, and influence social behavior. The American Association for Pre- and Perinatal Psychology and Health (APPPAH) and the International Society of Pre- and Perinatal Medicine (ISPPM) are membership organizations that support ongoing education, research, and dialog to highlight the impacts of untreated birth events on society, children, and families. They offer resources for healing and for exchange of theory and ideas related to supportive social education and change.

Birth as a mystery of life and death

Exploring perinatal imprints often reveals unfortunate medical ignorance, or the reality of difficult birth circumstances that demanded life-saving interventions. Ignorance occurs in delivery rooms when a woman is placed on her back to birth. Back placement puts the entire weight of the baby upon mother's biggest blood vessels and limits mother's ability to respond through movement. It predisposes births to be difficult, and often sets the stage for pain medications or delivery interventions. A baby must rotate its head in order to exit the pelvis. A mother in a squat position, on all fours, or able to move can use her large sacral illiac pelvic joints to respond to birth pressure, and best support her baby to exit the birth canal.

It is important for the reader to remember that most birth physicians and birth providers are doing their best to be helpful. Unfortunately when parents expect doctors or midwives to guarantee a live birth outcome, they are creating an impossible double bind and liability issue for the physician. Birth is a mystery, women's pelvis' are shaped differently, and even under the best of care there are circumstances where birth becomes a question of life or death. Necessary emergency interventions are the blessing of managed labor. However, not understanding that birth itself can impact later behavior contributes to continued use of protocols and interventions that create later developomental problems relating to social or learning abilites. Elective C-sections and the standard delivery of pain medications interrupts the connection of the infant to the mother during this enormous rite of passage, and does not support conscious birthing and secure attachment.

Parents often feel powerless, angry, afraid, or disconnected from each other following a difficult birth. It is common for a mother, father, or client to experience emotions of guilt, rage, fear, or blame. Getting help to resolve these emotions will bring more potency and success to parenting and to healing. Transforming guilt to healthy anger and acceptance provides the potency to work toward resolution. Release of internalized terror coupled with body-based re-patterning provides long-standing relief. Parents who process their feelings related to the birth experience reclaim potency and connection with each other, and are more able to help their children. Repairing the collective nervous system of birth helps parents and children befriend the experience, release body shock, and have more ease in their physical and social connection.

Western culture is at a disadvantage when dealing with the experiences of the impacts of birth, especially when the birth results in death. Indigenous cultures have rituals to support the life/death possibilities of birthing. Perinatal therapy sessions can help western parents and mothers to develop their own rituals related to birth. Supportive midwifery and obstetrics, educated parents, adequate training of the impacts related to difficult births, and more natural hospital birth room settings can return birth to a more organic and natural process.

Note to reader

Exploring prenatal events can bring uncomfortable experiences to the surface. It is highly recommended to seek individual qualified therapeutic support or form a study group facilitated by a prenatal therapist.

If you become uncomfortable while reading, it might mean that pre-cognitive memories are being triggered.

Take a break and do something that helps you to integrate, muse, and explore what might be triggered. Write, dance, listen to music, or go for a walk in nature. This helps the psyche and soul express and integrate experience. Be kind to yourself in this exploration and remember to breathe deep!

Movement and awareness of sensation is both the primary language of infants and the cornerstone of this work. As a Somatic Psychotherapist, I utilize body-based methods and work with implicit memory stored in the cells and tissues. Somatic clinical work involves re-educating clients to sense, feel, and perceive without applying previously established filters of meaning. Such work provides a reclaimed ability for clients to stay socially present while experiencing sensation.

How Does Pre-cognitive Story Telling Produce Lasting Change?

Clinical sessions where clients unraveled early stories related to overwhelming sensations of birth convinced me that infants are impacted by birth, and that children and adults retain perinatal imprints for many years. Such imprints can form a template response to stress that can last a lifetime and is encoded both in body tissues and emotions at the limbic and brain stem levels. Successful treatment lay in working with early brain states where responses to overwhelm can be treated and resolved.

I call this method Applied Neuroplasticity®, which means using the brain's ability to re-pattern. Through mirror neurons, reflective function and the ability to recognize "brain states," therapists and parents can help a child or client slow down sensations that normally escalate into disorienting chaos that interrupts the ability to process incoming information. To dismantle ingrained survival strategies, one must understand what events created traumatic imprints. Accurate naming of events coupled with compassion and understanding reorganizes the nervous system and produces a coherent narrative of life. Previously un-named stories surface through the body tissue, are told, listened to, and put to rest.

Hundreds of hours of clinical sessions and over 35 years exploring, teaching, and treating has helped me develop this working model that meets the brain where it is most plastic and able to change. My method combines neuro-science, kinesthetic science, movement, and the art of story. Learning to listen for these stories, and how to recognize them when they surface is essential. Applying body-based psychological interventions reduces fear, doubt, protective withdrawal, and selfish anger. Such interventions return emotions to present time and bring out the best in children, lovers, spouses, and families. Bringing awareness of pre- and perinatal imprints can help couples maintain intimacy, continue to enrich their growth, and provide interconnected support for each other.

This method was developed in response to my need to unravel my early incubator impressions and the interrupted bonding. Finally realizing the impact this had on my adult life caused me to seek a broad base of support. I was fortunate to have superb teachers and trained in BMC infant development and body systems, as well as somatic psychology beginning in the late 70s. I spent 12 years in perinatal psychology studies, including 5 years assisting David Sawyer in prenatal and birth trainings, and received certification from Myrna Martin's 2 year perinatal program. These studies culminated in a doctorate degree in Pre- and Perinatal Psychology.

What Do We Listen to and Why?

We listen for held stillness in the body, fear-producing events, and escape strategies encoded in the body and emotions. Whatever dangers were experienced in the past are held in associative memory, and behavior that worked in the past is expressed in the present, even if it doesn't really make sense. The bodymind does so because it likes to be efficient. It is better to run away and be safe than to wait and find out if the danger is hurtful; especially when we are holding a story of a primitive, life-threatening event. This is why behaviors can seem out of context or appear confusing to others. Someone over-reacts even when danger is not present. Neglect, abandonment, inundation, or over-stimulation creates a perceived lack of safety in the brain, and complicates perception. Understanding how cellular memory and nervous system responses shape internal body communication helps clinicians understand and treat behavior. Knowing how medication, interventions, or birth chemicals impact an infant helps parents listen in a new way to difficult behaviors. Perinatal treatment can bring relief to nameless anxiety, dissociation, tactile defensiveness, hyper-activity, and identity beliefs that are inaccurate and pervasive.

Early encoded stories are pre-cognitive, occurring in the timeframe of 0-18 months of age. Later events can encode as shock, such as parental tyranny, raging, sexual abuse, misuse of power, or any life event that produces overwhelm in the bodymind. When treating, it is helpful to observe escalation of the body and thought. Speeding up is a sure sign one is getting excited. Will this excitement be expressed in a useful way, or will someone jump to habits of survival behavior as an attempt to regulate intensity? Sometimes a persons bodymind has a hypersensitivity to sound, smell, touch, hunger, or stimulation. People can appear vacant, get depressed, go into hiding, or become grandiose. They can tease or confront others, be controlling, or go into hyper-drive in an attempt to manage excess stimulation, arousal, or fear.

When we become curious about how the body responds, we have more clues to whether someone is activated. Are they breathing, do you feel uncomfortable around them, are you getting confused in a conversation? Whenever things start to get incoherent or chaotic, it is a time to pay attention and look for earlier stories that have not yet been told. When someone is relational, able to handle stress, and adjust to having needs that differ from their partner, they are not telling early stories, but able to be in present time. Successful coping means the nervous system is free to process incoming stimulus, rather than pulling up the old "roadmap" and applying it.

Parents and therapists can help children and clients to breath, use movement to help process emotions, learn to pay attention to sensations, and speak about feelings. Intervening at this level helps repair life-long patterns and supports children and adults to reclaim their natural intelligence. This allows for new perceptions, and for more pleasure and satisfaction in life.

Birth's Hidden Legacy: Volume Two offers many useful interventions and treatment props that support the sharing and healing of early stories. It is available on-line at www.bodymindsomanautics.com.

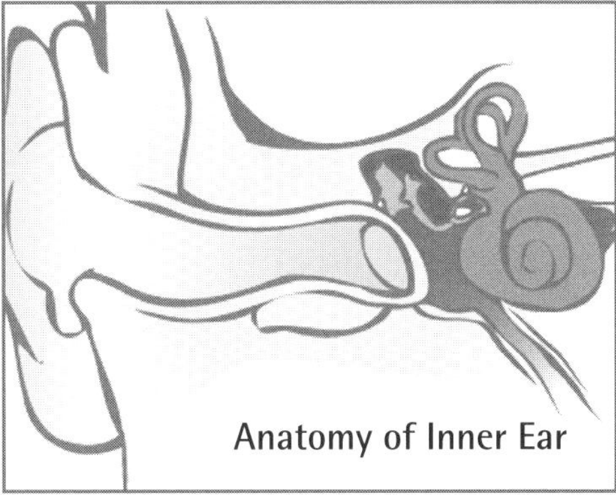

Anatomy of Inner Ear

"The first nerve to myelinate is the vestibular, which helps one to orient through movement and balance. The [prenate's] first language is one of vibration and responsive movement."

— Bonnie Bainbridge Cohen,
School for Body-Mind Centering

The three basic questions of early perinatal existence

- Is the world safe?
- Will I survive?
- Will I survive in relationship?

"These seem to be the underlying questions of the nervous system and govern child and adult relational behavior under stress"

— *Annie Brook*

When someone does not regulate sensations and responses well, they develop strategies which can be assumed to be personality, but might actually be un-named or unprocessed sensations and memories. The amygdala of the brain is awake during prenatal time. It is the security chief and its job is to register danger or social safety relating to survival. Clinicians who know how to re-establish social safety can help this part of the brain to relax and to take in new information.

Seek support for behaviors that become "labelled or diagnosed." Diagnosis can produce relief for parents as they realize something is going on with their child that is not a direct reflection of their parenting skills. I often see with adoption, that very well intended and skilled parents are getting worn down by children with a pre-determined construct of threat layered deep in the primitive brain stem. While a diagnosis brings relief, do not stop there. Seek treatment to resolve early impressions. It is most useful to utilize diagnosis and seek a skilled therapist who uses interventions that address the body and neural plasticity of the brain. This early intervention will provides changes before behaviors become habituated over many years of development. If available, aquatic attachment work in a warm pool can repair the early nervous system and re-establish a sense of safety.

Identity and Esteem

Adults come to sessions who struggle with internalized criticism or obsessive self-attack thoughts. Children have brought me drawings of themselves as infants where they labelled themself as "bad baby." It is sad to see identity and esteem affected by events that happened to an infant; their attempt to make meaning of overwhelming "bad" events often includes an internalized identification that they are "bad." Rather than believe that bad things were happening, which would be too scary to acknowledge or integrate, it was easier to see themselves "at cause" rather than as a victim. This is smart to do in a primitive way, as at least there is some locus of control and a way to orient rather than dissolve into chaos. Unpacking such identity beliefs and helping a client or child understand what happened repairs and reduces such self-attack thinking and deeply ingrained identity constructs. It brings a relief from self-destructive thinking and restores confidence.

Perceptions Decide Behavior

Difficult behaviors have clinical names, such as hyperactivity (ADDHD), autism spectrum behaviors, or sensory processing difficulties. Unprocessed sensory overwhelm of birth can leave adults and children susceptible to melt-downs, control issues, struggles with transitions, and difficulties processing sensory input. Learning to see how someone is perceiving and processing is one step in the direction to understanding behavior.

Re-patterning perception filters and the ability to uptake sensation is the next step. Find out if your child or client is looking through filters of fear or anger. Notice if they actually take you in through their gaze or if there is a type of deflection. These subtle cues will help you know if they are neutral or already "pre-sensory" focused.

Pre-sensory focused means their nervous system is focused on survival rather than remaining open and curious. Learn to help your child identify sensations by naming them aloud and talking about them. "Oh, you are scared! Do you feel fluttery in your belly or your heart?" With infants, name aloud what you see. "That was a noisy dog barking! Let me pick you up." You are teaching your infant and child that when she is in danger, the body will respond, and she can notice sensations, there is help that comes, and she can relax back into safety.

Helping a child or client to befriend body sensations interrupts the orienting to arousal and escalation, and use of chronic defense patterns. Help clients settle, fold children back in against your body, and use verbal and body awareness support. Work with facial recognition of emotions. Name behaviors and other choices of ease and safety. These are all tools that teach the ability to regulate.

Reactive behaviors can be a "pre-motor" focus, meaning a previously utilized movement response that was planned to alleviate earlier stressful imprint, rather than the current situation. Notice if your client or child's behavior is exaggerated or doesn't match the situation. It is likely that he or she is "pre-motor" focused, and about to use a non-helpful neural pathway. Once you see this, you can use movement and reflection of events to interrupt these perception-response sequences and get new results.

Birth's Hidden Legacy: Volume Two, contains advanced theory and useful interventions to support how to make such behavioral changes. The next section of this book, *Birth's Hidden Legacy: Volume One* introduces some of the themes related to prenatal, birth, and post-birth themes. This will support the reader to understand more specifically the way that early impressions influence behavior.

Know the Importance for Infants of a Sense of Safety

Parents who provide social smiles, safety, and touch help their infants develop a body sense of ease. This is extremely important for their later social development.

– Annie Brook

An infant needs a felt sense of a "good enough" world with "good enough" parents. This means they sense that their needs will be met; they cry out and someone comes who can bring relief. Learning this is the basis of discovering that they can meet their own needs as they mature. However, that learning curve is a developmental progression and develops over time.

Parents are confused both by literature and recommendations from others about whether they are "spoiling" their baby by going to him when he cries. The concern is that the baby will "manipulate them." A young infant needs you! Under the age of one year, and some would say 18 months, an infant is truly helpless to self-regulate without support. Helping an infant to discover and trust a safe world is of primary concern in this early time where the neural pathways are being programmed for future use.

Engaging in right use of power and finding safety is the task underneath a toddler exploring whether they can manipulate their parents. Near the age of two, having limits set by a parent actually establishes a sense of safety for a child. Knowing this developmental time line makes it easier to care for infants, regardless of other's opinions. Support those infants through smiling contact, touch, and interactive verbal play. A supported infant will bond, discover how to use their body, and come into relationship with you. Your gestures, dialog, and responsiveness help them feel met. Infants learn the interdependency related to need; that they need others for help and that help comes! With help and attuned support, infants discover the ability to relax in close contact with you.

It is important to allow infants to explore their environment. An infant placed on their tummy has greater access to brain development and an integrated body. They can push down against the earth and feel themselves through the proprioception of the body. This helps them to feel safe in the world. Pushing builds strength and resiliency. They can look and reach, taking hold with their attention, and then with their fingers. They can measure with their arms and muscles how far away objects are! They are practicing orienting spatially through the body.

Please do not sit babies upright surrounded by toys in easy reach. This dulls their seeking ability; it limits integration of core strength by demanding outer muscles hold them upright, rather than finding their way to sitting through intrinsic spinal muscles closer to the core. Infants learn an awareness of themselves in relation to gravity, which supports their ability to find a healthy yield, and push. Learning to "sit up" rather than be propped into sitting is a hugely important developmental task for the body and mind of an infant.

Verbal dialog helps an infant discover "feelings." When parents name their baby's expression aloud, such as "oh, you heard the dog bark and that scared you!" or "your diaper is wet and you are mad! Are you cold? Let me change you," or "Daddy had to leave for work and you are sad." This provides verbal reflective function, and helps your infant learn what mad and sad and scared feel like in the body. They learn empathically as the mirror neurons of their brain engage with your voice, facial expressions, and heart vibration. Safe and heart-felt care help the infant to grow and become secure emotionally and in their social world. Your baby is learning how to exist and to explore its world with curiosity, comfort, and pleasure.

Help Children Integrate the "Story" of Birth By Creating a "Baby Book"

Discovering we were pregnant

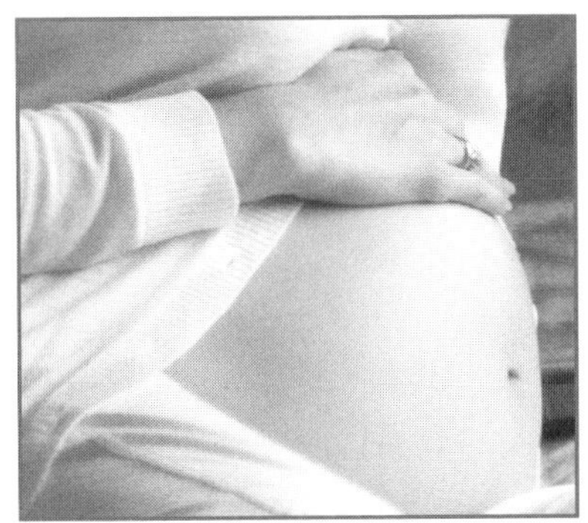

Mommy listening to you

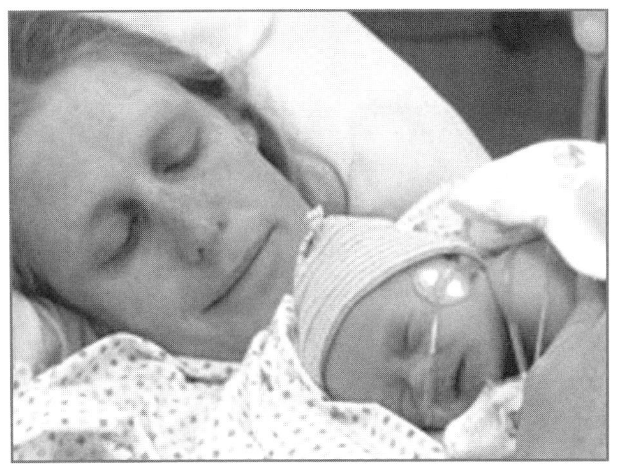

Tired from Birth
Sleeping with Mommy

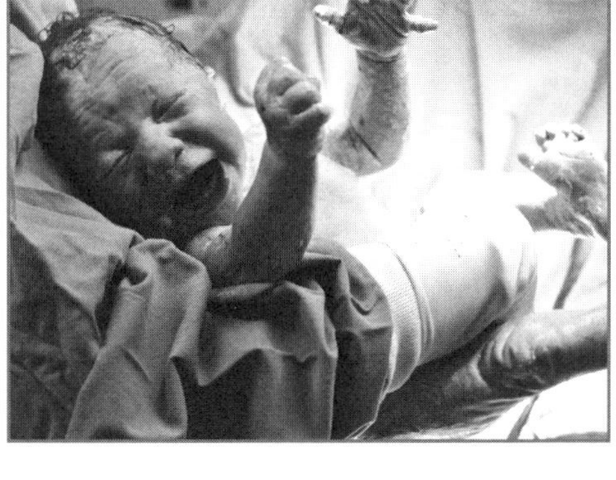

Your first cry

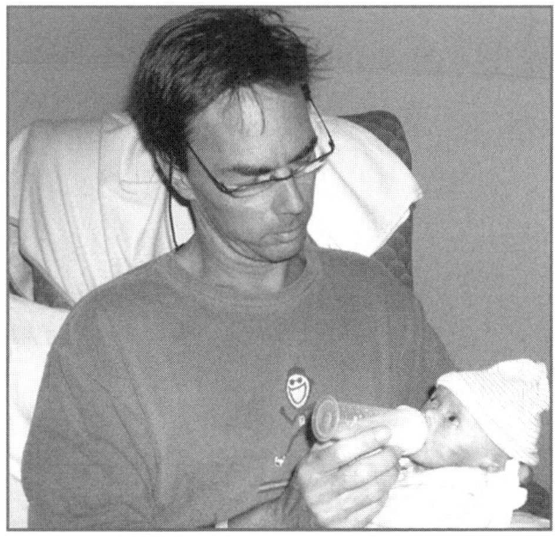

Daddy feeding you!

above pictures courtesy of Emma Sayge, age 6

Create a baby book that includes the entire narrative
Help infants integrate birth and prenatal events

Include pictures of:

- Mom and Dad in an affectionate moment (pre-conception)
- Pregnancy picture
- Birth pictures
- Early attachment experiences
- Movement transitions during early baby movement learning (rolling, sitting up, crawling, creeping, walking)
- Images of play and love with baby and Mom, Dad, grandparents and siblings

Hiding under the blanket

Creating a Baby Book Gives Children a Reference Point

A Baby Book helps your child ask questions, explore feelings, and integrate the rites of passage that birth entails. If you don't have photos, you can draw pictures, or use pictures taken from magazines. These are not as personal, but do introduce the topic of birth and infant learning and development. A baby book can be a way parents can ask questions when their child shows curiosity, such as, "what do you think you felt in this picture, or what do you think this little one was thinking and feeling?"

Laughing with Mommy!

Learning to lift your head

Daddy loving you

Enjoying the outdoors

Tips for Integrating Early Events of Life

- Slow down your vocal and movement pacing when there is escalation with children.
- Make eye contact, and bring spaciousness when things get intense.
- Help a child to "know" their arrival story in all its complexity.
- Release any guilt and find your potency so children feel your presence as support for being safe.
- Always remember to breathe.
- Widen rather than narrow your focus, while maintaining contact.
- Help your (and your child's) pent-up energy to move through the whole body in a safe manner.
- Relax muscle tension, find support and power through your core (organs, fluids, nerves, and bones).
- Help babies born in C-section to feel their joints through compression.
- Schedule BodyMind Centering® sessions to help with brain development and integration of rotational birth patterns, release of shock, and healthy sequence of compression.
- Schedule Osteopath or Cranial Sacral sessions following a difficult birth.
- Help your child draw or color in their experiences of birth... their cells remember.
- Listen and learn... find the stories of your attachment style.
- Show videos of healthy unassisted, midwife-assisted, and hospital births to prospective parents.
- Listen for the story beneath the behavior.
- Get qualified help sooner rather than later.
- Encourage Kangaroo Care for newborns. (See Kangaroo Care DVD in resources).
- Get support with adopted children. An inability to settle, hyperactivity, a need for extra attention, or a stiffening in the body can be a sign of fear deep in the nervous system. Again, get help sooner rather than later.
- Use humor and playfulness to help develop safety and trust.
- Don't take your child's behaviors personally when they are in trauma loops.
- Find the source of overwhelm and help it to unravel.

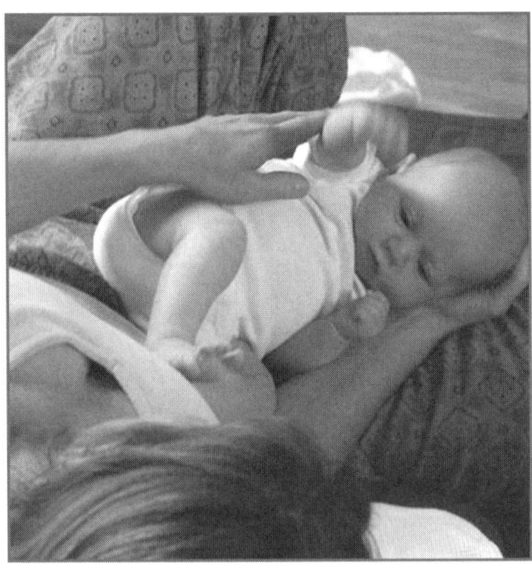

Listen with no agenda
Babies respond to body sensation

- Settle your own body
- Maintain empathy
- Track the baby's cues

Connection with the parents is most important
Teach the parents how to "hear" birth stories

- Help parents listen without guilt
- Help parents feel empowered
- Help parents integrate their feelings
- This helps the baby to settle

Use movement resources
Help parents learn to play and use touch

- Teach the value of flexion, folding the body in to itself
- Teach baby handling that does not lift the infant by holding their underarm ribs
- Lift from supported bottom with flexion of baby spine
- Show compressive touch support
- Teach about baby's cues
- Show the value of "tummy time"

Teach pacing
Help care-givers to slow down!

- infants process 6-10x slower than adults
- Teach caregivers to use 'infant time' and to pause for self-regulation

Periods of Human Development

Below is the anatomical and medical terminology for understanding prenatal development

Human Prenatal Development is subdivided into 1st, 2nd, 3rd trimesters

Periods of human embryology in Standard Terms of Embryology

Period of the egg: the time of fertilization through implantation plus 1 week
**Period of the embryo:* begins at the end of the first week after implantation.
Period of the fetus: the end of the 8th week continuing to birth.

Purpose of each embryonic period: In Prenatal Psychology, therapists address issues of energetic forces of conception, implantation, cellular growth, twin loss, plus the source energies of sperm and egg imprints. This is due to client reported memory of such impressions, which are existential in nature and influential to perception on a primitive level. See case studies.

Period of the egg is subdivided into:
Zygote: (fertilized egg): for the egg and sperm to unite, join chromosomes, and create new identity. This is an intense period of creativity and includes cellular streaming, folding, movement, and tissue organization.
Morula: (zygote divides by mitosis into a cluster of cells, encased in the zona pelucida). Cells increase in number but not size due to this protective membrane. This rebalances the large egg cytoplasm to nucleus ratio; bringing this ratio back into proportion within each cell. Therapists address issues of twin dynamics and Vanishing Twin from this time. *Note: E. Blechschmidt, M.D., and R.F. Gasser, Ph.D., believe humans do not go through a morula stage due to metabolic movements of change. (See Biokinetics and Biodynamics of Human Differentiation in resources).*
Blastocyst: (cells plus a large fluid filled central cavity). Allows supportive tissue as well as the embryo to keep developing. Therapists address issues of nourishment, contentment, a good enough world.

Chapter Two gave an overview of perinatal psychology theory and supportive methods. The next chapters begin the perceptual journey of the prenate and are divided into themes of pregnancy, birth and post-birth. Knowing Perinatal themes helps therapists and parents to accurately mirror and attune to emotional needs of children and clients. Processing early events clears the brain and body for clear thinking. The Case Studies section found later in *Birth's Hidden Legacy: Volume One* demonstrates how themes appear and are worked with in the context of clinical sessions.

The next chapter will elaborate specific prenatal themes occurring during the time of pregnancy.

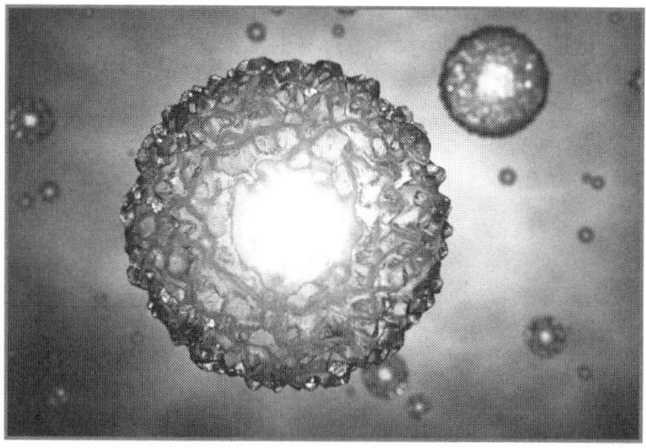

Zygote

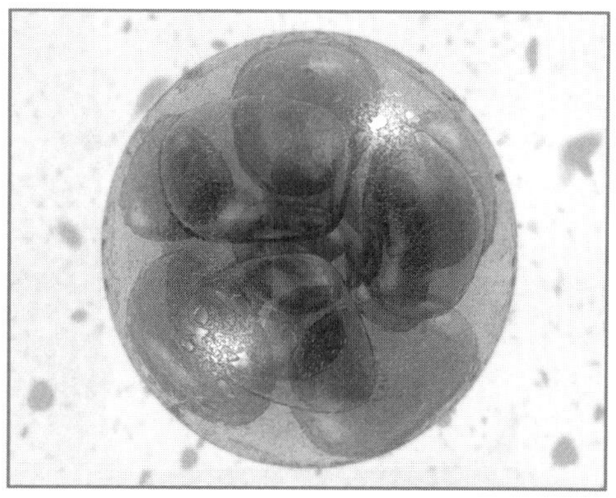

Morula

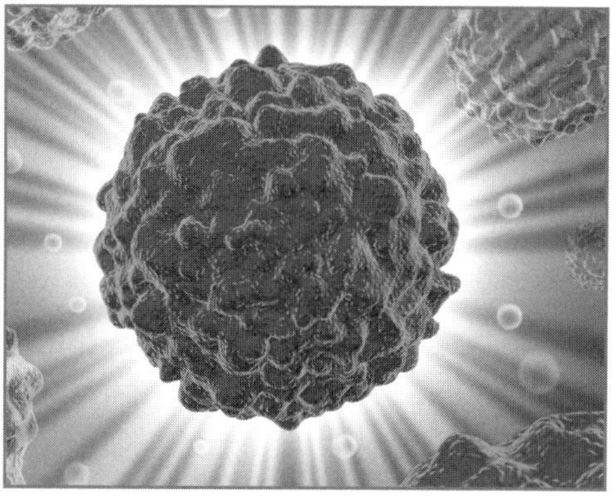

Blastocyst

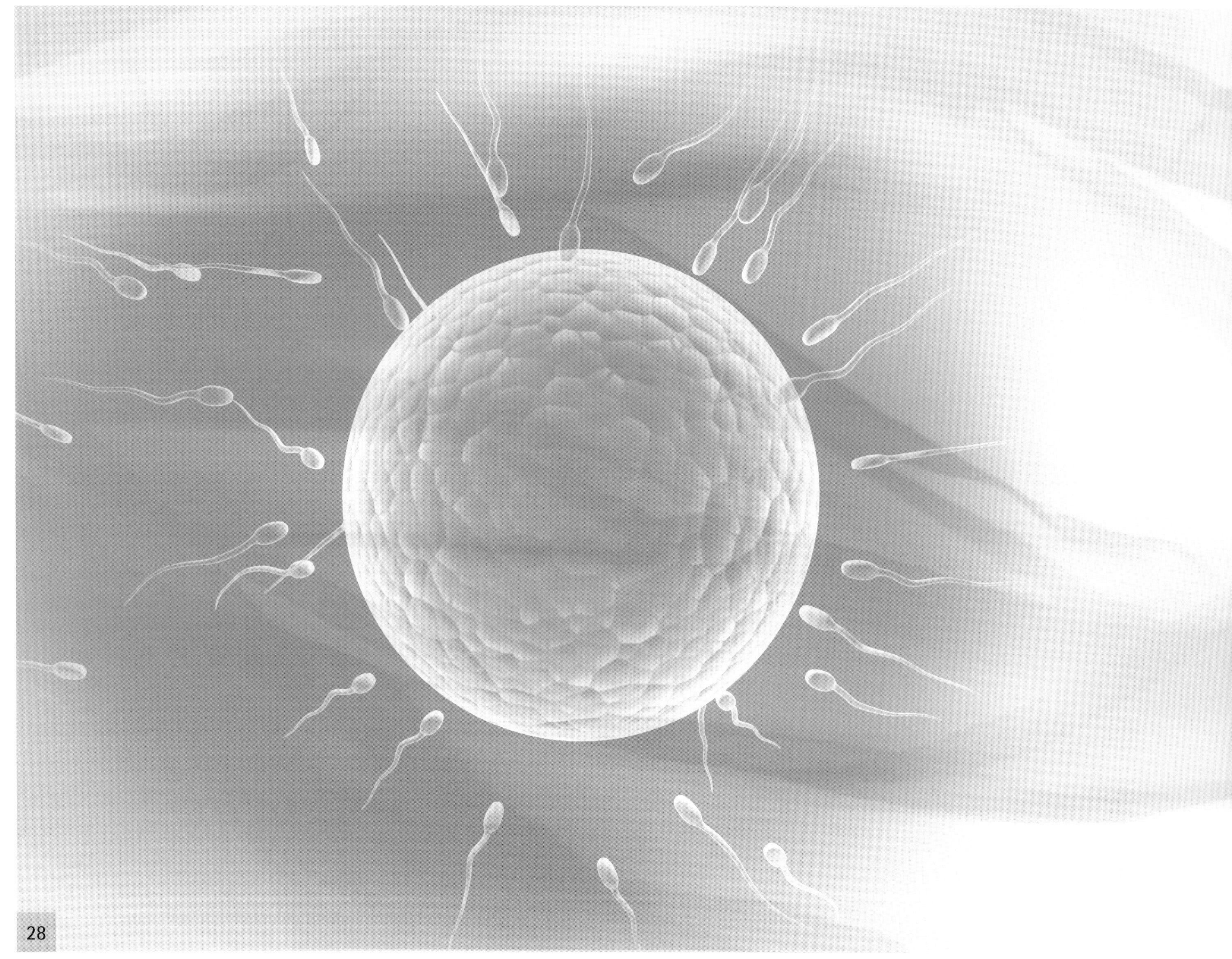

Chapter 2

Prenatal Themes

Influences on conception, the Zygote, Embryo, and Fetus prior to birth.

This chapter explores the earliest of themes which hold an existential quality. Treatment is spatial, delicate, and demands a listening into the unknown. Prenatal time reflects an arrival of self into body. The sense of self is delicate; influenced by vibrational energy, mothers movements, nutrition, hormones, and the emotional waters of both parents and the surrounding environment.

Implicit cellular memory

Implicit memory is pre-cognitive. It is the recording of events found in the consciousness of cells and tissues; the amygdala of an infant brain is awake during pregnancy and registers events relating to safety and survival.

It is this implicit memory that is accessed for pre- and perinatal treatment. When implicit memory becomes explicit and is then shared in an empathic setting that allows for participation, healing occurs. New neural pathways become available that create new behavior. *(based on personal comments of Dr. Alan Fogel, former head of Infant Research Laboratory, University of Salt Lake, Utah).*

This next chapter contains common prenatal themes that have surfaced with clients during clinical sessions. This includes adult and child clients, and listening to parents' stories of pregnancy or generational history when working with an infant. Early themes are cellular and existential, and shape part of one's perspective on identity. These are the important things to know about early themes; that they actually influence identity, and are based on a very existential body perception of self. The goal is to dismantle conflicting messages and threat triggers that don't affirm a person's sense of self in the world. Adults access infant cellular memory by recalling scenarios that are snapshots-in-time based on stories they have heard, plus body sensations that arise when they are speaking in session. I track the somatic and brain state cues which inform the treatment. With children, I use props and toys, and follow the child's play to identify themes. *Birth's Hidden Legacy: Volume Two* has specific guidance on how to surface these memories.

Any stories of chemicals during pregnancy, violence, heavy grief if Mom recently lost a parent, extra family stress related to other children or Dad's work, etc. can encode as perception for a prenate. Prenates are influenced by a couples' emotional dynamic and resonance, as well as directly influenced by mother's hormones and diet. Prenatal inquiry helps clients interrupt false beliefs that were rooted in pre-cognitive existential perceptions. Be sure to review the case studies chapter to see how these themes are utilized in treatment.

It's important to view prenatal experience simply as experience and release any guilt, remorse, or regret. Those are natural emotions to have; however, they don't further treatment. The most helpful thing to do is to treat early events as experiences that shape perception and bring compassion and curiosity to how these events shaped a sense of self and social behavior. Parents can help their child the most by processing residual emotions. This helps the child's emotional body to be seen and cared for, and gives parents the clarity needed to help their child make accurate meaning of those times. Children become curious about the early stories; when those stories are shared with them by their parents and worked with therapeutically, children will access emotions, integrate them, and find relief.

Theme descriptions are discursive and purposely succinct; included are common perinatal themes for classification and learning. The case studies chapter highlights clinical treatment and shows how themes appear and are worked with in the context of clinical sessions. For quick reference, themes are presented in a chart format at the beginning of each chapter.

Common Prenatal Themes

Pre-Conception	Some clinicians explore the influence of existential realms.
Conception	The energies of the mother and the father (sperm and egg) come together. This includes artificial reproductive technology influences (ART).
Free Fall	This happens twice. Once, when the spirit Free Falls into matter and takes form at conception, and secondly when the fertilized egg Free Falls from the Fallopian tube into the uterus on its way to implantation.
Incarnation shock	This is existential shock, and occurs at the earliest connection to the parents' energetic field. A deep sense of being in the wrong place, or not being seen, can lead to one resisting a full engagement with life. This often leads to a divine homesickness and longing to return to spirit.
Vanishing twin	Science now tells us that 50-80% of fertilized eggs arrive as twins and that one vanishes early in the pregnancy. It seems nature's way to ensure species survival.
Implantation	Approximately 8 days after fertilization the zygote burrows into the tissue of the uterus in order to attach, and then resurfaces in order to grow.
Discovery	The time when mother discovers she is pregnant. This is approximately 4 weeks after conception when the mother misses her menstrual cycle, but can be much later, producing impacts of feeling "seen or heard."
Annihilation issues	Overwhelming shock, such as abortion attempts or ideation. Physical abuse of the mother during pregnancy. Any event where the prenate perceived itself in danger of annihilation. *In-Vitro* removal of other eggs (ART).
Toxic womb	The environmental conditions inside the womb that negatively affected the developing fetus. Nicotine, alcohol, recreational drugs, chemicals, constant and excessive stress or worry, or if baby were hated by one of the parents.

Clients with complex issues that have not resolved through other methods, or who have already had years of therapy often find relief when exploring prenatal themes. The recurrence of non-useful behaviors or symptoms indicates that the nervous system brain states have not yet been resolved and brought back into balance. Prenatal work repairs hidden identity beliefs that interrupt the ability to to settle ones nervous system and help one orient to satisfaction and learn to thrive.

Common prenatal themes continued

Mistaken gender	The fetus is not the gender of the parents desire. This affects both prenatal life and birth events. One feels somehow inherently wrong.
Haunted womb	The prenate who follows a miscarriage or abortion feels unprocessed death, grief, and loss of those who came before.
Ancestral influence	These appear in the 3rd trimester when the baby is in more contact with the womb tissue. Influences can be supportive or not supportive. Explore both positive and negative factors. Negative times create shock memory where ancestors were dis-empowered, abusive, in life-threatening situations, exhibited fear-based behavior, or experienced trauma through natural disasters. Also explore issues of nonsupport from parents due to chemical dependency, mental illness, suicide, or murder. These influences extend two or more generations back and include ancestral cultural genocide, deaths in the family, and other cultural influences.
Prenatal death of twin	When a twin dies in utero.
Prenatal birth position	Attempts to turn the baby and baby being "stuck" in the birth canal or in a painful position for long periods of time.

Incarnation Themes

In an ideal world, parents would be excited and happy to start a family and they would have the support of their friends and community. Incarnation would be a welcoming event with plenty of nourishment and support for the busy job of growing a self. However that is not everyone's experience. Conception can occur during an alcoholic rampage, a rape, a one night "fling" or as an attempt to "save the marriage."

When working with incarnation themes, a parent or clinician has to take a wide view. Understanding how these earliest forces create an existential perception and affect development occurs through listening to a client's or child's expression with existential awareness. Knowing these early themes helps one recognize and assess behavior patterns. Incarnation themes have a different felt-sense than later developmental imprints due to the existential timeframe of occurrence. There is less of an established differentiated self experiencing events and responding to impact. Clinical observation and hundreds of hours of treatment point to the importance of treating at the incarnation level, and the reality of such perceptions.

The following pages highlight issues of shock at the time of incarnation. Some of these themes start prior to conception. Others occur after implantation. The reader will benefit most by remaining curious about three things: 1) How early experience records as cellular memory, 2) how meaning is made from this experience, and 3) that both adults and children have the capacity to access this pre-cognitive memory by attending to sensation which evokes brain states of consciousness.

Prenatal cellular memories surface at odd moments, and under stress. They influence unconscious behavior until resolved. Integration occurs when emotional support is coupled with reflective function and accurate naming of pre- and perinatal themes. Behavior expressions related to early body stories are more likely to be recognized when teachers, therapists, and parents suspend judgment and remain curious.

A cognitive map of this pre- and perinatal territory is helpful, and ideally combined with a felt-sense of brain states that occur through dissociative shock and fragmentation. This allows for deeper recognition and treatment. (See Body-Based Interventions for Healing Shock and Trauma in *Birth's Hidden Legacy: Volume Two*).

Early impressions express in a non-linear fashion that is also non-chronological. There might be very early events that surface, then later events, and then you go back to earlier events. The client or child will guide you through their experience in the body. Working at this early perinatal level and learning to help clients process clears very deeply encoded brain states. Therapists can learn to recognize the echo of early impressions as underlying current behaviors, and how to work with the overlapping impressions of a client's experience. Learning to do so provides clarity around the complexity of certain behaviors and brings relief knowing there is actually a reason your child or client is behaving in such a manner. The next pages are about the transition of awareness into an incarnate body. Take some deep breaths and prepare yourself to enter the watery world of impressions via sound, vibrations, and emotions.

Case Study Example

The case studies chapter highlights how these themes appear in clients' personal experience. See Case Study #7 on Incarnation Shock.

Note to reader

Treatment is not linear but based on how material presents in sessions. Often prenatal imprints arise after birth themes are addressed and cleared. Clinicians will gradually learn to recognize how various themes present.

Knowing the entry point for treatment comes with experience. However, using primary scenarios can provide that entry point and help a client engage the inquiry of early distress imprints and implicit memory (see Volume 2 for those tools).

Egg Journey

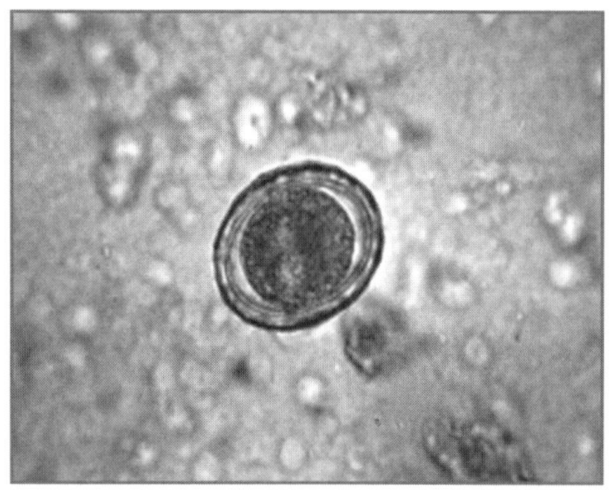

Cells appear to have awareness, choice, and ability to re-choose at a membrane level whether to brace or relax and feel support. This is felt through hands-on tissue work, and also through brain state of return to relaxation. See Body Resources chapter and Body-Mind Centering work.

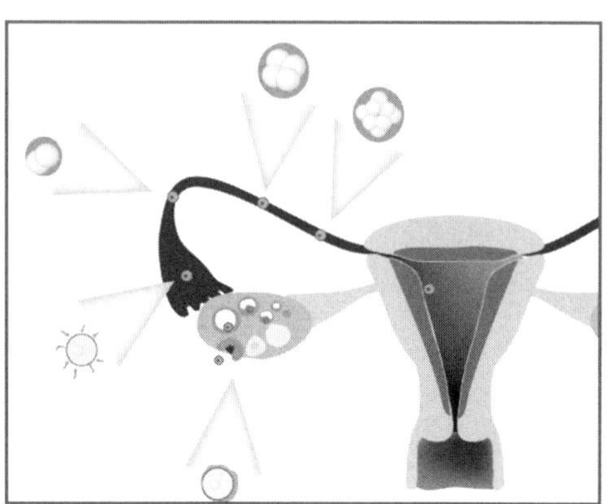

The biological necessity of life causes ovaries to ripen and eggs to gather cytoplasm. Egg memory is experienced by both men and women, since we come from the union of the egg and sperm. When ready, ovaries are hormonally induced to rupture. They are brushed open by the fingers of the Fallopian tube which gather the ripe egg and draw it inside. Descriptions of ovary memory experiences vary. For some clients, the sense of the ovary was comforting, as if being in a safe nursery and feeling connected to a sisterhood. Some describe a feeling of not wanting to leave; a sense of loss at leaving others behind. Others describe a sense of positioning, having to vie for their place in line. "Will I be chosen, whose turn is next?" Still others feel a sense of rightness that it's their time and they deserve the attention and focus. Their egg journey was enjoyable. "I was ready and it was my turn!" These clients expressed a happy acceptance and comfort when they were willing to align with a sense of being chosen.

Regardless of the felt-sense experience, the greatest support tool is to help clients to orient towards a sense of healthy emotional connection and physical safety during their time in utero. The egg enjoys receptive patience, potency and protection. If that were not available you can teach them to orient to the "great mother" and to imagine what that types of support would have felt like. Warm water pool sessions are excellent for reclaiming a sense of safety in the womb like container, and I train water therapists to provide this support. Water sessions are an excellent repair for adopted children and their new mothers.

Appreciating the gift of life is another resource. Clients in your office survived! No matter the conditions of pregnancy, their life force was strong. Make sure that clients and children do not retain a sense of being the victim of prenatal times; this is really important for a right connection to a sense of personal power. Appreciate the despair, release the depression in the tissues, and focus on the vitality of the instinct of life. Anyone who's in your treatment room obviously wanted to be here in some fashion, or they would have died in utero. That is a form of resource and strength.

With depressed clients who wonder why they are alive, helping clear prenatal imprints can clear the depression and help them find potency. I only met one adult male client who "didn't want to be here." It turns out that he was resuscitated at birth. As he healed the body shock of invasion due to resuscitation, he could return to enjoying his incarnation and release his confusion of whether he "wanted to be here." Early shocking imprints interrupted his desire; clearing them allowed him to reclaim his excitement for life. He began to engage with life in an empowered manner rather than hold resentment and rage.

Teaching clients to orient toward satisfaction and to accept the biological reality of existence as proper support can release attachment to emotional imprints. The seduction of distress can be dismantled with cognitive support and reflection about early experience. Clients who orient toward satisfaction; learn to feel content, supported, and happy for the gift of life is the repair of incarnation shock. (See chapter on the "Satisfaction Cycle" in my other book, *From Conception to Crawling* available at www.anniebrook.com).

Trusting I will have a turn and taking that turn

Issues of self-worth, ability to receive attention, feel confident, and naturally entitled without superiority can be traced to the egg journey. Reminding clients of the biological success of their egg journey allows them to release emotional baggage related to the feminine, mothering, and to the choice to engage in life without resentment. Finding trust in the basic process of life without having to be in charge all the time is a supportive ease gained from doing this work. Such work returns a sense of trust, flow, and ease to the body and nervous system. Fear patterns are released at a tissue and brain level. Another benefit from revisiting this time is that many clients have reported better connection with and enjoyment of their siblings after having revisited and repaired egg journey imprints.

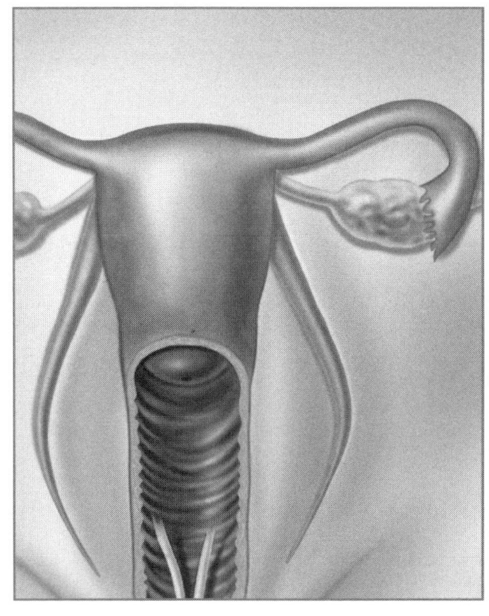

Egg Issues of Support and Identity

Suspension and waiting

- How do I wait?
- Am I impatient?
- Do I trust the outcome?
- Will I allow support?

Being chosen

- Do I accept my destiny?
- Am I willing to stand out?
- Can I say goodbye and move forward?

Nourishment and receptivity

- Can I support and influence outcome?
- Can I trust accurately and without naivete?
- Can I follow through without getting lost?
- Can I stay focused and not self-abandon?

Assessment of social behavior

- Is connection easy?
- Do I feel ready?
- Do I let myself receive attention?
- Do I enjoy this, crave it, or fear it?
- Can connection be simple and enjoyable?

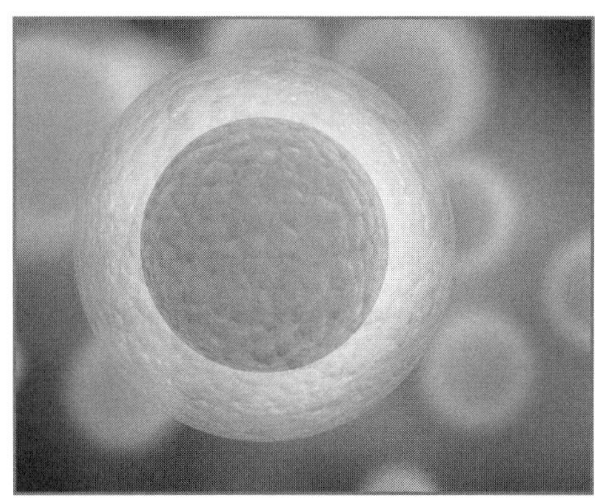

Sperm Journey

Whether male or female, we have all been on the sperm journey and have a relationship with the successful energy of the sperm. Only the strongest sperm in the 5 million that are ejaculated produces a child; we are by nature of our existence successful in the energy of sperm. This supports a sense of internal potency which is useful in life.

Contrary to the eggs which gather cytoplasm, sperm cast off cytoplasm in order to be ready to travel. They become more crystaline in nature. To prepare, sperm mature and rest in the Vas Deferens. They are supported by male nurse cells until they mature. The head of the sperm carries the chromosomes while the tail is filled with mitochondrial energy packs. These fuel the long journey to reach the egg.

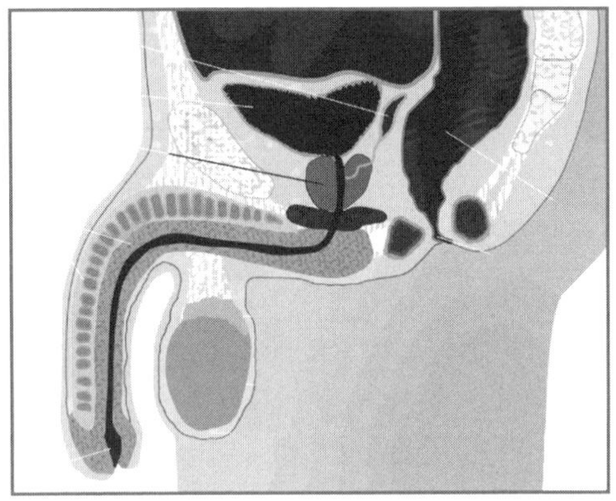

Sperm have an arduous task. They enter a hostile acidic environment when they spurt into the vagina. The acidity keeps out bacteria and self-selects the strongest of the sperm. Sperm navigate through these acidic fluids and choose the right or left Fallopian tube; only one tube holds the egg. Many enter the wrong tube and die. The ones that enter the correct tube must find the egg and be invited into the egg. Many sperm arrive to the egg and tap upon its its protective zona pelucida surface, which supports an awakening. However, most often only one is chosen by the egg to enter. The non-chosen sperm create a fluid spinning vortex through the movement of their tails. This vortex of energy may support the the merging of 23 haploid chromosomes to become 46 diploid during the 6-8 hours it takes for conception. This is the successful hero's journey for the sperm.

Case Study Example

See Case Study #10 for sperm donor and egg themes in treatment.

Power, potency, and success

Every living person has found potency and the ability to find one's way. Orienting to this personal power of the sperm can be a resource. Questions to ask include: How did conception take place? Was the sperm awake, confused by alcohol, or donated by someone else? If donated, the sperm might have been frozen midway through its journey. How does that impact life force? Without a juicy exchange between the mother and the father, how would one's sense of sexual pleasure and potency be impacted?

Clients can repair difficulty with male energy by reclaiming their sense of the sperm journey and its success. It is important to acknowledge sperm potency and use that to differentiate from abuse or emotional impotency carried by one's father. Help clients remember they have the potency and power to succeed. Teach parents to allow the vitality of sperm energy in their children, and not to squash it but direct it into useful behaviors. Sperm energy and potency is a valuable asset. Allowing the energetic success of creative life force to circulate through one's cells reduces a sense of being a victim. Help clients whose fathers were unknown or abandoned the family to reclaim a relationship with their own successful masculine force. Help them find gratitude for the basic life force carried within sperm; this allows them to interrupt self-attack or crippling shame. They can release emotional baggage with the masculine and identify with a positive male forcefield.

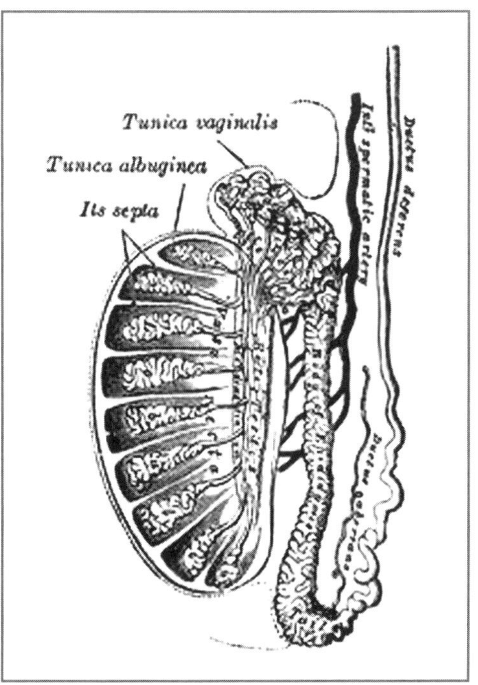

Potency and Purpose: Sperm Energy

Gathering energy and releasing excess material

Sperm condense and concentrate energy

- Do I build potency for success?
- Do I rest and recuperate as part of preparation?
- Do I wait for the right timing?
- Do I work well with other men?

Issues of social support

Sperm go on the journey together

- Do I utilize support from men?
- Can I find my way in a crowd?
- Will I continue even if others are struggling?

Orientation and Behavior

Sperm orient toward and make the goal

- Can I call forth my successful sperm energy when needed?
- Do I let my potency show? Do I enjoy it?
- Can I stay focused on the goal regardless of obstacles?

Assessment of sperm energy and healthy warrior behavior

- Do I accept responsibility?
- Am I a team player?
- Do I have what it takes?

Some couples pray for the arrival of their baby, and some mothers feel the soul nearby prior to conception.

Choose Health

We cannot change the past
Perinatal inquiry must not be used to pathologize or victimize oneself. Many functional people have been perplexed at the tenacity of certain internal struggles, and seek this work because they have not found relief elsewhere. Relief can come from understanding but not carrying forward any dysfunctional energy of our parents choices.

Why do some people have a good sense of esteem and others feel lost and wandering? Conception is the first vibration of welcome. Based on clinical treatment, conception experience apparently impacts identity. This occurs more as a field vibration awareness rather than as solid sense of self. Resolving existential angst of self brings relief for later developmental tasks. Clients shift behavior. They no longer spin under pressure, or hold back vitality, or freeze when they need to take action (due to donor sperm; see case study #10). Finding vitality and integrating the experience of conception is the goal of this level of treatment.

Energy Medicine: The energies of the two parents influence identity
How did conception occurr? Exploring this can dismantle identity issues. Were parents juicy, connective and joyously passionate, or unconscious and inebriated? Was lovemaking pleasurable or from a sense of duty, boredom, or violence? Connected loving parents will have a different vibrational field than parents who were detached or violent. Healthy physical lovemaking creates a different field than reproductive clinics where workers energetic vibrations are picked up, as is the vibration of other fertilized eggs that were dissolved. Inquire about the energetics persent during conception.

Is there a lack of self-worth, sense of incompetence, spinning under pressure, or resentment of others? Does a person seem lost, feel insubstantial, gravitate to spiritual aspects, rather than adjust to healthy conflict and the reality of intimacy and life on earth. These are the existential consequences related to conception.

When the emotional/physical/energetic environment of conception is not nourishing, a form of incarnation shock can occur. Energies of confusion or rejection are felt and can be mistakenly personalized by the existential self. A false identity that one is too much or not good enough can form due to the emotions found in the conception and discovery environment.

Differentiating the self from events surrounding conception helps release negative beliefs formed at the inception of life. Imagine what occurred, name what was true for the parents, and then differentiate from those circumstances. Maybe there was much love and lots of alcohol, or intercourse was forced. Sometimes the only good news at one's conception was that they found life. Perhaps conception was a special celebration, a romantic summer evening, or maybe one chose this family to learn some important lessons. To heal incarnation shock, help clients push away environmental alcohol or toxicity encountered during this early stage. Doing so clears the space for later detoxification and clarity.

Musing about conception events clarifies a personal narrative. Regardless of actual circumstance, return to the potency of conception to help clients find a sense of purpose, destiny, and desire for life. This builds relsiliency and supports one's life journey. Release any "fight" with God about destiny. For children, name events in child friendly ways, such as "oh it was a wild beginning!" or "even though Mommy was hurt, it was not your fault." Healing conception relaxes existential angst and struggle.

Questions for Conception

- Was the conception planned?
- What circumstances surrounded conception?
- Was it a loving experience?
- Was it a forced experience?
- Was playful, loving, healthy sexuality present and expressed?
- Was the environment supportive?
- Was the couple relaxed?
- Were the parents open to each other?
- Were they ready and desiring a child?
- Can I allow the potency of life to flow in me?
- The soul arrives into the force field of life. What was that field like?
- Is it OK to be me?
- What was the parents' motivation for conception?
- Was it to save a marriage, take-care of a parent, or to create a replacement child for a sibling who died?
- How does this task of conception create pressure in one's life?

Tips for Healing

- Make peace with what happened
- Feel emotions as they come
- Forgive
- Take responsibility
- Feel Welcomed
- Feel at Choice
- Re-create sense of Purpose
- Celebrate your life
- Find your destiny
- Enjoy
- Share
- Appreciate your unique nature (Both egg and sperm surrender "identity" in the transformation of conception)

Vanishing Twin Theme: Morula Stage of Embryology

Unhealed vanishing twin issues can drive the seeking energy and need for there to be a "twin flame." See Case Study #1.

50-80% of zygotes have a twin which vanishes sometime before implantation. (personal commentary, David Sawyer)

Why are some children, more so than others, concerned with a magical and invisible "special friend?" Why are some adults "lost in longing" and constantly seeking a "special partner," insisting that life is meant to be shared at an impossibly intimate level? Their partners are never quite "good enough."

Vanishing twin may explain these behaviors. Recent findings show that 50 to 80% of people have a twin following conception; this "twin" is lost before implantation, but perhaps part of a biological intelligence of survival of our species. Cells divide and rebalance the cytoplasm/nuclei ratio during the Morula stage; this dividing would be a ripe time for "twinning." The journey down the Fallopian tube lasts approximately 8 days. Cells feed from an internal food supply which is being depleted. Once that food is gone, the fertilized developed zygote must implant or die. Shortage of resources could cause one twin to "vanish."

I first heard of this theme during my 5 years co-teaching with David Sawyer. I was highly skeptical, yet observed that addressing the vanishing twin theme consistently brought relief to a number of trainees. Many years of research with adult and child clients produced enough anecdotal evidence for me to realize that a "vanishing twin" is a real occurrence. Clients who explored this theme made significant changes. They were more comfortable with loneliness, no longer felt so "abandoned," and gave up the unfulfilled obsessive longing for that perfect "beloved." As they reduced inner confusion and abandonment fears, they settled into life as a separate and differentiated adult and their partners became "good enough." Children who said goodbye to their "special" friend were better able to relax and fall asleep at night.

Confusion of identity is a strong imprint of this developmental phase. Due to the symbiotic sharing of cells in the morula it is easy to get confused and existentially shocked. Vanishing twin loss produces an uncanny connection to the spirt world which is not always useful; one can be confused as to "who" stayed and "who" left. Such loss is emotionally unfathomable. Adults appear overly seductive of others and often jump into partnership, as if they had known each other for a lifetime.

The easiest way to work through this theme is to role-play the vanishing twin. During this play, clients describe a felt-sense of danger as "the food" supply dwindles. They demand that the "twin" stays and often grab me and try to shake me back to life as my "energy" diminishes. They are heartborken and reluctant to say goodbye. There is a fear to inhabit this life "alone" and often a sense of being betrayed. Clients offer to be a martyr and "die" instead. Resolving the reality of "who" stayed and left, and saying goodbye brings relief. This can take a few sessions to resolve.

Relational fears are latent in vanishing twin theme. Behaviors can include excessive flirtation, especially if they find another with the same unresolved theme. Survivors guilt, feeling betrayed, that one's potency is too much, or an unwillingness to connect deeply with another can occur. Cases of gender identity confusion can appear when the loss was of an opposite-gendered "twin." Be sure to look for this theme and help clients resolve it. Doing so will bring relief and a greater sense of a capable self.

When addressed through clinical role-play methods, clients often express confusion about who stayed and who left. Adult, children, and teen clients consistently grab and shake the "dying twin," demanding to "not be abandoned!" Often they burst into tears as the inevitable loss becomes conscious.

Empathy is needed for the confusion of identity related to "Who am "I," when "we" formed the "I" of me?" The twin that stayed must navigate an existential loss where the sense of self is so rarified. People respond with an inconsolable grief that is life threatening and vast. Incredible emphasis is placed on seeking the "lost other" rather than moving forward with one's own life.

Vanishing twin fears and complications of identity

- Confusion about who stayed and who left (went back to spirit)
- Possible gender identity confusion if the opposite gender vanished
- Unexplainable grief and fear of loss of connection... a sense of perpetual abandonment
- Longing to be overly connected to the spirit world (often expressed as a strong heart connection and link to the dolphin species)
- Continuous longing for that special other; seeking the "twin flame" partner
- Inability to allow intimacy with one's partner; not accepting them for fear of loss, not accepting them as "good enough," insisting they be "special!"

Lost in longing

Too much identification with the spirit world keeps one separate from life and never satisfied. Living in magic, dissociating, demonstrating an inability to have boundaries, or to say "no" to others may point to relentless twin seeking. Healing comes when one actually says goodbye. If the twin vanished close to the time of implantation, an infant may "twin" with the mother and feel overly responsible for her well-being. The key is to acknowledge the loss, differentiate, experience being alone and surviving, and reclaim curiosity for life in this world. The helpful task is to embrace life from a full self instead of a half-lost longing.

Important Clinical Note

Sometimes what might appear as sexualized behavior is an attempt at "twinning." A 12 year old boy was brought to treatment by a wise mom, following concern of inappropriate touching of younger siblings. This boy had experienced inappropriate touching during his kindergarten years by another child, and his mother was concerned to get to the source of current behavior.

To assess this boy's impulses, I held a number of pool sessions with him, getting a sense of his potency and basic nature. He was not engaging sexually but playfully. Having worked with sexually abused foster children, I had a perceptive sense of inappropriate developmental "arousal states" in children. This boy was not engaging that energy. However, he did appear to be longing for the "twinning" feeling.

When I asked his mother about her pregnancy, she reported she thought she had twins but had some early bleeding and the sense of twins went away. She hadn't mentioned this to her son.

When I role-played "Vanishing Twin" with the boy, he begged me to stay and dragged me over to his mother sitting on the pool ladder. I "left the pool" and he just sat under the ladder rather than play in the water. When asked why, he reported, "I was too lonely." This existential twin loss can be confused with a seeking of sexual contact and reek havoc on adult relationships unless understood and dismantled.

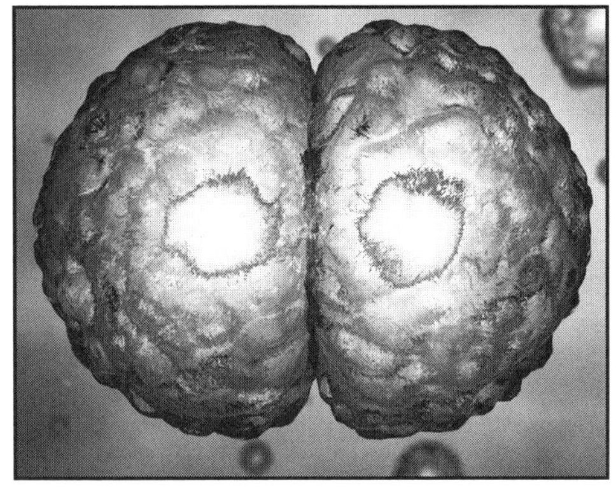

It appears that cell division during mitosis sometimes results in twins

Case Study Example

See Case Study #1 that explores many themes, including vanishing twin.

Lost in longing, continual seeking of the special other

Frozen longing

- If only they had stayed!
- I will find them in a lover
- My life will never be the same!
- I will stay in the spirit world in order to be with them.

Meeting death, loss, and feelings of abandonment

- Did I do something wrong?
- My power is too much for others!
- There is something unacceptable in me.
- I am angry at having to do this by myself!

Survivors guilt

- I should have died.
- Confusion about who stayed or who left.
- I won't ever act strong again so I won't hurt someone.

Life is such a mystery. Scientists were recently in awe that a mother produced offspring with genes that didn't match her own. (*Scientific American Journal*, 2011). Genetic tests seemed to indicate that the mother was not the creator of her own child because her DNA did not match her offspring! Further investigation determined that early in pregnancy, twins had merged to become one child. Their combined DNA resulted in a DNA different than the mother's genetic pattern. If we add the psychological awareness of developing identity to this biological curiosity, it is a time rife with possibility for identity issues. The development of self becomes a grand mystery and must be treated with continual respect and curiosity.

"Oh, That Twinning Feeling... "

People who have experienced a "vanished twin" are often unconsciously seductive, especially to each other. The early "twinning" experience produces a felt-sense of intimacy that is hard to match, unless one is lost in the same longing. Twinning issues can get confused with adult sexuality and pleasure and create false sexual elation and bonding.

As a clinician, learn to recognize the look of "twinning." It is a distortion of psychic connection that feels almost magnetic and is highly pleasurable. Twinning behavior elicits a glandular rush that is ungrounded and unsustainable when met with real life pressures. "Twinning" appears in issues where people seek immediate intimacy, unrealistic closeness, and feel they are so connected that they read each other's minds and thoughts. Unaddressed vanishing twin imprints can lead to strong projections that are mutually enacted in relating.

Assessment: twinning issues

Do you?

- Push and criticize yourself as if you have to prove your right to exist?
- Go into a "touch trance" or quickly fuse and bond in relationship?
- Overly sensualize and energize conversations?
- Hold yourself back as in survivor's guilt?
- Resent others for not fusing with you?
- Believe in lack at a spiritual or existential level?
- Chase spirituality?
- Live on Crumbs?
- Sabotage your success?
- Seek the specialized other at risk of losing those who do care for you?
- Treat your partner as if they were "never enough!"
- Minimize your accomplishments?

"Free Fall" Themes

Free Fall occurs two times in the prenatal journey. The first is the fall from the spirit world into conception. This is the existential free fall journey of embodiment. Some clients describe this as "being kicked out of heaven" or "abandoned by God." The second occurs when the fertilized egg free falls out the Fallopian tube on its way to implantation in the uterus. Both involve the threat of "succeed or perish."

Free Fall happens to us all...

Free Fall teaches one to go with the flow, to accept, to surrender in a useful way. People who struggle with this experience often feel dis-empowered and a victim. Clinicians can help clients recognize the power of choice in incarnation. You can remind clients that many babies die in utero and leave in a miscarriage. However, they have obviously succeeded as they are here in your office! Help clients to accept their choice to live and engage in the journey of their life, rather than resist their existence. Clients who release this existential struggle reclaim a sense of destiny and desire for life. People who accept life and choose to live seem able to meet life pressure more successfully and find enjoyment.

Free Fall themes and treatment

If a person orients to life as a victim due to the forces of their incarnation and implantation, they lose a resilient "yes" to life. Free Falling is disorienting. If they cling to this disoriented perspective, they lose sight of a through line of action and a sense of accomplishment. Sometimes people self-sabotage to "get back at God!" Support the biological reality of successful arrival and encourage clients to engage their destiny. Sort through any felt-sense of a spinning confusion related to Free Fall. Help clients find relationship with their potent life force that carried them beyond the fall. Doing so supports the ability to orient and get needs met. Such potent clarity allows the journey of Free Fall to become a success.

Free Fall 1: existential suspense of conception

Bring awareness to choices

- Did your spirit choose to arrive?
- How can you find safety in that choice?
- What allows you to feel empowered?
- How can you let go of blame and revenge? (may appear as self-sabotage)
- Explore beliefs about life and release issues of mistrust

Free Fall 2: prior to implantation

Issues of Survival, Disorientation

- Help client orient to potency and arrival
- What were the conditions at implantation?
- Help clients orient to direction. Use body support in the spatial planes (see *Conception to Crawling* by this author).
- Use sensations to track health in the body
- Find security in one's path and intentions
- Practice doubting one's doubts

Assessment: Free Fall issues

Do you?

- Get disoriented just before success?
- Sabotage crossing thresholds of transition?
- Resent those who welcome you and enjoy you?
- Withhold your true nature to loved ones?
- Have trouble staying in one geographic location?
- Easily or often appear lost and dreamy?
- Feel vengeful about life?

Case Study Example

See Case Study #10 that highlights imprints related to sperm donor conception.

Addressing Parents Reluctance

Parents are often reluctant to tell children of an ART-based conception. However, an aspect of the child's psyche already knows. Using child friendly language and addressing loss of "siblings" from dissolved eggs, or that "Dad is your Dad, and you had another man help you to be here too" can clear up deep rooted confusion in a child. I have seen children relax, mother's release guilt and grief, and ultimately relief of anxiety and identity fears when children are supported to "say goodbye" or to know the reality of their beginnings. They may ask a number of questions following a session; coach parents to stay guilt free and to speak clearly and not too technically. It is helpful for a child to know that "Mommy couldn't take care of so many babies." Children seem able to integrate these realities when shared in a non-defended or exaggerated manner.

The influx of ART technology on identity and internalized fear has yet to be studied. However, clinical treatment shows that ART has an impact. ART technology extends to sperm donor, egg donor, and *in-vitro* fertilization. Each has its own unique form of impact that appears in sessions.

A surprise to mainstream thinking is that children and adults have cellular memory that "remembers" conception events and adapts to these experiences. As a clinician, it is important to sense for ART influences. I have seen internalized freeze responses and panic at loss of siblings that only resolved once I considered ART influences.

In regards to sperm donor: I treated one client (see case study #10) who had an internalized freeze response that appeared to have no "origin." However, when I contemplated how the sperm energy is centrifuged and flash-frozen, I began to get results in treatment. This adult client was able to repair on a body level (once she realized the origins of her freeze) from an event that happened prior to conception!

In regards to *in-vitro* fertilization: I treated at separate sessions a 4 year-old and a 12 year-old child. Both had been conceived from *in-vitro* fertilization. It is common for *in-vitro* fertilization to have "multiples" and for some of them to be dissolved. The 4 year-old placed all the round hand balls in my room around her and snuggled into the cushions. The 12 year-old carried two hand balls at all times, and was in a panic when she could only find one of them! Both children helped me to realize that children cellularly "remember" their "vanished" siblings.

This 12 year-old's internalized terror expressed as a need to save the 2 siblings that had been eliminated. The 4 year-old returned to comfort and settling when all her siblings were still around her. For both, saying good bye with mother's support (Mom not feeling guilty), allowed each child to settle. Often Moms had to "say goodbye" as well for the experience to integrate!

Treatment of ART

The treatment goal is to digest the past. For these children, it helped to have a chance to "say goodbye" to their lost siblings and send them on with love. We did little goodbye rituals, with picture drawing and waving goodbye. For the adult client with sperm donor experience, it meant coming into gratitude for her initial life force from the donor, and appreciation of the life-long support of her actual "Dad" without regrets for how conception was managed.

Each person will be unique in their needs. It is important to support parents to release any residual stress from that experience, such as feelings of impotency, jealousy, or incompetence. Doing so clears the field so parents are able to support the child to have closure, using child friendly language. Doing so will free the nervous system and reduces internalized "anticipation" fear in children.

Personal sharing on Artificial Reproductive Techniques (ART)

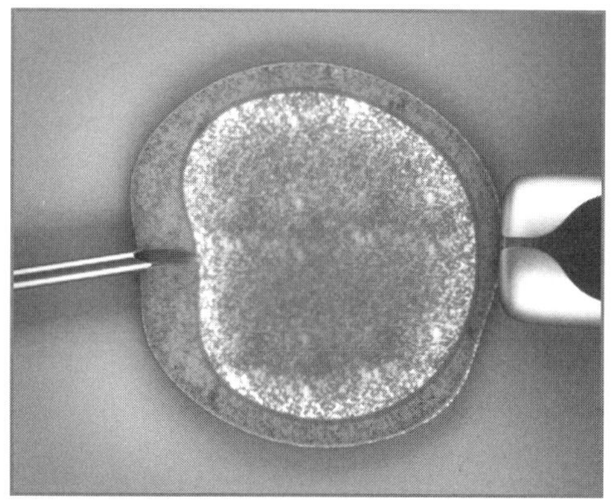

A colleague in the prenatal work has generously shared some writing on her experience of being conceived through artificial insemination as support to help clinicians and parents to better understand the complexity woven into this experience. While each person's experience is unique, it is important to realize that there is an experience and template set at this early time that can have impact on identity and sense of self. Integrating this experience can bring relief and a sense of personal freedom.

My conception journey by PQ

I first touched ground somewhere between the "turkey baster" (or whatever they used in a medical setting) and my father's shame. The way I see it, I was looking for the strongest presence to attach to, and the prevalence of shame was unmistakable.

I was conceived by artificial insemination because of my father's emotional and sexual insecurities. I was the contact between my parents, quite literally. My parents were not in the same room during my conception. I have a felt sense of the distance between them inside myself, a distance that was there long before my arrival. The relationship between my parents was both loving and confused. They both brought big wounds to the relationship and spent a lot of their eighteen years together living them out. My parents both idolized each other and didn't feel worthy of the other.

The absence of physical contact and sexual lovemaking in my conception has always been significant to me. I felt the impact of it most acutely as a teenager when I was trying to find my own way sexually and couldn't find intercourse anywhere on the map. Others have pointed out that not all conceptions are loving, and that's true enough, but ALL natural conceptions do involve physical contact between the parents, and mine was different. I also believe that the positive side of this space is a specific kind of differentiation from my parents, and the space to both see their choices and make my own.

Knowing my conception journey has normalized the ways I feel different in the world, and the many moments when my unique perspective is appreciated or challenged and often met with "wow, I never thought of that!" To the extent that I choose this journey, my choice to incarnate in this manner makes more and more sense to me with each passing year.

Implantation Themes

A well-nourished Mom can relax and support a new baby to come into existence. Implantation is one of the first milestones of pregnancy. It is also the first sense of tissue contact with one's mother. This theme is less existential than the previous themes. Implantation provides our "first touch," and after a long and arduous journey, one would want to feel welcomed with a nourishing and comfortable place to eat, rest, and relax.

However, the reality is that zygotes arrive and implant in all kinds of conditions. The will for life is strong; and addressing implantation conditions helps clients to deal with issues of basic need, ability to accept nourishment, and sense of safety. Some clients are reluctant to "take too much" because they felt their Mom's womb was exhausted from so many previous children. Other clients carried a sadness that did not belong to them but was based on the loss of their "siblings' in previous miscarriages.

Early Beliefs Based on Perception and Earlier Themes

Prenates arrive in the fluid-womb environment of mother's hormones. Implantation can be felt as welcoming and nourishing; however, this journey follows the earlier themes which may have layers of shock. The blastocyst is struggling to connect and receive nourishment; an implant or die imperative. "Am I welcome, is there enough for me, is it safe? Can I make it?" Relational beliefs and issues of mistrust can form during this phase when there are minimally adequate or dangerous womb conditions. Clients have felt omnipotently "at cause" for Mom's exhaustion, or carried core beliefs of being "bad, unworthy, at fault, or too needy" based on implantation conditions. Such beliefs interfere with secure attachment. Clients must be helped to differentiate their identity from their perceptions of the womb conditions, and supported to find comfort and nourishment in connection with others. The "self" at implantation is minimally developed and rarified but becoming more tangible; treatment requires listening for themes of connection, early need, and willingness to take in nourishment.

Tissue Tone and Educative Touch Can Begin the Healing of Implantation

Touch to the forehead can reveal the quality of a client's implantation; I often ask them to lean toward my open palm and observe if they are reluctant to allow connection. This dialog begins the process of working through limits to receiving nourishment. I suggest clients take in the energy of my palm, and their body settles when this occurs. For clients who "blamed their Mom" for being toxic and refuse to connect, I remind them that there is an embryological "tissue bubble" that grows around the implanted blastocycst. No matter what the condition of mom's womb, they can take in nourishment. Moms don't have to be perfect and clients can appreciate the gift of life and establish a safe enough implantation.

Implantation repair can be a resource; taking in through the forehead aligns with early suckling. Creating receptivity supports the social aspect of the Autonomic Nervous System, and brings parasympathetic ease and sympathetic seeking into balance. Success with implantation imprints allows one to relax and have needs in the company of others.

Help clients differentiate and repair identity beliefs

"I am not welcome"

becomes

"Mom just had too many children already!"

"I must struggle to get my needs met"

versus

"Even though Mom was tired, I made it fine and here I am!"

Energies of miscarriage and loss

"Those aren't really about me. I have a right to be here".

"My needs do not take away from others. It is OK to feel supported and nourished."

Repair connection issues for social health and enjoyment

Surveillance of others based on implantation shock and un-met needs creates discomfort in social settings. The above seeking and nuzzling exercise repairs "first touch" implantation wounds and supports the social aspect of the Autonomic Nervous System, bringing parasympathetic ease and sympathetic seeking into balance. Success occurs with implantation imprints when one learns to relax in the company of others. Repair of implantation establishes a safe enough social connection.

Dispel "Need Shock" (the fear of needing without being met; needs become "dangerous")

Implantation is the first level of tissue connection between the mother and arriving self. Womb tissue may contain mothers energetic beliefs about the world and relationship. Quality of womb tissue often underlies dysfunctional triggers about safety and survival. A person with implantation shock can feel resentful of others success or feel overly entitled to nourishment. They can project or recreate scarcity easily in life.

Self-deference, being outwardly focused on the needs of others, or a reluctance to have needs of any kind might be an implantation imprint. Clients may express "survivor's guilt" if mother had previous miscarriages, or be afraid to take hold of support from others when needed.

Release excessive care-taking and fear of success

The attaching blastocyst appears able to sense the energy of the womb, and can tell whether mother has enough energy for its needs. If mother is depleted, one might feel at risk and develop an unconscious care-taking strategy, "giving to get" rather than taking nourishment directly. This strategy is manipulative; however it was a forced manipulation due to the circumstances. Inability to take in nourishment or a reluctance to take what one deserves (one's fair share) can imprint at this time.

How a client or child interprets circumstances is key. Behavior will show this. Fear that there is not consistent nourishment can stem from an overworked mother with an exhausted womb due to many pregnancies. "The world is really unsafe. I better not rock the boat!" could explain a womb that contains grief or shock from earlier miscarriages or abortion. Awareness of prenate sensitivity to implantation can help clinicians support clients to eliminate underlying anxieties and re-establish a sense of trust and safety in the world. This is especially important if one implanted following an abortion.

Treatment of implantation "Need Shock"

Remind your client that miscarriage loss or a previous abortion was not specific to them. Remind them it is imperative to "need" for life to continue. Help them release their need to care-take, do without, be self-diminishing, or need to be grandiose in order to be noticed.

Releasing implantation shock can support a natural healing of abandonment or invasion issues. Need shock works at many developmental levels, from prenatal through early childhood. Unraveling shame, understanding early needs, and re-patterning healthy body responses is essential for well-being. Refer to *Birth's Hidden Legacy: Volume Two,* for more information on "Need Shock."

Discovery Themes

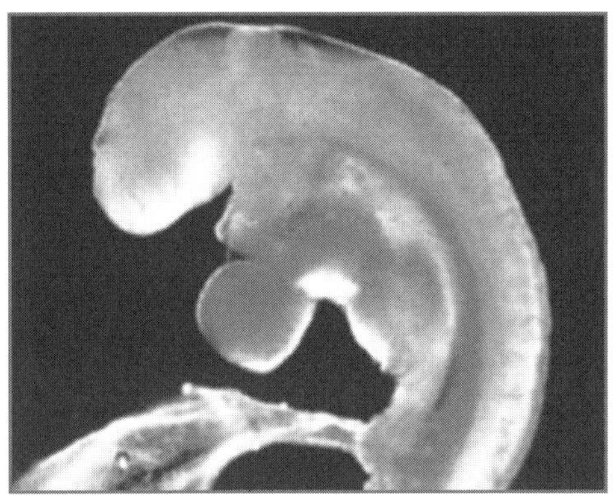

Embryo at 4 weeks

The heart is almost "outside" the body at 4 weeks and most vulnerable to the impressions of Mom's emotions and thoughts as she adapts to being pregnant.

A fertile woman expects her menses at approximately every cycle of the moon. She begins to suspect she is pregnant if menses is late. How mother responds at this time is felt deeply in the vulnerable heart of the 4-week old prenate. The embryo's heart is almost as large as its head at 4 weeks and is out in front of the body covered by a membrane. It has not yet rolled into the protective internal space of the prenate torso.

Such a vulnerable placement of the heart predisposes prenates to be shocked if mothers are surprised, ambivalent, or anxious upon discovering they are pregnant. Mothers can have a full range of feelings from excitement to despair. A vulnerable prenate interprets this personally and "takes it to heart."

Deeply rooted identity beliefs about self-worth are formulated in relation to discovery shock. Babies translate a mother's "oh no! I am pregnant!" to "there is something wrong with me. I must be bad in my very core since mother does not want me!" Help such beliefs to surface and remind clients that mother's feelings had nothing to do with their essential nature but were related to her concerns. She didn't yet "know" them as a person. Helps clients titrate the existential sadness out of the tissue of the heart area.

I have seen highly successful people struggle with low self-esteem because they had personalized mother's ambivalence or fear of pregnancy during the discovery time. Differentiating one's capacity from mothers feelings can heal this lack of self-love and sense of being never good enough, not wanted, and not welcomed.

Discovery themes and identity repair

- "I am not welcome" becomes "mother was not ready"
- "I did something wrong but I don't know what it is!" becomes "There was something wrong in the field. It was not about me."
- I am no good at my core" becomes "Mother's feelings were not about me. She didn't "know me" yet!"

Late discovery

Late discovery is a significant theme that produces issues of confusion and a sense of disconnection from the body. People repeatedly felt "unseen." Mother is not attuning to her own body accurately, nor to her developing fetus. Clients have reported 4 and even 6 month gaps before there were "known about," rather than the normal 4 weeks. One doctor kept insisting his patient was not pregnant and ordered her a colonic! This mother abandoned her biological sense of self, and a prenate will learn to do the same.

Late discovery can feel isolating and lonely. If mother thinks she is gaining weight rather than pregnant she may go on a diet. This can imprint a lack of nourishment, and lead to eating disorders and difficulty with food regulation. When a little one feels unseen, and not celebrated, she can feel unwanted and unwelcome. Clients report a chronic undernourished life. Lack of proper nutrition due to late recognition can create a premature birth. Double bind behaviors of "emanding to be seen or heard" can conflict with a sense of "I need to stay invisible." Secure attachment work is very helpful to repair late discovery beliefs.

A growing fetus can feel things. Help children or clients to make accurate meaning of events that occurred.

Discovery Differentiation of Sensation and Thoughts			
Mom (and Dads) feelings are theirs	Track the sensation of those feelings	Release any imprint in your tissue	Accept and forgive
They are not about you	They didn't know you yet	You are just arriving	Feel your own essence
You are just fine	Don't collapse	Regain potency	Feel your own worth

Starting to show

While mothers may have reasons to "conceal" it is hard on the prenate to not be welcomed and recognized when pregnancy is obvious. I have treated clients coming to terms with a sense of living on the periphery and hesitant to show up in this world due to late recognition of pregnancy. Trying not to show can create confusion for the fetus and a disconnect with Mom and her body.

Concealing pregnancy

Many people try to conceal their pregnancy due to judgment, how it will influence their career, or to avoid shame. This is common in celebrities, and unfortunately supports concealing pregnancy. Concealing robs women of the joy and enagement with a supportive sense of pregnancy.

Celebrities are pros at hiding their pregnancy to avoid the dreaded bump.

A popular social magazine speaks of the "baby bump watch" and highlights fashion that supports concealing.

"Pair a poncho with black skinny jeans to further camouflage the fact that you are expecting—make sure it is a shorter necklace—so not to draw attention to your belly!"

Most women show at 12 to 18 weeks. If a plus-size, you may not show until much further along. Some [very thin] women show much later and wear normal clothes throughout 2nd and sometimes even 3rd trimesters

(web research... google pregnancy showing)

Case Study Example

See Case Study #1 for toxic womb issues and impact on prenate. See Case Study #4 for Haunted womb theme and impact.

Ideally the womb environment is nourishing. Usually it is "good enough," and mothers must be counseled not to expect perfection. However, some womb conditions are highly toxic, others are "haunted" from energies of previous miscarriage or abortion. Addressing these imprints with children or clients can being relief. Chemicals have an impact, whether they are ingested chemicals, such as nicotine, drugs, or alcohol, or even stress chemicals due to excessive worry and adrenalin. Fear, stress, anger, and worry "hormones" are carried in through the umbilical blood supply. Stress corticoids register in the infants' immune system and can produce nameless anxiety or fear.

A toxic womb environment can be cleared. Help clients feel and digest the "felt-sense" of any chemical, while discharging the "felt-sense" of toxicity. If mother's used recreational or abusive substances during pregnancy, counsel them to accept the reality of this impact on their child without reverting to self-blame. Appropriate grieving, remorse, and acceptance is more supportive to her child than self-attack or guilt. Such guilt robs a mother of her necessary potency and diminishes her ability to parent.

Examples of Toxicity			
Nicotine	lowers O^2	increase heart rate	draws blood away from extremities
Drugs	influences baby's rhythm	interrupts nourishment	patterns fluid rhythms
Stress	high cortisol levels enter baby's blood	creates adrenal rush	results in nameless fear or stress response

Toxic Womb influences baby's sense of the world

A developing infant wants to feel safe. Toxicity is felt as invasive and life threatening; and there is no escape. Prenates can feel trapped, poisoned, and that Mom is not listening to their needs when mother ingests substances or allows too much stress. Fads of the time play a role; in the 1950s many women smoked. Doctors suggested a glass of wine to relax, ignorant of the onset risk of fetal alcohol syndrome or the sense of disconnection and confusion alcohol causes for the prenate. Doctors even prescribed diet pills. Such ignorance about chemical influences creates havoc on a developing prenate's nervous system and can result in premature delivery. I was born premature from the combination of nicotine and diet pills; however, I also learned to clear my system through this perinatal work, and doing so relieved chronic cold hands and feet, and a hyper arousal in my nervous system.

Common Substance That Create a Toxic Womb

Nicotine effect

- Both speeds up and then depresses the nervous system; a common cause of premature delivery
- Usable oxygen level in blood is lower; baby's heart beats faster to accommodate this condition
- Blood is partially shunted from limbs to make more oxygen available to the heart. This often underlies tendency for cold hands & feet later in life and glandular conditions prone to activate a startle response.

Alcohol

- Perceived as spinning under pressure
- Disorienting
- Reported to feel prickly to the skin
- Produces issues of loss of control
- Fetal Alcohol syndrome is a reality; it is irreparable due to absent or reduced brain folding.

Cocaine and other hard drugs

- Chemicals effect development. High risk factors
- Cocaine imprints create difficulty with transitions; interrupts child's ability to release agendas
- Hyper fragmentation of thought; can appear as incredible creativity/dissociation
- Inability to contain and go inward
- Hyperactive nervous system: obsessive focus, inability to switch train of thought.

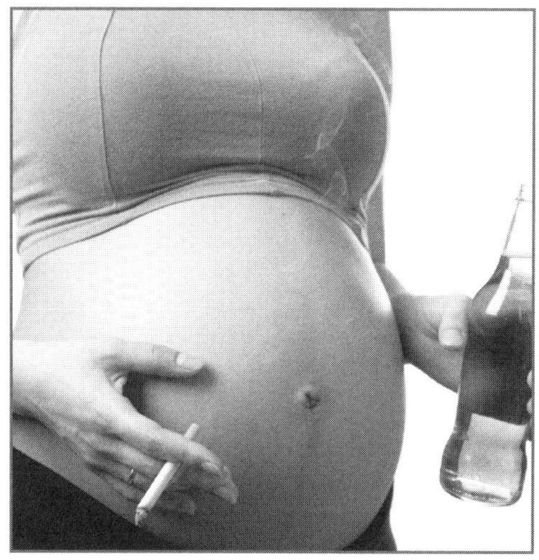

In addition to substances, mothers can be conflicted as to proper self-care and then add "self-attack" energy into the mix that the prenate perceives.

Emotional imprints that Contribute to Toxic or Haunted Womb Themes

- Adrenaline due to worry or fear
- Mother's anxiety produces corticoids
- Stress Corticoids enter baby's blood as an irritant
- Mothers stress makes it difficult for prenate to relax
- A baby unable to relax into mother's body has a greater difficulty to bond
- Baby cannot tell "who" is worried or the source of concern. Creates nameless fears and anxiety

Excess grief due to death of a relative or loved one

- Mother's grief depresses both her and her infant's immune system
- Baby feels grief and depression
- Grief makes it difficult to bond as Mom is distracted
- Helpful for Mom to exercise and boost oxygen levels in blood
- Helpful to name cause of grief out loud to baby in order to differentiate

Possible infant beliefs based on uterine events and conditions

Implantation Beliefs

- Womb tissue energy is low = "I better not need much!"
- Womb is too soft; many previous births = low chi or potency. "Mom needs my help!"
- Womb is hard and mother is too stressed or busy = "I won't take much from her!"
- Womb feels engulfing = "I will be swallowed up and cannot get my needs met!"

Previous birth/miscarriage/abortion imprints

Third trimester issues emotional & energetic imprints from mother's womb tissue

- Unprocessed grief: low immune function, less potency = "Am I too much?"
- Fear of abortion or miscarriage = "Am I scary to Mother?"
- Too many children already = "I am a burden to Mother!"

Messages from Mother that affect an infant self throughout pregnancy

- This baby will save my marriage = over-responsible, never capable or good enough infant
- A replacement baby = "never seen for who I am, cannot let you really get close because you won't like me!," or "there's something wrong with me!"
- If Mother substitutes infant love for un-met needs from spouse = too much pressure on infant for contact = inordinate fear of intimacy, or identifying intimacy with engulfment or loss of self.

We cannot change the past but we can better inhabit the future as emotions process, stories are told, and guilt is released. Accurate reflection, body pacing, and social connection with the therapist, and/or family is essential for brain rewiring and repair. It is especially important to assess and address ancestral cultrual or genocidal conditions that may have been carried forward.

Associated effects of heavy marijuana use during pregnancy *(http://aspe.hhs.gov/hsp/cyp/drugkids.htm)*

- low birthweight
- merconium staining and complications in delivery
- a shortened gestational period
- neonatal neurobiological abnormalities

Cocaine exposure

Ages 4-10: Prenatal cocaine exposure was associated with greater externalizing behavior. Several studies have found that hyperactivity and externalizing behaviors are increased among prenatally cocaine-exposed children... prenatally cocaine-exposed boys having more behavioral problems, particularly hyperactivity, than non-exposed boys... an effect of prenatal cocaine exposure was found for symptoms of oppositional defiant disorder.

(The Effects of Prenatal Cocaine Exposure on Problem Behavior in Children 4-10 years, by Minnes S, Singer LT, Kirchner HL, Short E, Lewis B, Satayathum S, Queh D., Case Western University, Neurotoxicol Teratol. 2010, Jul-Aug;32(4):443-51. Epub 2010 Mar 20.

Physiological emotional imprints

Studies have shown that consumption of illegal drugs during pregnancy can result in miscarriage, low birth weight, premature labor, placental abruption, fetal death, and even maternal death. (http://www.americanpregnancy.org/pregnancyhealth/illegaldrugs.html)

How does marijuana use affect pregnancy?

What happens when a pregnant woman smokes marijuana? Marijuana crosses the placenta to your baby. Marijuana, like cigarette smoke, contains toxins that keep your baby from getting the proper supply of oxygen that he or she needs to grow. (ibid)

How does secondhand smoke affect pregnancy?

(http://www.webmd.com/baby/smoking-during-pregnancy).

- Secondhand smoke ... is the combination of smoke from a burning cigarette [(passive environmental influence [sic] and smoke exhaled by a smoker.

- The smoke ... from ... the end of a cigarette... contains more harmful substances (tar, carbon monoxide, nicotine, and others) than smoke inhaled by the smoker.

- If you are regularly exposed to secondhand smoke, you increase your and your baby's risk of developing lung cancer, heart disease, emphysema, allergies, asthma, and other health problems.

- Babies exposed to secondhand smoke may also develop reduced lung capacity and are at higher risk for prematurity (this author's note) and sudden infant death syndrome (SIDS).

RDSP (regulation disorder sensory processing)

Substances tend to affect a baby's brain and ability to regulate. Infants and toddlers with (RDSP) may continue to have mild to intense difficulties in some areas of their sensory, motor and behavioral regulation throughout their childhood. *"Cocaine easily and rapidly crosses the placenta, and is not significantly metabolized during maternal-fetal transfer."* See *Understanding Regulation Disorders of Sensory Processing in Children*, by Pratibha Reebye and Aileen Stalker. Research does suggest that these children will have *"difficulty with self-regulation and impulse-control"* [Mead, Colleen. *The Effects of Substance Abuse on the Development of Children: Educational Implications (Askin, 2001*).

Brain rewiring *"The Neurobiology of "We" by Patty de Llosa, Parabola Newsletter, Nov 2011.*

The good news is that while our earliest interpersonal experiences may have created detrimental repetitive patterns, new patterns are formed all through our life span. We can liberate ourselves from those old patterns through new neural connections... The regulation of energy and information flow is a function of mind as an emergent process emanating from both relationships and brain. Relationships are the way we share this flow. In this view, the emergent process we are calling "mind" is located in the body (nervous system) and in our relationships...

The study of neuroplasticity is changing the way scientists think about the mind/brain connection. While they've known for years that the brain is the physical substrate for the mind, the central mystery of neuro-science is how the mind influences the physical structure of the brain...

Interpersonal relationships that are attuned promote the growth of integrative fibers in the brain. It is these regulatory fibers that enable the embodied brain to function well and for the mind to have a deep sense of coherence and well-being. Such a state also creates the possibility of a sense of being connected to a larger world. The natural outcome of integration is compassion, kindness, and resilience.

...Siegel believes interpersonal relationships are key to new forms of mental flow that shape the focus of our attention and what we envision. Since the mental processes of attention and imagination change the firing in the brain, the brain can be changed by the mind.

Support mothers and fathers skillful parenting by addressing the past and dealing with reality

I continue to remind parents that "you did the best you could at the time," or "you just didn't know," or "you were just unconscious at that time in your life." Otherwise the guilt, blame, shame, or regret interferes with the forces for healing. Helping the true story be told relieves both the child and parents. With children, I use stuffed animals who "speak" the story in child-friendly language that clears confusion and helps both parents and children to relax and connect around difficult events from the past.

Toxic womb is not just "mother-dependent," but also influenced by the surrounding environment. If Father smoked, was abusive, overly worried or "toxic" to Mom, he would contribute directly to "toxic womb" by his impact on Mom's adrenals via her anxiety or worry. If Mom refused to follow good prenatal care guidelines, Dad's worry could activate and influence the field. Telling the accurate story of prenatal time doesn't condone behavior, but relieves guilt and relieves the residual shock imprint. When Mom can apologize without guilt, her child realizes Mom was afraid and did the best she could. Realizing Dad was worried and expressed it through his behavior brings relief for Dad's too, and can help parents rebond if they have been holding on to that stress.

Approach Toxic Womb with curiosity rather than guilt. That is the most helpful thing parents can do for themselves and their children. Coach parents to express regrets that arise so they don't have to be "superhuman." This will help them release held emotions and be supportive for any triggering material for their child.

Umbilical cord abnormalities are numerous, ranging from false knots, which have no clinical significance, to vasa previa, which often leads to fetal death. As prenatal ultrasound becomes increasingly sophisticated, many of these conditions are being diagnosed *in utero*. However, many are not apparent before delivery, and the only forewarning is related to their association with certain conditions such as monochorionic twins and placental abruption.
(Medscape: online article)

The navel cord is an infant's gateway to the surrounding fluid environment. Natural hormones as well as toxic chemicals enter through the blood of the umbilicus. It appears that infants will create a tissue tension and bracing in the cells at the navel in order to keep out harmful substances. I have seen pictures of infants squeezing the umbilical cord, and in one instance it appears the infant tied their cord into a knot and subsequently died. The mystery of transmission of conditions and later beliefs surrounding the umbilicus is important to explore.

Sensitive bellies

Foreign chemicals and stress are not digestible by the prenate. Prenates respond to chemicals by bracing in the muscles and organs at the umbilicus; this protective impulse at the navel has repercussions. Full flexion (the ability to fold inward in order to digest information and rest internally) can be compromised. Think of the umbilical area as the first organ of perception. Help clients soften and release tissue around the navel. Clients report that belly tension they had endured for a lifetime dissolved when umbilical affect issues were explored and resolved.

Case Study Example

See Case Study #4 for an infant with severe cord wrap. Note that cord wrap can also occur around the ankle, and impact the connection to the hips and ground.

Helping parents to grieve a prenatal death Umbilical difficulties can lead to death. Help parents take time to grieve, and to process the overwhelm and confusion of prenatal death. One grieving mother adopted a foal and raised it; creating a channel for her heart as she cared for this young one. Grief takes its own time, and heartfelt listening goes a long way. Offering a form of existential support for the larger mystery of the cycles of birth and death can be useful, such as encouraging clients to create their own rituals and ways to grieve. Support from other traditions can be utilized. Buddhist perspective of the karmic wheel of birth and rebirth views prenatal death as a completion of a turning of the wheel, however brief. Perhaps the soul of the prenate only needed to feel wanted, or to reconnect to the mother for just a moment before completing its karma. Mothers have reported sensing this deeper knowing as well. Especially important is to help mothers and parents to forgive themselves and surrender to the mystery of birth and death in order to return to an integrated sanity due to umbilical affect and prenatal death.

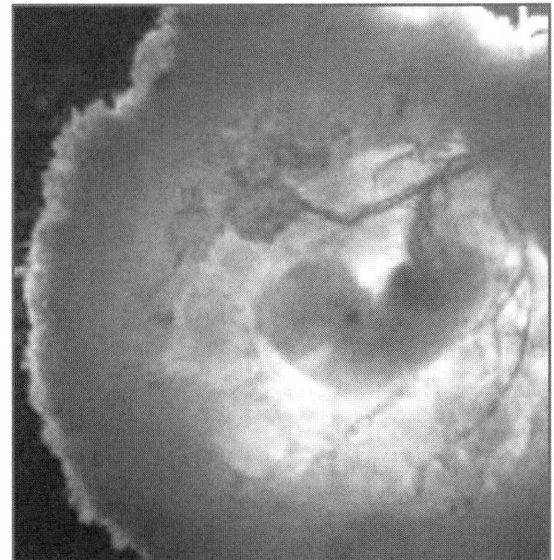

The baby receives information through the Umbilical fluid

- Excessive worry, fear, or rage from the parents
- Fear, Anger, and Worry create stress hormones
- Relaxation is important for pregnant parents
- Previous pregnancy losses must be grieved in order to detox the womb environment

Toxicity due to prenatal chemicals

All Chemicals are carried through the blood

- Nicotine, excessive coffee consumption
- Alcohol
- Drugs of any kind
- Diet pills

Toxicity due to birth chemicals or procedures

Imprints of invasion and annihilation

- Anesthesia imprints of any kind
- birth induction drugs, such as pitosin

Moms: Unnatural beliefs and restlessness

"My movement endangers baby, let's be passive together."

Invasive monitoring by nurses, invasion by chemicals prescribed during bed rest.

Baby's identity beliefs

"My movement is dangerous, I am too much, I need to be still to survive, I must be vigilant."

Prescribed Bed Rest

Everyone wants a full-term baby; they are the most healthy and resourced, and bed rest is the common prescription when there is fear of early miscarriage or premature labor. Babies born prior to 7 months are at high risk due to under-developed lungs. Working through the residual emotions of a necessary bed rest is helpful both for mother and baby.

Knowing the consequences on relationship and sense of self supports treatment. Mothers can become restless and frustrated due to forced inactivity. Prenates can misinterpret the forced stillness to mean that their basic liveliness was dangerous to mother. They interpret their natural vitality as unsafe.

Mothers can become hypervigilant and worried that any motion they make somehow hurts their baby. Yet movement is important for prenates. Babies locate themselves through movement and develop spatial orienting abilities. The Vestibular cranial nerve is the first to gain its fatty coating, which is called "myelination." This means the Vestibular nerve is necessary early in development, and that movement is baby's first language. Prenates orient to mother's moving body, and movement is both a dialog and rhythm of exchange between Mom and baby. Movement increases brain development and is essential for survival.

Treating Bed Rest Adults clients recalling bed rest memories say they were startled and disoriented. They made up the belief that they were "too much" for Mom, and learned to sit still rather than take action. When treating a child, review memories of bed rest with mother. Help her release any unprocessed emotions, vigilance, or worrisome attachment patterns from that time. Doing so eases the distress of the child in treatment. Bed rest can set up a care-taking quality between mother and child that is not healthy; Moms are often overly attentive because they became programmed to worry about their child during the bed rest times.

Some clients with prenatal bed rest imprints are hyper-active or court the extremes through sports and daring activities. They are proving to themselves that they can keep moving; and their movement is flooded with the adrenalin echo that the mother carried as she worried about her baby's health in the womb. Other clients are overly passive. Activity is a defense against forced stillness and passivity is deemed necessary to maintain the relationship with mother; so people can be too passive in relationship simply because that was the relational rhythm established early on for safety. Clients with bed rest imprints can vacillate in an unusual manner between activity and rest; they remain still when it would serve them best to take action, and then are afraid to slow down to rest as it brings back the encoded fears awakened in Mom during that time. Treating bed rest themes helps a child or client come back into relationship with their own natural impulse and rhythms.

Physical implications of bed rest

The sensory-motor loop is a natural nervous system information exchange. It helps Mom and baby to orient to each other as each responds to the other's movement dialog. (see Sensory-Motor Loop in Body Resources section, Volume Two of *Birth's Hidden Legacy.*) Inhibition of natural movement impulses during bed rest can lead to vigilance and a freeze response whenever energy or excitement arise. Healthy rest can be interpreted as forced immobility and avoided by clients afraid they might spiral into a hopeless sense of despair. Clients with bed rest imprint may be overly vigilant to their partners movements in intimate relationship and exhaustively monitor their activity and rest.

Drugs are often prescribed to prevent premature contractions. Chemicals are toxic, mothers describe the procedures to administer them as invasive, and that they feel they must surrender to the chemicals, yet often resist them. A five-year-old client's response to chemicals and bed rest appeared as hyperactive and overly vigilant behavior, both in self play and cooperative play. He felt there were attackers interrupting his sleep and he needed to defend himself. He created games of alien invasions, and insisted we create "land mines" to blow up the "aliens," which he delighted in activating during sessions.

Over time, we were able to identify these "aliens" as the chemicals that were uncomfortable yet perhaps necessary for his survival. Mother reassured him that she made the choice for chemicals in order to protect him from being born too early. He described the sensation of his memory of these chemicals as "prickly and dangerous!" With her awareness and normalizing of his distress origins, his vigilance settled.

"A veritable obsession with prematurity has led many doctors to advocate an aggressive preventive attitude. In many countries, bed rest is commonly prescribed to guard against premature labor, yet not one study has been able to demonstrate that bed rest has any such effect. We therefore remain quite sceptical about the effectiveness of such a prescription. This policy against bed rest is also motivated by our worry that prolonged immobilization may lead to fetal sensory deprivation by limiting input to the vestibular organ—the inner part of the ear—which processes information on the body's position and eventually ensures proper balance. In addition, the vestibular organ possibly affects the fetus's orientation in utero, and deficiencies in its function might result in breech or shoulder presentations. From our point of view, the common prescription of bed rest can only be viewed as yet another example of the intrusion of obstetrics into the birth process: women are told to lie down not just during labor, but for the whole pregnancy as well."

"Along the same lines, we also question the practice of prescribing drugs that inhibit uterine contractions to prevent premature birth. First, these drugs—which women may take for days, weeks, even months—have intense, adverse side effects such as palpitations, dizziness, and overall malaise."

— Birth Reborn, Dr. Michel Odent

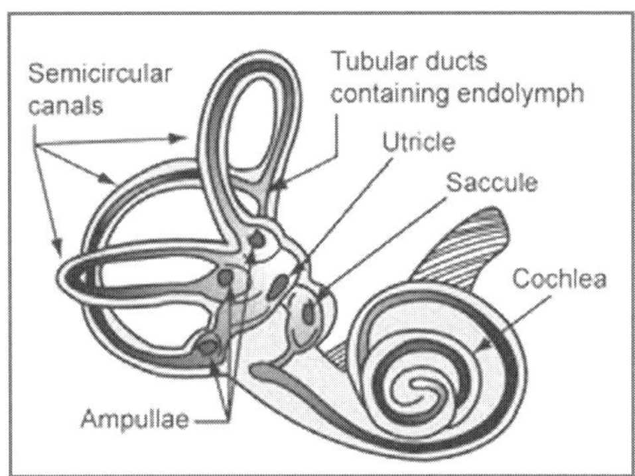

Impact of Bed Rest on Spatial Orientation

Function of vestibular nerve

This nerve controls balance and eye movement. It helps to integrate the faculties of vision with balance, and stabilizes eye movement with head movement. The Utrical of the inner ear controls linear acceleration, and the Ampula of the inner ear senses gravity. These are necessary vestibular perceptions for orienting.

The vestibular system serves as the gyroscope of the inner ear

Movement supports the baby's spatial orientation, ability to readjust when off balance, and to appreciate surprise with a sense of confidence and delight. The first nerve to myelinate is the vestibular, and movement during pregnancy is essential for early development. Bed rest is a forced "freeze" for the mother, and she often worries when she moves due to fear of miscarriage. This freeze impulse can be adapted by the prenate to be vigilant rather than relaxed during movement. Vigilance reduces accurate brain connection with the cerebellum and movement can be stilted. A child who devlops a freeze response relating to the inner ear will be more emotionally guarded and less resilient in adjusting to changes in the environment.

Repair of bed rest imprints

Scan for an awkward pacing between movement and stillness. Look for contrasts in energy during interactions, such as high arousal followed by flat affect or passivity. Notice if energy is allowed to increase and flow naturally or appears interrupted and awkward.

Help the client or child access internalized messages relating to potency or vitality. Find the body response coupled to their belief and work with them to repair both inhibition and fear of movement. Use Primitive Reflexes to repair nervous system imprints of held stillness (see Body Resources chapter Volume Two, or *From Conception to Crawling*, by this author). Primitive reflexes interrupt passivity and re-establish spontaneity as natural movement pathways are reclaimed. Teach clients and parents how to apply reflex practices at home. Remembering that movement is "safe" and reclaiming the pleasure found in vitality challenges the lingering belief that one is "too much" for others. Releasing bed rest imprints returns a healthy sympathetic-parasympathetic balance to the autonomic nervous system and brings pleasure and ease to movement and transitions.

Third Trimester Issues

By 3rd trimester, babies are fully formed, and simply growing. This means they have more free attention, and are susceptible to absorb energetic transmissions of womb tissue. These include: previous miscarriages, stillbirths, abortions, plus ancestral events of the parents, grandparents, and great grandparents. Third Trimester babies encode a minimum of 3-generations of ancestral wishes, fears, and imaginations. This includes societal imprints during that time if there is large overwhelm in a culture such as starvation or genocide.

Baby's physical space becomes limited as she grows; less physical movement allows for more "mental" movement. This supports creative imagination. In psychology, the development of early imagination is known as the "Imago" time. As the internal visual center and mind move, creative imagination, dreaming, and fantasy awaken. However, mental imagery can contain demons if the events surrounding the womb-time were life-threatening.

Why prenates pick up 3-generations of information

- A developing female fetus develops germ cells *in utero*
- These are dormant but aware cells that become eggs; they are the future fetus of their mother, who is a prenate inside her mother.
- These cells experience three generations because the ovaries within the prenate contain the eggs of the next generation.
- The existing "mother" becomes the "grandmother" of the dormant eggs.

Ancestral Influences can evoke nameless fears, phobias, and uncommon behaviors

Infants are innately loyal to bloodlines and pick up influences of previous generations as ancestral themes. Family constellation theorists think babies do so in a loving attempt to heal their parents' past. (personal commentary, Burt Hellinger). Past murders, genocides, aggressions, acts of wrong doing, abuse, and high drama set templates for confusion and angst in the infant's nervous system. These become ancestral patterns carried forward from one generation to the next unless released through naming and processing.

It is impossible to process energies of the past that are not based in personal experience. Help clients to find the support or special facilitation to become freed of the burden of nameless worry, grief, or angst carried forward from earlier generations.

Ancestral themes

- Family secrets: shame, aggression, sexual abuse, suicides
- Health Themes: mental illness, health issues, depression, rage
- Cultural themes: genocide, war, deprivation

Case Study Example

See Case Study #4 where the child was born the day after 9/11 and the Twin Towers fatalities in NYC. This study also addresses impacts and treatment following an abortion.

Cultural Imprints

These are also picked up in third trimester, and include issues such as cultural genocide, devastation and war, and any "field" that was overwhelming or produced fear in a community.

Treatment of ancestral influences

Help clients identify how ancestor influences impact their current life. Examine how their relatives' needs for protection and secrecy do not need to be carried forward. Don't forget the ancestors, or minimize their reality; but choose life. Help clients release any burden they cannot process; pay attention to current conditions, but don't escalate or lace them with exaggerated fear. Empathize, and differentiate the influences and beliefs made by ancestors in response to horrific circumstances.

- Infants carry energies forward in an attempt to heal the family lineage
- When awareness is brought to emotions and they do not release or resolve, they are most likely not related to experienced events, but to an energetic ancestral imprint
- Name the stories and differentiate. Take energy back to the past and leave it there
- Track sensations, release emotions, find the body midline, orient toward health
- Carrying things forward does not save Mom or Dad
- Create healthy boundaries, release overwhelming horror, terror, rage, or grief

4 steps to ancestral health

- Name the prior conditions
- Imagine emotional/identity impacts: loyalty, despair, needing to rescue or safe, survivors guilt
- Differentiate self from environment
- Reclaim vitality and choice for this life

Abortions

- Prenates wonders if you will terminate them?
- Prenates may remain overly still in utero; create no waves to get into trouble.
- Reassure prenate that you are ready now to be a parent.

Please don't blame yourself for earlier circumstances. To clean out the echo of an earlier abortion simply tell your prenate that you are so happy and ready to be a parent now. In treating children in session, demystifying that earlier echo is very helpful. Mother let her 4 year-old know that his sibling did not stay because it was an unhappy time and mother wasn't ready. We used child friendly language and a stuffed animal to represent "baby despair." Telling this story made a profound impact on the child; he finally relaxed into his mother's body with a deep sigh of relief. He had somehow "sensed" this story, even though mother had never told him. When she grieved her own loss and explained it to him in a manner he could understand, he could relax.

Miscarriages

- Grief and death remain a felt-sense within womb tissue
- Processing grief prior to next pregnancy is ideal
- Reassure prenate that they have a right to live even if others have died
- Support children to say goodbye to unborn siblings and release survivor guilt
- Orient prenates or children to enjoy their potency and power

Previous Baby Was Given Up For Adoption

- This is felt in the field of the prenate through cellular imprints
- Explain out loud to your prenate or child (using child friendly language) the previous adoption situation and why it happened without guilt or defensiveness
- Release any guilt from the past choices
- Reassure prenate that they are not responsible for the other siblings journey or death
- Let baby know that you will keep them with you

Prenates "sense" the energy of earlier womb experience. Telling children these stories in a child friendly way brings health to their nervous system; naming events relieves them of survival fear and re-establishes parental trust.

Previous Stillbirths

- Babies met as eggs in the ovary "nursery time" and can feel the loss of siblings
- Process previous grief and fear of such loss
- Differentiate mother's fear from baby's capacity for life
- Release fear of stillbirth so it does not cloud current experience
- Reassure baby that they are not responsible for the earlier lost sibling

Baby Replacement Themes and Mistaken Gender Issues

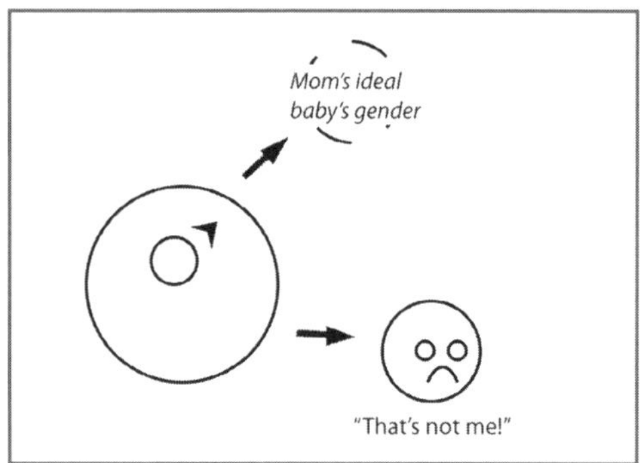

Replacement Baby

Compensated Behavior Beliefs

Confused Thinking
Heightened mistrust of others!

Having a baby to fulfill a parent's need creates confusion and places a burden on an unborn child. Both conscious and unconscious parental wishes are felt energetically and cause prenates to feel inadequate. Since they are not "the wish," but their own self and identity, there are never good enough. Prenate's want to be welcomed for who they are, rather than as the object to fulfil their parent's dreams. Such unconscious parental thoughts cause a prenate to mistrust their basic self; they feel they are not good enough, that they are a disappointment to their parents, and that their true nature must be hidden away.

"Mistaken Gender" issues

The baby is not mistaken about its gender. However, parents who strongly wish for the opposite gender set up a hopeless double bind for their prenate. Gender wishes are conveyed energetically, even if unspoken. If Mother delights in the idea of having a girl, yet the prenate knows he is a boy, he cannot please her. If Father wants a boy while the prenate knows she is a girl, she can never be enough for Dad. Such prenates learn to put up an emotional wall so as to hide their true nature, yet resent the fact of not being welcomed for who they are.

An arriving infant can feel the father or mother's disappointment at birth. Even if the parents are accepting, a doctor's remarks of, "Uh, oh, its' another girl!" can dismay the sensitive new infant who wants to be loved as they are. Mistaken gender issues are fraught with despair, defiance, self-doubt, and hopelessness. People feel the need to prove themselves all the time. They are afraid to let anyone really get to know them because they believe they are irrevocably flawed due to these imprints.

Gender and identity: an assumed flaw of self			
I will hide	I can't let them discover me	no one can get close I will build a wall	no one can really know who I really am
I will fight	I will prove I am good enough	I will fight for my rights	I will fight to be someone different than who I am
I will be confused	I will feel split	I will be non-committal	I will pretend to be different than who I am

Basic belief with 'mistaken gender'

These are internalized thoughts I have heard clients identify when working with "Mistaken Gender." "There is something wrong with me! It is something I cannot change. It is my basic core self. My parents do not want this. They do not want me! I have an inherent flaw that I must keep hidden for the rest of my life. I must work forever to keep proving I am good enough!"

Such thought patterns can be exhausting. Such thoughts of self-identity produce despair, rage, hopelessness, and secrecy. Help a person differentiate between the parent's wishes and the reality that a baby can not be "wrong" in this case. Support clients to take center stage and become visible as they are.

Replacement Baby

Infants and children sense when they have been given an impossible task by their parents. This can start prenatally with the parents wishes for their unborn child. Parents who conceive and raise a child as a replacement for a lost relative or their lost dreams are not seeing their child's true nature. The infant is going to be "just like uncle Fred," or the "little ballerina" Mom never was, or replace a child who died, or be the savior for a faltering marriage. The prenate or child senses these thoughts and interprets this pressure to mean that he is not "just right" as his natural self.

Parents who wish for a person whom the prenate can never become cause a prenate to feel they are never good enough. The prenate starts early on with adaptive behaviors; he or she learns to hide, devalue, or constantly feel the need to prove themselves in order to feel loved. They can feel underneath all this effort the hopelessness of every being good enough.

Here is how this dynamic is created:

"Mother or father sees me as 'the special ___________' (athlete, uncle Fred, ballerina, the one to save the marriage, their boy, or girl). I am not that person, yet that is what mother or father wants. I will pretend to be that person (which I know is impossible). I will hide my real self behind a wall so no one will know. Yet I know, and I am hopeless to change this!"

Often there is deep shame involved as well. "I will not let people get close, and I will stay in control. If someone tries to do something nice for me, I will sabotage it! Obviously they are not really doing it for me, but only who they think I am. Since I must hide my real self, this is a hopeless situation. I want to be known and am terrified of being known at the same time."

Prenatal Compensations

Mom's or Dad's energetic focus is on "imagined baby," not their actual baby. They are already mis-attuning during the pregnancy. Prenates begin a pattern of beliefs and compensate their natural impulses of behavior.

- Oh, she wants that!
- I better be that!
- I can't!
- I better not let others know the real me
- They will reject me if they do!
- At this developmental stage rejection is seen as life-threatening!

Case Study Example

See Case Study #6, where the doctor's comment at birth had a significant impact on self-esteem.

Resolution of these themes

Identifying the resistance to be known, as well as the hopelessness of being good enough is key. Also making sure clients process any residual anger at the injustice of "not being seen" is essential. Moving this through the bodymind, naming the double bind created by gestating in this field and returning to potency produces the best results. The goal is always to digest and assimilate what happened and move on to a thriving and productive life.

Identifying and releasing such pre-cognitive beliefs frees the path for forgiveness, release of resentment, and return to vitality. As always, parents beliefs and rejections were not about their actual baby, but related to the parents own thinking. Encourage clients to explore who they "really are;" what impulses they would have if they were not managing themselves at this core level.

Also encourage parents to admit and dismantle this tendency by communicating to their child. "oh, your uncle had died and I was so missing him, I was hoping you could be just like him. But you don't have to do that, I love you for who you are!

Summary of Prenatal Themes

This concludes the chapter on prenatal influences on behavior. As always, observe behavior and treat what you are seeing rather than assume someone has prenatal issues. However, do explore these themes and learn to notice them if they arise. Knowing Prenatal themes brings a refined attunement and ability to provide accurate reflective function as a therapist or parent. Listening to these "hidden stories" and providing the attachment and bonding repair is what changes the nervous system habits that orient to threat, fear, vengeance, or need for protection. Repairing this earliest and almost existential sense of self can repair compensated protective behaviors that seem out of context, as well as establish healthy esteem and identity for children or clients at the very core level.

Chapter 3

Birth Themes:

Influences Encoded on the Nervous System Related to the Transition of Birth

Imagining birth from the infants perspective can help repair shock and align parents with their infant for more success with early attachment. This chapter addresses common impacts from circumstances of birth.

Chapter Overview

Birth is a miracle and a mystery, and every living person survives it. This chapter is included not to create distress but to relieve impressions of the nervous system based on the physicality of birth and how infants make meaning of this experience.

Birth is an intense physical stress and a ritual of intense physical initiation. The Buddhist Sutras refer to birth as *"the crashing of mountains."* (personal communication from Buddhist monk Gin Hzi). The pressure of birth provides the necessary sensory component to help a baby feel and know its' own body. Pressure records in the proprioceptive sensory nerves and allows one to adjust to sensations. Birth rotation under such pressure helps one organize perceptions into time, space, and orienting ability based on directions of right, left, up, down etc. The pressure of birth prepares a baby to move from a watery environment to a gravity-based world. Awareness of sensation is key to establishing a sense of self.

A newborn needs to pay attention in order to gain the benefits and resilience that a birth provides. Drugs, back placement, and birth interventions all interfere with sensation feedback from the pressure of birth. Baby's attention is drawn away from the task at hand, which is to rotate through and out of the birth canal. A mother placed on her back during birth cannot help her infant rotate when her pelvic joints are immobilized. This lack of mobility in Mom's pelvis causes baby to be stuck in the birth canal and leads to more medical interventions, including pain medications.

The most supportive birth is a cooperative experience between mother and baby in meeting pressure and succeeding. Mother is awake, baby is awake, and together they find the interactive movement responses to birth. Birth supports an inner dynamic of trust when infant and mother can meet the initiation of birth together; this trust and love is further supported in post-birth bonding by the birth hormone Oxytocin. It appears that this supportive hormone is masked by pain or induction chemicals administered during labor.

Treatment Goals The goal is to understand the impressions that influence behavior on both a body and an emotional level. Exploring the following themes and gaining understanding of their impact can bring relief and changes to protective or struggling behaviors. Issues of timing completion, struggles at transition, willingness to take risks and be visible, and to follow through and find completion have an echo in how one organized the impressions of their birth. Unfinished attachment dynamics that began following a difficult birth often set up an ongoing difficult relational dynamic and must be processed to return to ease.

Birth Themes

Issues of invasion and disempowerment	Forceps, Vacuum Suction, breaking of the waters, induction drugs, anesthesia. Need of the midwife or physician to enter the uterus to push the baby back in for re-positioning.
Issues of abandonment	Anesthesia, ether, Demerol, epidurals, laughing gas or Twilight Sleep. Mother's attention being distracted by the doctor or hospital staff.
Issues of potency loss Related to cord wrap or anesthesia or C-section	The umbilical cord is wrapped around the baby's neck or foot at birth and compromises forward movement. The baby loses movement ability due to anesthesia.
Issues of loss of support	Early amniotic fluid loss and skin sensitivity due to a "dry" birth, primary loss of support for mother during delivery, secondary loss of support for father during delivery, loss of contact between mother and father, and loss of attention on infant sensibility during delivery.
Non-vaginal birth	Operations (Caesarean-section births).
Influence of birth position	Breech births, transverse position, anterior presentation or "sunny side up."
Birth of twins or multiples	Issues of worry or stress related to multiple births. First baby set aside for second birth.
Sensory Overwhelm	Invasive lights, bulb suction, cord cut, and auditory startle

Case Study Examples

See Case Study #2 and #3 for treatment to support sensory repair.

See Case Study #5 for sensory overwhelm related to auditory startle; a nurse dropped a metal tray just as the infant was lifted away from Mom during a necessary C-section. Subsequent challenges and control issues appeared in response to auditory startle that freezes the brain stem and affects auditory processing .

Birth is a great initiation and rite of passage. Strengths are developed that become a resource for the personality and for life tasks. However, difficult births encode into associative memory in the nervous system and can produce primitive survival response under stress. The nervous system reverts to earliest adaptations, including collapse, fight, withdraw, or escape. One can over-identify with the birth template and appear pushy, passive, withdrawn, excessively controlling, develop obsessive behaviors, or be resistant to taking action.

Such behavior is unconscious, linked to survival needs, and wreaks havoc on intimate relationships. Arousal and primitive association memory hijacks the nervous system by producing reactivity. This escalation or escape prevents one from releasing birth imprints.. Behavior options are limited and less nourishing for self and others. Perinatal session methods can help a person unravel reactive behavior and find balance in life.

Process a birth experience so it integrates and the nervous system settles; processing even many years later still brings effective behavior change

It is often easy to mis-attune to an infant post-birth. Remember that an infant's experience of birth can be very different from the adults perspective. Physicians and parents might be busy celebrating the successful arrival while the infant is still traumatized or drugged from the experience. This misattunement can set up a conflictual dynamic from the beginning. This is especially true if the umbilical cord was highly compromised, or forceps, vacuum suction, or medications were used. Activation and accompanying dissociation is especially prevalent during C-sections. Parents can unconsciously set up a conflictual dynamic with their child simply by not attuning to the possibility that their infant was stressed and had birth trauma. The good news is that this "trauma" and conflictual dynamic will release with the accurate naming and processing of birth events through perinatal and educative touch sessions.

In difficult births, Mom's adrenals will flood the baby with stress hormones. An extremely long labor where mother was hungry and baby was stuck in the birth canal might feel like near-death to the infant. Many clients expressed a sense of dying at birth due to "umbilical cord wrap" where every contraction diminished their sense of oxygenated blood supply. Whatever the context, any experience that overwhelms one's nervous system will imprint as a life-threatening stress coupled to survival. Take the time to process this early event and bring relief to the nervous system sense of life and safety and support. Parents who are seen as "never good enough" by their offspring can suddenly have a child restore affection and trust. It is heartwarming to witness this repair of bonding during clinical sessions.

Behavior triggers

Triggers are physical/emotional behaviors based upon associative memory responses to present time events. These responses are not in correct context to the situation, and amplified due to the associative previous fear of life-death threat. Identifying triggers is key to finding the underlying cellular imprint.

An example of a trigger is an activation related to a sense of near-death at birth. People with this imprint may meet life with unnecessary aggression that is directed at others or at self (through criticism, overwork, or self-punishing behavior). Aggression is a force of fight that supports surviving threat, whether real or imagined. Infants, children, and adults often display early survival stubbornness that helped them survive a difficult birth. This stubbornness is retained and surfaces under duress, creating power struggles in current life decision making and relationships.

Keys for healing birth imprints

The key for healing is to become curious about what lies beneath will and stubbornness. A therapist must coax clients to explore this as no one willingly suspends a survival response when stressed. The body just does not want to do so. Yielding appears life-threatening!

Yet unless one suspends the fight/flight response, they will not access the parasympathetic depression that lies beneath the fight-flight-freeze. A lost part of self remains trapped in this pre-cognitive brain state experience. Slowing down in order to get to the "bottom of the parasympathetic" allows clients to realize they survived. The fear dissipates and the "great void" or "emptiness" recedes. They are then reunited with an aspect of self left behind at that impressionable time, and become fully integrated, and thus able to meet life. Therapists must be highly trained to support clients at this level because the depression is so pre-cognitive and overwhelming to the body. Most clients either take medication or have cyclic bouts of depressive occurrences (the BodyMind Somanautics advanced training teaches therapists to develop this skill set of working with depression).

Bringing past fears to the surface allows them to discharge through the body tissue. This cellular release of fear opens a more keen awareness of sensation and helps clients distinguish natural potency from will-based energy at a tissue level. People discover and reclaim awareness of internal power and the sympathetic and parasympathetic systems re-balance. There is deep relief in the neurocellular consciousness when one recognizes that they have survived. Defensive strategies are minimized and one can access the relaxation needed to engage in social contact with inner ease.

These next pages highlight specific birth themes and their implications on behavior response and possible identity formation.

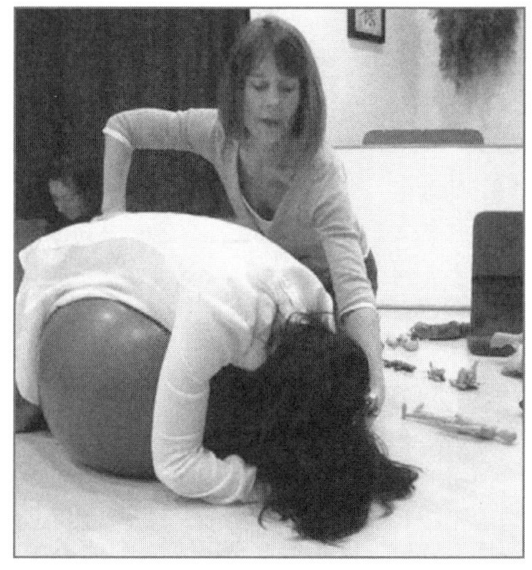

*The BodyMind Somanautics advanced training teaches therapists to develop this skill set of working with depression.

Nervous system response to near-death		
Parasympathetic Stress		
immobility	die	death brings relief
Sympathetic Stress		
mobility	fight or flight	fight brings survival
Social response in mammals		
seek help	interact	contact + protection

Case Study Example

See Case Study #9 that explores death of a twin at birth, and how mother's meeting of death at birth impacted the surviving twin's sense of shame and identity.

Near-death imprints occur prenatally, (as in toxic intrauterine conditions or abortion ideation); during birth, (as in umbilical cord wrap, forceps, or complex interventions); or through post-birth experience, (as in a sense of abandonment due to adoption, NICU care, or interruption of contact with Mother).

Infants who come close to death have a distinct pattern in the nervous system. Parents who don't realize this can be confused as to why their child has nameless fears, or is bossy, bullying, withdrawn, or controlling. Aware parents or clinicians can help others release near-death imprints that have formed a template that affects day-to-day behaviors; support children and clients to release these stories. Couples struggles are based on such imprints; including abandonment fears, depression, and deep mistrust at the core. Clearing imprints will support couples to engage more fully and find safety within relationship.

Shock patterns can imprint as life or death threat

The body's last attempt at survival is primitive. From conception to 18 months is the time where the nervous system lays down its first response behaviors. A perinatal near-death experience produces dissociative shock; and a person may have bonded with dissociation as an aspect of self. It is important in assessment, to determine whether a person has returned psychically and emotionally following a difficult birth. People with near-death imprints often remain both dissociated (parasympathetic shock) and fragmented (sympathetic shock). Treatment must address both aspects for full integration and healing.

The parasympathetic shock response of immobility and catatonia is an attempt to prevent death. Some forms of addiction and depression are rooted in early response to overwhelm. Within the collapse toward near-death, one finds a portal back to the sympathetic fight and will to live. This is fortunate, yet often prevents successful treatment for depression due to will getting in the way. A skilled clinician can help one suspend the "will to live" just enough to pick up the dissociated self lost in depression.

The need to escape

The brain releases natural opiates at death that provide a painless exit. My theory of dissociation, based on clinical research, is that opiates flood the brain in perceived "near-death" experience. Infants who receive a "natural high" of opiates, are imprinted to seek escape when under stress. Escaping inhibits the ability to meet pressure and ultimately to find a successful life. Children and adults with this imprint numb out; through a false sense of spiritual bliss, substance abuse, an inability to focus, or simply going numb. This behavior might be linked to an unprocessed parasympathetic dissociative response at birth.

An internal biological fight between collapse and mobility is a simultaneous sympathetic and parasympathetic shock. This results in double-bind thinking. The sympathetic will to live inhibits the ability to reach the bottom of depression. Not meeting the near-death memory leaves ones' psyche hopelessly trapped in past fear and present-time activation under stress.

Treatment for meeting death at birth

Being curious about near-death with clients can help to unravel compensated behavior. If I have a felt-sense during treatment that this might have happened, I will wonder aloud with a client, saying, "gosh, that was extreme for your little one's body. I wonder if you thought and felt you were going to die?" I then track the somatic cues the client or child presents. I help them to slow down their nervous system so that they can process emotions and track sensation.

If there is a grain of truth that near-death happened, mixed emotions will appear in a client. Often there is grief, fear, anger, and resentment. Beneath that can be collapse and a giving up that leads to dissociation. I am continually surprised at how often a near-death imprint has occurred, and the personal adaptations that compensate for such overwhelm. Without naming and resolution, triggers remain and non life-threatening current events are perceived as if they were highly dangerous. Such imprints remain linked to survival and govern confusing adult or child behaviors. Such behaviors do not heal at the core until pre-cognitive memories are included in treatment.

Clinicians now believe that prior to 6 months of age, an infant does not know it exists separate from the mother (private commentary, Myrna Martin). A pre-crawling baby is truly lost in space if placed alone. Hospital events as common as early umbilical cord clamping and cutting can be perceived by the infant body as a life-threatening blood loss. Cord cut followed by nursery care away from mother cycles an infant into shock, terror, rage, and despair. It is out of the protective womb surround, exposed to the emotional suffering of other nursery babies, has no ability to sense that mother will ever return, and has no ground of existence. Imagine the infant's confusion!

Although midwives reassure mothers that cord-wrap is common and not significant, numerous clinical sessions confirm that there is a dissociation for many people. It appears that cord wrap heightens a temporary loss in oxygenated blood during the pressure of contractions, and that some people blacked-out or dissociated during those contractions. Others identified the cord as a monster, and thought of themselves as monstrous. Cord wrap can feel like near-death and abandonment. People with cord wrap often link their potency to fear. They unconsciously hold back on ambition and living from vitality. Their power is under-utilized, there is no appropriate risk-taking, and personal apathy can result.

As a clinician, it is important to ask about possible near-death imprints and to assist them to unravel. Near-death produces the most primitive of all fears, and is the key that unlocks later emotions and behaviors. Clinicians may need to work backward through other imprints to help clients access this annihilative terror. The near-death imprint will not readily show itself until there is a bond of trust in the therapeutic relationship. The client must know that the therapist is able to meet their emotional responses and to face near-death with them without exaggerating or minimizing the experience.

Interrupted Timing

Wait for the baby's time... it is usually the right time

Get support

- understand fully all procedures
- relax and go with the flow
- help baby move by moving yourself

Question your birth provider

- what methods will be used if baby becomes "stuck" in birth canal
- what alternatives are available?
- Be prepared for these alternatives in a calm "unrushed" fashion

Tune into your sense of things

- get support for what you want
- work collaboratively with baby and birth provider
- talk to the baby so they know what procedures will be used

Interrupted timing interrupts the baby's sense of personal power and their ability to withstand pressure. Interruption is also frightening. Induction methods, such as stripping the membranes, breaking the water, and use of pitosin are invasive. Babies feel out of control and unprotected. Templates are set in place for struggles with timing and pacing. Such children will "melt-down" during transitions when they are not in charge of the timing of events, or if the pace is too fast. Clients resist, escalate, or ignore transitions and fail to meet deadlines in school or work.

Think about interrupted timing in advance

If the birth is on its way and there is not time to travel to hospital, it may be best to take charge and settle in for a home birth. Remember that the female body is designed to give birth and that birthing is a natural process. Although not their first choice, many couples have successfully delivered at home while unassisted. Being prepared for this event can be as helpful as preparing for hospital birth.

One client's parents resisted the baby's timing and rushed their new baby to the hospital just as he was being born at home. The baby was placed in quarantine and isolated for 6 days simply because the parents were Russian! This 40 year old client is just now unravelling his fear of rejection and defensive behavior under stress. Another client who thought her power was "too much for mother' realized she created that belief in response to Mom clamping her legs together during the long ride to the hospital. This client interpreted Mom's resistance as resisting her and often found herself in situations where she felt resisted by others. In both instances, mother resisted the timing of birth.

Talk through a possible home-birth scenario with your husband and support team so you are prepared for this situation. Once an infant has settled post-birth, help them process the birth impact by telling the story aloud. This reduces shock and the drama becomes integrated into the family experience. Sometimes a child will not settle until the story has been re-lived and emotional interruptions repaired.

Induced labor

Induced labor is common practice in many hospitals. Induction interrupts the attuned movement dance between mother and baby that is part of vaginal birth. A baby can sense with its head and uses it to feel spatially when not filled with pistosin. The baby discovers which direction to turn, as Mom adjusts her hip, leg, and the angle of her pelvis in resopnse to pressure. Both infant and mother work in cooperation to navigate the birth. Cooperative navigation of pressure is a very important training for their future relationship and interdependency.

Finding the way out of the birth canal is a creative act for the baby. It is important not to rob an infant of their experience of interaction with the mother, the spiral rotation, the ability to meet pressure, and the felt-sense of knowing their timing. Uninterrupted vaginal delivery allows babies to feel and sense naturally. It supports their inner sense of strength. Meeting the pressure and pacing of birth helps children meet later thresholds without added fear.

Induction

With induced labor babies feel unprotected. "Stripping the membranes" or "breaking the water" involves entering the babies womb space. When the chemical Pitosin is used, contractions are overly muscular, forced, and have a mechanical rather than natural rhythm. This type of pushing is physically painful on both the mother's pelvis and the baby's cranium. Baby and mother may have instances of bone bruising.

Induced labor interferes with a mothers ability to feel her baby. Some mothers reported jumping off the birthing table in pain and astonishment when pitosin was administered. I have seen induced infants afraid to crawl forward in normal patterns due to induction. Pitosin is powerful and influences muscles. Babies can have a jerky mechanical muscular rhythm and high tonicity in their muscles. Other successful methods that bring on labor have been to support a couple to be romantic during the birth though kissing. Pitosin should only be used when there is life threatening emergency rather than for convenience of scheduling.

If a person has been induced...

Clear the chemical imprints from the organs, and the emotional impression of urgency and loss of orientation under pressure. Explore the resistance to crossing thresholds, finishing projects, or bringing things to completion. Have mothers schedule a skilled cranial or BMC session (ideally with a clinician aware of the impacts of birth trauma) for both themselves and their infant to help relieve residual inner bracing, fear-based high tone, and bone pain. Work with internalized fear.

Interrupted labor

Labor can be interrupted for many reasons. Hurricane Donna interrupted my brother's birth. The hospital birthing staff was afraid of power shortages and gave all birthing mothers chemicals that stopped labor for 3 days. My brother was very anxiously attached. At 10 months he still screamed in terror and with a deep sadness any time Mom was out of his sight.

Interrupted labor may be necessary to save lives. When this occurs, please remember the impact on the infant and help them emotionally repair imprints related to their interrupted potency or sense of connection with mother.

Case Study Example

See Case Study #5 that explores C-section labor.

The only "right" answer is to stay relational with the infant

Midwives and hospital staff are trained to do their best. Birth is a mystery and emergencies happen. The simplest way to minimize risks to an infant is to educate obstetric practitioners and support personnel about the impact of interventions on a baby's nervous system. Birth attendants can then attune to the baby even in the midst of necessary interventions.

Maintain an emotional and mindful connection to infants even if they have been drugged. Even under anesthesia, infant cells are recording events and coping to survive. Mother needs to stay connected to this baby, and so does father. The gesture of contact reduces polyvagal activation and helps the nervous system.

When a birth interruption is about to occur

- Talk to a pre-birth baby
- Let them know the reason for interventions
- Understand their tremendous imperative to be born
- Stay connected to them
- Let them know what to expect
- Let them know you will use chemicals to help them get out!
- Chemicals are foreign to an infant
- Identify the confusion due to chemicals
- Understand the dissociation
- Help them find their way back to connection

Unwrap the neck and find the breath!

It is not uncommon for the umbilical cord to be wrapped around baby's neck. Midwives or doctors slip their fingers under the cord and slide it over the baby's head. However, if there is severe tension or pressure, a baby may feel strain and anxiety due to being pulled back while being pushed forward by the tremendous birth force of contractions. A template forms around power and collapse. The neck may brace against pressure. In addition, oxygen levels of the blood are measured by carotid bodies, which are glandular tissues located adjacent to the carotid arteries in the neck. With cord wrap, the carotids may still hold a shock imprint and be overly taught.

Thoughts on cord wrap

I included the below paragraphs so readers would understand the medical view. However, therapuetic clinical experience shows clients with cord wrap imprints do have a significant emotional impression of this event, even if not so "physically" dangerous. Be sure to treat the emotional/physical aspects.

"The placenta and umbilical cord are an amazing creation of both form and function. The placenta acts as a factory for hormones to support the pregnancy, a filter that acts to bring in good things, remove waste, and provides a reserve of blood and oxygen to support the baby through labor. The umbilical cord brings sugar and oxygen via its two veins while through its one artery passes the waste by-products of growth.

About 35-40% of normal term babies are born with the cord around the neck at least once. It can also be wrapped around the body or legs or even at times have a true knot. The baby does not breathe through its throat and, therefore, cannot choke. The cord is well equipped to handle temporary squeezing as the 3 vessels are cushioned by a matrix called Wharton's jelly and the surrounding amniotic fluid.

In labor, sometimes after the bag of waters breaks and fluid leaks out, the cord can be repeatedly compressed with contractions. This is not uncommon and is not, by itself, a sign of distress. Your practitioner or nurse can listen to or interpret the fetal heart rate pattern to know whether any intervention is necessary. And the compression of the cord almost never is an emergency or a cause for the tragic death of a baby inside the womb. When that tragedy occurs we all want to know why and often, mistakenly, we are told it was a "cord accident". Compared to the number of times I have heard this mentioned by patients or news stories the real truth is that this is a very rare event." *edited portions of article by Stuart J. Fischbein, MD, FACOG, BAC.*

Case Study Example

See Case Study #4 that explores cord wrap issues.

Life-threatening push and pull of cord wrap
Creates difficult dynamic with Mom
cord is part of Mom
cord gives me trouble
mistrust and push-pull dynamics with Mom
Treatment
work with empowerment
work with the tissue of the neck
unwrap the cord through play and simulation
Explore emotional mistrust
lessen the withdrawl pattern
collect potency and find pacing
practice pushing, resting, and going forward without speeding up or creating panic

Physical/emotional aspects

Babies don't expect to be pulled backward while they are moving down the birth canal. If the cord gets wrapped around the baby, either at the foot or more commonly around the neck, the pulling can feel life threatening. Cord wrap is a secret theme in that it happens without the doctor or Mom knowing the problem as it occurs. I have worked with adults and children who appear to have dissociated and even blacked out during the birth and later engaged in consistent struggles with Mom as the enemy.

"You are all pushing me to be born and I am being pulled back and strangled. As I lose oxygen, I lose my power. Maybe I will die! Somebody help me!" If the baby pushes they are in increased trouble. A baby's sense of power and ability becomes confused and unconscious anger at mom can start here. One client was pushed back in due to cord wrap and then had a c-section. This confused her sense of potency and purpose.

There is terror in the push pull of cord wrap and especially in the perceived black-out state if the oxygenated blood supply feels interrupted. Cord wrap must be met emotionally and sequenced through the body for true settling to occur. It can show up as heightened neck tension and anxiety when needing to make choices. It can also appear as continued and relentless power struggles with Mom or therapist.

Expressions in session

Umbilical cord wrap is not uncommon, and it is useful to consider possible shock imprints. These can appear in the neck and throat area as hypertension, avoidance of touch to the neck, and appear in dress as a consistent use of turtleneck blouses and shirts or wearing of scarfs. There can be an emotional tendency toward anger, and to avoid interdependence.

I have worked with numerous children in non-directed play therapy who express signs of cord wrap stress. They seek out my play snake and tie it around their neck, want to wrap the snake around my neck and pull me around, build cages for the snake, and exhibit a heightened avoidant response in working with the throat area. Neck tissue feels extremely tight. When I show how cord wrap happens with the doll and cloth pelvis, children with this issue are often overly avoidant or anxiously engaged.

Supportive treatment

Due to the vulnerability of the throat area, this imprint demands skilful intervention. Hands-on bodywork is extremely helpful. However, first encourage a client or child to touch their own throat, and scan for discomfort. Next have them touch their hand with their throat so the throat tissue is making contact rather than withdrawing. This guides them to motor through tissues that may have remained frozen due to fear. When there is an emotional readiness, use your hands to skilfully touch the throat and neck in order to release the layers of tissue. Always make sure the client is touching you with their throat. Touch and movement supports blood flow in the neck tissue and crossing through the brain stem. This can greatly relieve tension and shock.

Mother's body releases natural chemicals during birth. A cocktail of oxytocin and adrenalin is released into mother's blood stream when baby's head descends to a point near her bladder. Baby and mother share this natural hormonal boost and it assists the labor and subsequent bonding.

Unfortunately women are often given labor drugs either to relieve pain or to speed up the birth. These interfere with natural oxytocin, make labor more difficult, and can produce children who are hyperactive and unable to settle. The mother and baby may become groggy or numb. At the very least, chemicals reduce presence in the body and the baby becomes frightened when it feels mother's numb withdrawal. If the chemical is an anesthesia, adults remembering birth have reported going through rage at the invasion coupled with panic before finally dissociating. People who experienced pitosin often report they are unconsciously pushy and hard edged under stress. This was their body's bracing to meet the stress force of pitosin.

Substance abuse has been linked to birth chemicals

When babies are given chemicals at birth, it appears they learn to seek ways to dissociate when stressed. In *The Effects of Anaesthesia on Newborns*, author Beverly Bird wrote that "A British Medical Journal study found that ["a significant proportion of mothers of addicts had received opiates or barbiturates, and nitrous oxide during delivery."] The study went on to find a positive correlation between duration and frequency of drug administration in mothers and severity of addiction in offspring. As anesthesia use in labor is on the rise in the United States, this could have widespread consequences in the future." [British Study: Increased Chance of Addiction Later in Life, released in 0, (Bertil Jacobson, et al.), Jun 14, 2011].

Young adults displayed a correlate link between type of substance abused and type of anesthesia used during birth that crossed gender and economic class lines in one study. If anesthesia becomes linked with survival, a cycle ensues where adults feel they need chemical support in order to withstand the natural pressures of life.

The natural life force "ignition" during birth helpsbabies push out through the birth canal. This is interrupted when drugs are administered at birth. Drugged babies cannot use their wisdom and sensibility to make it out. They become inert, trapped, and require interventions to be born. Often they are in shock and not able to bond. They have been both abandoned and invaded. This sets up a difficult attachment pattern. There is almost no awareness of boundary of self. Psychologically, this can create an Oral/Schizoid pattern (see Character Styles chapter of this book) which is one of the more difficult styles to treat due to "no self" able to process energy. The sense of "self" has to be reconstructed. People with this style often have high needs for contact yet are energetically unable to hold a charge necessary for connection. They can feel overbearing with neediness and unable to hold a sense of self.

Alternative methods to chemicals

Birth Position: not on the back! All fours, squatting, ability for mother to move the joints of her pelvis.

Natural progression support

kissing with the father induces sexual support for birth. Opens mother to that state of energetics and pleasure.

Warm water labor

Some mothers stay more relaxed when there is a warm pool that they can use. Some mothers give birth in the water and some use it just for pre-labor, preferring to be out of the water for the final pushing.

Birth hypnosis methods

Mothers have reported ease in staying present while enduring pain. I witnessed such a home birth. The mother needed no anesthesia for birth or even for stitching a birth tear that occurred. Baby was in her arms during the stitching.

Talking to the baby

Some mothers reported they told baby it was going to get really difficult if the baby didn't go head first to engage and find it's way through, and the baby turned from a breech to head-down position.

Case Study Example

See Case Study #1 that explores anesthesia effect on physical digestion and emotional safety.

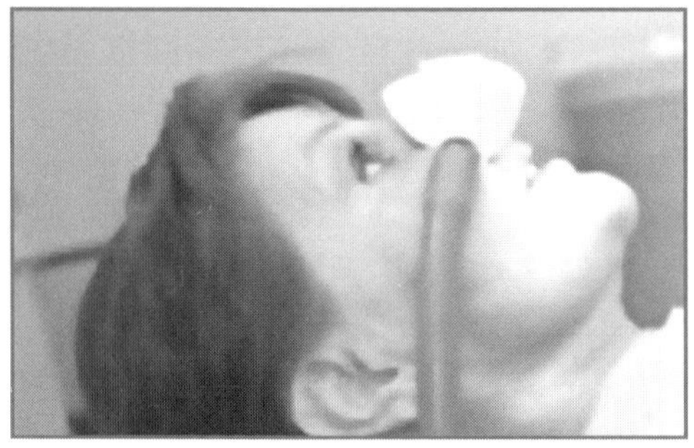

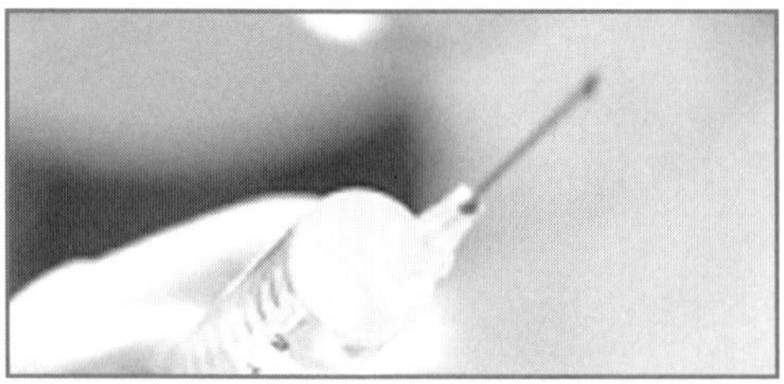

"Of all the bitterly contested obstetric treatments of the past 160 years, the administration of anesthesia for labor pain has prompted the longest-lasting disagreement! WIlliam T.G. Morgan inadvertently sparked this discussion when he demonstrated the miraculous use of Ether before an enthralled audience at Massachusetts General Hospital in Boston in 1846. Within a year, James Young Simpson exhibited the anaesthetic properties of chloroform to similarly enthusiastic colleagues in Edinburgh, Scotland. In the wake of these two exciting discoveries, doctors almost immediately began using ether and chloroform during childbirth as well as surgery."

-Jaqueline H. Wolf, *Deliver Me from Pain*, 2009

Different types of birth chemicals have differing effects

It is helpful for clinicians to be able to distinguish the differing "look" of anesthesia imprinted during birth. Differing chemicals produce differing responses, and a different look and feel when clients are releasing chemical imprinting. There will always be a kind of forced dissociation. Clients often flicker in and out of presence without knowing it. This is an invisible handicap for school learning, social friendship, and intimate relating.

The emotional impact is a disconnection from Mom and feels like abandonment and invasion. Birth chemicals are often the first non-natural physical impression on the cells. This can result in an instinctive bracing of the tissues and cells when a person becomes alarmed.

Types of birth chemicals

twilight sleep or laughing gas

Gas produces total misattunement as Mom is "flying" in a blissed-out state. Mom often self-administers. She loses touch with her pregnancy, the act of birthing, and is totally disoriented. It is normal for infants to "follow their mother." Clients who fused with this state of intense emotional drama become lost in a dark zone, and use self-soothing touch in an attempt to orient. One client described a terrifying sensation of "falling back in her head and down her spine." This imprint often carries a deep sadness associated with contact with mother (see http://www.medicinenet.com/script/main/art.asp?articlekey=10238).

Ether

Common in the 1930s, ether seems to evoke a seduction to shamanistic experience. Clients exposed as infants exhibit a rigidity as well as an emotional anger and loyalty to intense forces. Ether creates a wild ride for the mother. One mother went into hysterical dream time and never recovered her mental stability. One infant slept for 3 months following birth and his mother literally had to smack his feet to wake him up to nurse. Learning to orient to the present, and not need shamanic dissociative intensity is key to processing ether imprints.

Demerol

Creates a type of spaced out orientation dissociative in nature but not very pleasurable for the infant or the mother. It just takes one out of touch. People appear glassy-eyed and there can be gaps in conversation. Without outside reflection, there is often little self-knowledge of this behavior.

A "cocktail" of chemicals

"The tragedy of these chemical experiments is that mothers were turned into raving psychotic animals without reduction of pain. In the 30s it was common to place a hood over the mother and tie her down with lambs wool so there would be no marks on her wrists or ankles "(see DVD, *The Business of Being Born*, See DVD, *The Business of Being Born*, available free from Netflix).

Time Line of Chemicals Used in Birthing

Jaqueline H. Wolf, Deliver Me from Pain, *2009*

Note that some chemicals were retained in use through later years, such as ether.

The Question of Necessity	The Question of Professional Respect	Developing the Obstetric Anesthesia Arsenal: The Question of Safety	Baby Boomers, The Question of Convenience	Birth reform, The Question of Authority	The Backlash, fading enthusiasm for natrual childbirth
1840s–1890s	**1890s–1930s**	**1900s–1960s**	**1940s–1960s**	**1950s–0s**	**0s–Present**
Ether and Chloroform	Anesthesia	Twilight Sleep, Anesthesia "Cocktails"			Due to stories of difficult births from women unprepared for realistic meeting of pain both emotionally and physically

Thoughts on Chemical Imprinting

Science tells us that cells are replaced in a natural cycle every 7 years. However, the imprints of those chemicals appears to be maintained. When chemical imprints are released, there is behavior change. Successful treatment brings sensations, smells, and tastes to consciousness.

Allergens trick cells and gain entry through cell receptor sites by mimicking healthy substances. With chemical imprinting, it seems the body continues to retain the "chemical effect" long after cells have been replaced due to an associative memory. Cells continue for years to pass along the "information" as essential to survival until the emotions are felt, the chemicals sensed, and the impressions released and integrated.

Treatment for Chemical Imprinting

Regardless of the chemical used, methods to support healing are similar. Use educative touch to squeeze the skin and limbs. This returns clients to tactile perception and ability to perceive sensation, and allows them to come more into relational contact.

Invite clients to squeeze their internal organs, as in squeezing a sponge. This image of squeezing allows clients to condense internally and sense inner organ movement. When they find the bottom of the squeeze, invite them to feel the sensations as the organs puff back out and to inhale plenty of fresh oxygen. Repeat this throughout the session. Ask clients to consciously exhale and cough, especially with nicotine imprint, and then inhale fresh air. It is especially important to squeeze the liver as it can hold residual chemical impressions due to its ability to filter and store chemicals.

With this movement, one should be able to observe clients shift from a "glassy-eyed numb look" into a state of aware presence. There should also be less flickering in and out of contact. Clients reported they are better able to feel inside their own body. Even children can do this squeezing and releasing. Note that it may take several days for sensations to clear.

For some people, releasing anesthesia imprints produces a feeling of nausea. Clients must be coached through the process to go beyond the discomfort by squeezing, coughing it out, and inhaling fresh oxygen until there is a sense of internal freshness and vitality.

A highly effective way to support clients move from numbness to potency is to treat using Aquatic therapy in a warm pool. They can discharge fear and kick and shake in a very satisfying manner. They can curl fully with their feet against the pool wall or ladder to squeeze out the last of the imprinted substance. As potency returns they can push you back through the water and feel their own body in a powerful manner.

"Baby Rescue" Themes

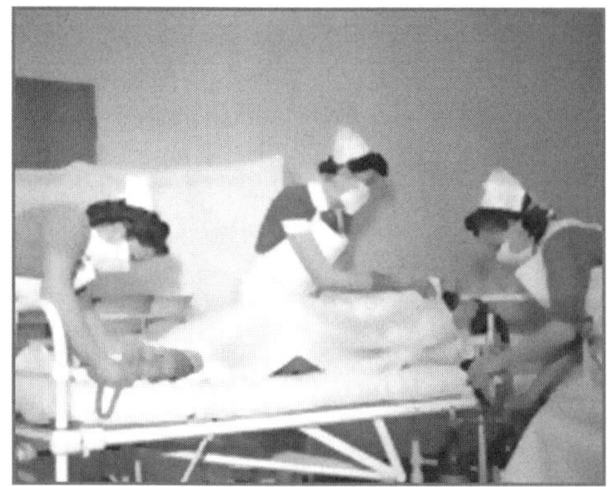

Sedated birth image

In a medical emergency, a baby may need to be rescued and is fortunate to be alive. However, babies are more likely to need rescue when mothers lie on their backs during labor. Back labor limits full range of pelvic movement, puts pressure on the mother's vena cava, and leads to use of pain killers, spinals, anesthesia and C-sections! It also unterrupts the sense of support and connection while under pressure.

Back labor was first introduced when King Henry IVX of England wished to see his children born. He was made comfortable at the expense of his wife, who had to lay down so he could observe her while seated at his throne! (personal commentary Myrna Martin). When a woman is placed on her back the probability of interventions drastically increases. When babies are rescued, listen for physical and psychological impacts. Rescued babies may bond with the doctor who saved them rather than with the mother who failed to protect them from invasive procedures.

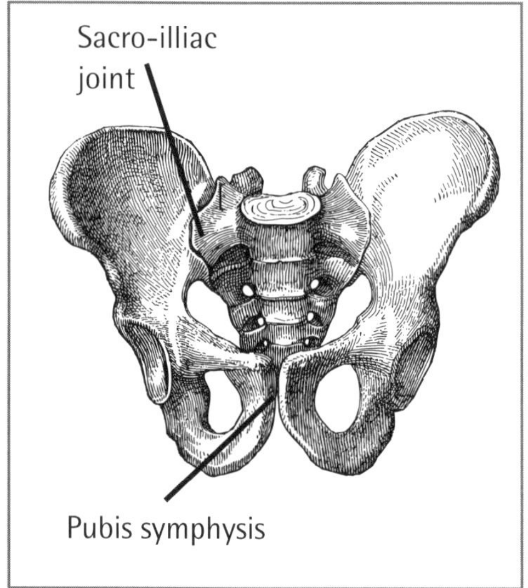

Back placement for birthing limits range of motion of the large joints of the pelvis and baby's get stuck, requiring interventions!!

A successful vaginal delivery is very impactful. This shared experience between mother and infant is created by a powerful ignition force that travels head to tail and tail to head. This Cranio-Sacral energy is a body-felt-sense for the infant and sets a template for success with risk-taking, task completion, and trust of one's power in connection with others. Feeling power, listening together, finding one's way under pressure, relief of pressure and then bonding are supported by the Oxytocin hormones released in non-interrupted labor. Address any form of birth interruption to re-establish a felt-sense of potency.

Impact of rescue themes on behavior

Babies "rescued" at birth show a variety of behaviors. Observe expressions of task completion, control and ease. Look for a dissociative overly contented response due to anesthesia and shock. When you hear a mother say "such a good baby, he never fussed!" listen for numbing shock response. This can lead various behaviors in later child development. Children may be overly controlling, edgy, extremely independent and precocious, or overly dependent and anxious. They often have tactile sensitivity. They will have mixed body tone, often with low tone internally coupled with a high tone externally. They may excel in athletic events due to "no one is going to mess with me!" or struggle due to imbalance in tissue tone. They may be hyperactive due to excessive adrenaline that flooded their nervous system at birth. Many develop night terrors of aliens coming to get them from C-section, can carry an unresolvable sadness, and may not rest into the comfort of Mom's body.

Baby's rescued at birth were the center of focused attention. Children and adults can demand attention and yet feel anxious when they get it; as it evokes anxiety about what is coming next. There is a body-felt memory of having no control. Clients complain of difficulty dealing with pressure, a fear of being interrupted, feel reluctant to cross thresholds (such as finishing homework, going for that promotion), and of struggles in intimacy with issues of control. When in compensation, they can be highly capable, even headstrong, yet struggle to trust. They avoid interdependency necessary for relationship and teamwork

Clients will have unique responses based on interruption of their "through line" due to a rescue birth. Explore double binds and help the birth imprint to resolve and the nervous system to settle.

Types of birth that create rescue

Forceps and vacuum suction

Forceps and suction apply pressure to the infant's head in an attempt to help them turn and exit the birth canal. Forceps create a directional pressure and produce clear vector force lines in the bones of the skull. A forceps imprint tends to create a pushiness that can feel like "head-butting;" seeking conflict in order to feel connection with an underlying sense of being disempowered. The cycle of experience can include anesthesia, forceps, being taken away from mother, and then left in the nursery with other unhappy babies. This creates an expected pain cycle. Please support clients to repair this imprint!

Vacuum suction is more nebulous than directional. A plastic cup connected to a pressure pump is placed on the visible aspect of the baby's head and the infant is pulled out. The sense of self can be "fractured" and newborns can feel disoriented and be in unrecognized pain post-birth.

C-section rescue

A C-section is a rescue operation where baby is removed manually. Such operations save lives and should be used when necessary, but only when necessary. The disempowerment and shock associated with C-section is held deep within the nervous system. C-section is one of the scariest forms of birth from an infant's perspective. The birth surgery is conducted in a room that is intentionally cold, sterile, and brightly lit. Doctors wear masks, gloves, and head and eye protection. The transition out of mom is rapid and babies lose the body experience of the squeeze of the birth canal. Vaginal birth helps develop necessary proprioception, flushes the organs, and supports the ability to meet pressure and navigate obstacles. This squeeze is an important survival imprint.

Additionally, mother is still in surgery following the birth and not immediately able to hold her child which further interrupts bonding. Fortunately some physicians are changing procedure so baby goes immediately to mother after C-section delivery.

Restore the sense of potency and ability

A rescue at birth organizes a person toward self-doubt. They may doubt internal instincts, be reluctant to take risks, unable to finish projects, and always seek extra assistance. I have observed "rescue at birth" to be the reason certain children struggle with activation when it is time to complete homework.

Repair of Rescue Themes

Hands-on sessions can relieve cranial pressure from the bones and brainstem. This helps a child or client regain physical potency. BMC or Biodynamic cranial work can help help clients work through fear, terror or anger held in the tissues and associative hippocampus. Help clients orient to an "I can do it!" sense of success that is sustained over time. Do so by naming the imprint difficulty, empathizing with the early event, and distinguishing between that moment in time and current reality. Remind children that there are always growing pains with new risks and skills. This helps them to normalize the natural pressures of learning.

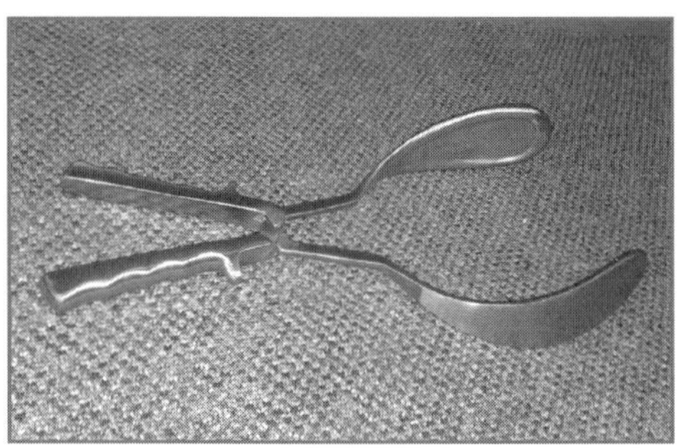

Use of forceps creates mis-attunement and emotional issues

Case Study Example

See Case Study #1 that explores forceps and anesthesia imprints.

The Push and Pull of Forceps

Forceps are metal "tongs" used to pull an infant out of the birth canal. The intent of forceps use is to save lives, but they are are painful and perceived by the infant as life-threatening. The pressure on the skull and brain is debilitating and often linked with anesthesia. The physician slides in one metal tong at a time, hooks them together like salad tongs, and applies pressure to "pull" the baby out.

Forceps can imprint in a number of ways based on the multitude of birth factors and post-birth experience following this imprint. I worked with one adult who carried huge self-doubt, even though she was quite accomplished. She didn't trust herself under stress. Through clinical work, we discovered she had been pulled out in the wrong spiral direction. Once this was discovered and repatterned, both the self-doubt and her neck-chin tremor disappeared. Adults who experienced forceps often have imprints laced with anger and deep annihalitive terror. Expressed externally as an aggressive "head-butting," or need to pick a fight, need to "be right," yet internally there is a sense of panic and relentless vigilance. If anesthesia were used, the body is dissociated and attacked simultaneously, and can have low tone inside with high bracing in ligaments of the spine. This creates incredible distortion of perception. The sense that "someone is trying to hurt me" is common with a forceps imprint, as is pushiness, a vigilant self-reliance, and a quick sympathetic arousal.

People can dissociate, and "wait to be pulled out" rather than face danger and successfully move through it. They can seek your help and push you away at the same time. Often people are afraid to cross thresholds, might wait to be rescued, or push themselves through in an intense manner. Such imprints can underlie the unwillingness to accept a promotion, to make a change, or express as a need to be in control. I have seen a kind of obsessive-compulsive behavior trait with forceps imprints.

Forceps as "first touch" Imagine how an infant would make mearning of this pressure. The body would brace internally to resist the sense of one's skull being crushed. Then, the force of being pulled would interrupt the natural integrity of the spine. Physicians cannot always see clearly which way the baby is rotating, and may pull the baby out contrary to the direction to which the spine is oriented. This creates internal confusion and doubt. Often forceps are used following anesthesia which alters the infant's perceptions and contributes to the magnitude of internalized alarm. An infant is meant to push its way out the birth canal. This push is halted, the head is crushed, and an unbearable pull exerted upon the spine, rather than an integrated spinal push. Even though anesthesia is masking consciousness, this overwhelming experience still registers in the body as an assault.

Additional Factors to explore with forceps related to the Birth Environment

The scene of the birth will impact a newborn's sense of safety. One client was born in a teaching hospital. She always felt "watched in life" as there were many students observing. In addition the doctor scratched her face with the forceps so she was born with a facial cut. She had an obsessive-compulsive need to distract herself from her internalized terror. Another client who was an OB-GYN realized her own birth shock contributed to her application of forceps. She grieved her brusqueness and lack of timing awareness of the infant's needs during delivery. Factors to explore include: a doctor's unresolved birth shock. which can lead to a sense of urgency or need for force; the alarm of other birth attendants, which is palpable to the newborn; the intense narrowing and focus of attention on the infant, which can feel threatening; the application of the forceps on body perception of safety, and the loss of spinal integrity and rotation.

Difficult post birth factors Post-birth factors can set the forceps imprint even more deeply. Baby's often have a slower recovery from anesthesia than Mother because they measure the amount of anethesia based on mother's body weight, which means the infant is really "over-dosed." Mother is ready to bond while her baby is still in shock, and she can feel disappointed and somehow not good enough when her baby doesn't respond. Infants are taken away to the nursery, where the loss of contact with the mother becomes an existential shock shared with other infants in pain. One client's head was so bruised from forceps that the doctors would not let the mother see her infant for four days. Nursery experience can become globalized as a cultural experience.One client had a strong need to rescue others, was extraordinarily tuned in to global suffering, and was "mad at God."

The main repair with forceps is to regain spinal integration and a willingness to inhabit the body. After such a painful imprint, there can be a sense that the body itself causes pain. With an interrupted spinal integrity, there is likely to be more pain! Another repair is to help clients to develop a felt-sense that their power is not too much for others, and that they are headed in the right direction. Help them learn to move forward without needing to pick a fight or make life too difficult. Hands on work with the skull and spine, as well as the organs, is essential for full-bodied integration. Repairing forceps imprints can help the body yield enough to begin a process of embodied curiosity about sensation rather than overriding sensate signals.

Use of Vacuum suction

This imprint carries many similarities to forceps and yet is different in temperament response. There is a fragmented feeling of skull integrity rather than a crushed feeling. For suction, the doctor places a plastic cup over the visible portion of the infant's head. This cup is connected by a rubber tube to a hand-held canister with a pump handle. The OB-GYN pumps to create the vacuum pressure. Unfortunately, the guidelines for amount of pressure applied are sometimes ignored. The force is intense and babies develop cranial bruising. Clinical treatment suggests that vacuum suction, while helpful, is not harmless. The infant experiences energetic confusion.

Heal Forceps Imprints
Cranial pressure was perceived as life-threatening
address parasympathetic + sympathetic shock
Relieve forceps memory in bone tissue with cranial or BMC sessions
Everyone was happy you arrived. You were in pain... a mismatch of emotions
Aggression in the Field
anesthesia is felt to be aggressive
forceps are aggressive and very hard on a newborns' skull
dispell the need to equate aggression with survival
Transform terror energy
fear is energy; slow down and feel it
know that you survived
discharge the energy; shake it out
Reduce the inner bracing

The indications for vacuum extraction are the same as forceps—and while both are safe if performed by experienced practitioners, vacuum deliveries are associated with less trauma to the vagina (and possibly a lower chance of needing an episiotomy) and less need for anesthesia. Babies born with vacuum extraction may experience some swelling on the scalp, but it is not serious, doesn't require treatment, and usually goes away within a few days.

http://www.whattoexpect.com/interventions/vacuum-extraction.

Impacts of Vacuum Suction

Suction creates an inability to orient due to the many force vectors on the skull. Unlike forceps which have an identifiable pressure, suction creates a globalized fracture of cranial integrity. One cannot identify the oppressive force, and the sense of self feels "sucked away." Overly nice" or "often irritated" are chronic behavior expressions. Responses vary. One client was "overly nice" and avoided conflic yet had an unidentified anger. Another thought she was born in a hurricane. However the hurricane happened a week after her birth. Her "internal vortex" was escalated and she was often irritated and felt pulled on.

Caught in the existential realms, people who experience suction can have a sweet presentation that is validated socially yet masks other feelings. They have no anchored midline of the body, which would help them express anger. Such internal contradiction sets an emotional double bind that guarantees little chance to get relational needs met.

A combination of hands-on work to repair cranial integrity, combined with the reknitting of the spine so there is a "push into reach" pattern rather than a "push, stop, be pulled" pattern is essential. Helping the brain state of confusion, annihilative terror, and disorientation to dissipate is necessary for effective resolution.

Forcep and vacuum suction repair

Spinal	Use hands on compression and integration so that spinal "push with the head" transitions to spinal "reach with the head"
Skull	Use hands on cranial release of vector force lines or fragmentation lines: find skull integrity and wholeness
Body	Release internalized bracing and frozen brain stem fear. Reach into contact. Unwind spinal rotation distortions and organ rotation distortions.
Emotional	Find ground for one's power, sense of direction, and relational ability to stay connected under pressure. Redevelop sense of trust in one's surroundings and ability to be met and cared for.

History of C-section

History & References (http://www.chiff.com/health/pregnancy/caesarian.htm)

Julius Caesar was said to have been delivered by the ancient method when his mother, Aurelia, was unable to deliver naturally. In ancient times, mother and baby rarely survived the primitive procedure, which entailed surgical removal of the baby from the mother's womb. Today the World Health Organization puts the acceptable rate of C-sections at 1-15% for countries in the developed world, saying that it is a major surgical procedure possibly fraught with danger. Proponents counter that vaginal birth is just as risky, and point to the ease and safety of Caesarean section, for both mother and child, using modern medical techniques.

C-section Factors

Birth is meant to be a time of transition for baby and Mom where both are awake, present, and engaged. Things have gone awry when C-section surgery becomes elective for mothers. C-section reduces liability and guarantees a live birth outcome. In 2008 the American Society of Obstetrics made C-sections elective, which supports an ignorance of the impact on behavior. C-sections imprint a threat response behavior, and parents are not informed of this risk. There are often sensory-motor difficulties, learning problems, and social-relational difficulties. This is a high social cost for an elective procedure!

Avoid birth physicians who speak only of ease, no stretch marks, and convenience. Doctors are easily sued for liability and put in the untenable position to guarantee a live birth outcome. The only way to do so is to make birth into an operation, no matter the emotional and relational consequences. Natural birth practices that allow for the mother's and infants timing and pacing are not as financially viable in institutions. Hospitals make more money per hour when they speed up the process of birth.
While mothers can avoid the pain of labor or the possibility of inconvenience, they miss the engaged meeting of pressure with the child. A C-section undermines a mother's sense of success in birthing, interrupts a baby's sense of potency, and effects bonding. Mother is often not able to hold her baby while she is being sewed up following the C-section incision.

When a c-section is necessary as an emergency procedure, it is useful to get follow up care. Ideal post-birth care for babies delivered C-section would be hands-on treatment to resolve shock from this type of arrival. Insurance companies likely would save money on overall expenditure if they reimbursed for post-birth early followup care. Parents would have less parenting struggles if they sought post-birth treatment.

Current available Web C-section statistics: World Health Organization
United States of America
1 in 4 births > 30.2%
60% increase 1996-2009
impact on culture and social emotional learning capacity-no studies
Brazil
80% private hospitals 35% public
due to fear of substandard care
impact on culture... no studies
Mexico
0.30 > 1/4 of public institution deliveries
consumes millions of dollars in public health monies
Denmark
8.3% - 15.2%
34% give birth at home
impact on culture... no studies

Reasons for this increase in C-section have been discussed profusely:

- The surgical focus of obstetrics and the need to train residents
- The low priority and few practical skills for supporting women's abilities to labor and give birth naturally
- A rigid view of the duration of normal labor
- A low threshold of definition for 'labor dystocia' (the justification for up to 60% of caesarean births).

Surgical birth is also a 'side effect' of interventions associated with actively managed labor: induction, artificial rupture of membranes, labor medications, and fetal monitoring. Policies against vaginal birth after caesarean (VBAC) and, increasingly, unsupported 'supply-side' justifications such as "baby seems large," also drive the trend toward caesareans. A recent report by the Lamaze Institute associates surgical birth with obstetricians' personalities—specifically their anxiety levels. (Medscare Ob/Gyn and Women's Health © 2009, Medscape LLC).

Modern C-sections are often performed for non-emergency reasons

"Caesarean section (C-section) is the most commonly performed surgery in the United States. The frequency of surgical birth has increased from 4% in 1965 to about 33% today, despite World Health Organization (WHO) recommendations that a 5% to 10% rate is optimal and that a rate greater than 15% does more harm than good. (Medscare Ob/Gyn and Women's Health© 2009, Medscape LLC).

The risks for birth by surgery have also come under discussion. Maternal risks include a higher overall death rate, rehospitalization for wound complications and infection, placenta accreta and percreta (both with 7% mortality rate), placenta previa, uterine rupture with subsequent pregnancy, and preterm birth, with its own set of risks and complications for the newborn."(Medscare Ob/Gyn and Women's Health © 2009, Medscape LLC).

Treating C-Section: Imagine the felt-sense of C-section imprint

Imagine a C-section. The text below is written in a style to help the reader understand the impact and convey that while sometimes necessary, it is a shocking experience. When reading, be sure to breathe and relax your nervous system, especially if you had a C-section birth as an infant or Mom. Your own material might become activated.

A C-section is an operation, not an engaged exchange between Mom and infant. It is by necessity rapid; it must occur within a few minute's time for the health of the baby. The mother is wheeled into the operating room, an incision done on her abdomen, and the doctor must then open the abdomen. The method most often used is to tear open the abdomen tissue rather than make a straight incision as this allows for stronger healing. Doctors must then find the baby's head, grasp his body, and pull him out. Anesthesia is always used on the mother; this appears to directly enter the baby, or at least the baby's felt-sense of their body, and the baby's experience of connection is interrupted.

Imagine the speed of pressure change alone. Going from a watery world into the bright lights of an operating room with no chance to squeeze through the birth canal is a scary movie at best. The intensity of this experience is amplified because the baby's body is under pressure to be born. Thus baby is primed to register birth events through the amygdala of the brain which monitors survival and terror. C-sections should only be used for medical emergency, not for convenience or fear of medical liability.

Simple post-birth interventions include hands on work. Body-Mind Centering sessions reduce startle reflex, develop proprioception, and reduce anesthesia in baby's system. BioDynamic Cranio-Sacral work rebalances the nervous system. Pre- and perinatal sessions help the entire event lose it's shocking impact for Mom and baby. Such sessions enhance the baby's chance at nursing and bonding. Later struggles in life would be reduced if post-birth practices were applied.

Possible complications in behavior and internal beliefs related to C-section
Extreme independence
Mother was gone at birth... I was captured by "aliens" = I will never surrender like that again.
Confusion! I will never let any one pull me out, but I need help to get out.
Life-threatening fear and protective response, yet needs help.
Inability to meet pressure in life
I get lost and disoriented and frozen
rapid pressure changes, no birth rotation = disorients under pressure
inability to cross thresholds
Out of sync responses to events
I never figured out how to find my way under pressure = I dysregulate
I am not sure how I got here = I zone out or lose my through line of action
I try and then give up under pressure
Physical complications
tendency to "zone out" with television or daydreaming
heighten tone in nerves, low tone in organs
core and joints were never activated by compression; they carry a freeze response

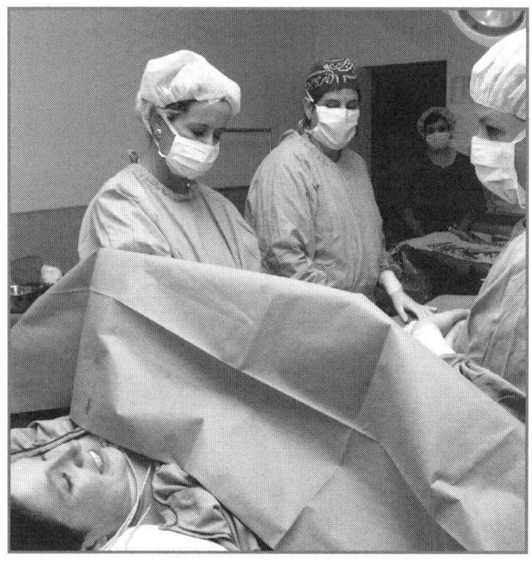

Case Study Example

See Case Study #5 that explores necessary C-section labor.

Education is available

Read and compare
Make an informed choice

Personal decision based on research informed consent

Help baby process the procedure out loud during birth

- Repair tissue imprints with squeezing and pressure and baby moving forward using power of midline
- Sequence mother's need to push
- Support for baby to find push with the head
- Repair emotional sense of failure
- Acknowledge choice
- Process rage and disappointment
- Identify strengths gained through experience
- Support choice from that time and reasons for surgery
- Work with forgiveness if needed

Treating C Section Imprints Assess what factors contributed to this procedure. Was it medically necessary or performed for doctor convenience? Was mother lying on her back in the common hospital delivery position, which then inhibited her from moving her pelvis? Was the pacing of birth pushed or induced? Was pain medication administered? How did that influence her labor, or her sensation of her legs and pelvis? Was the birthing environment chaotic or supportive? There are many influencing factors that create a cascade of interventions prior to the final outcome of a medical emergency procedure. Distinguish each one and name it aloud. Help mothers to complete the unsequenced push. Place their feet against your hips or shoulders and let them push. Meet them emotionally as they explore reclaiming their "push power." The birthing push is a powerful and potent impulse. Mothers who were numbed-out for a C-section operation need to reclaim this energetic potency. It will help them be more grounded as parents. To heal C-section imprint, couples must move past disappointment, blame, guilt, and anger. Unravelling the incidences of the birth story and processing residual emotions helps the event to be digested and the family can move on, integrating and releasing the birthing shock.

Planned C-sections versus emergency C-section

A planned C-section carries less shock than a medical emergency C-section, but still is not desirable. Planned C-sections are initiated before the baby's head is fully engaged in the pelvis, thus reducing the strain on the baby's spine and neck when it is pulled out. In emergency C-sections the doctor must break the suction between the baby's head and mother's pelvis. This pulling imprints as a sympathetic arousal pattern of terror in the baby's nervous system and can underlie nameless night terrors in children and adults who experienced C-section births. There is an incomplete Morro reflex (startle reflex) that continues to pattern the terror.

Talking to babies during the C-section may help them to be less afraid

Aware obstetric physicians can reduce the emotional impact of C-sections. A video clip of a Duke University obstetrician had the tone of supportive cooperation rather than medical emergency. The doctor communicated with both mother and infant the entire time she was operating. She maintained verbal and emotional contact with the infant, informing her of what would happen next prior to any assaultive procedure. She asked the infant to "help me locate your head so I can bring you out safely and place you with your mother." Viewers observed much less stress present in the mother. Such aware medical care is rare but will increase if requested. I encourage you to ask for this verbal and emotional support if a C-section is needed.

Help mother complete her birth push Once surgery has healed, help moms clear anesthesia from their systems using the hands on techniques described. Certain flower essence or homeopathics can help with this. Then work with mom's legs and pelvis connection. The "airplane" game of weight bearing can help mom release her emotions, anger and any push energy needed.

Protection Game

Helping the infant and mother re-establish a felt-sense of connection, safety, and protection is imperative in healing C-section imprints. Infants are often mistrustful deep in their core that mother let "the strange doctor" take them away! Mothers are often caught in grief at the loss of a desired vaginal birth.

The Protection Game was introduced to me by colleague Mryna Martin and is very helpful in rebalancing the nervous systems of children and their parents following a C-section. The game is a role-play of safety and is described in-depth on page 43 in *Birth's Hidden Legacy: Volume 2.* I play it with all ages, from infants to adults. The game re-establishes both a sense of power for the father and a sense of safety for the mother and infant (or child). The entire family matrix repairs. A mother can feel protected by her spouse, an infant by both the father and the mother.

Having the father fight the danger rather than danger being inside the mother and infant's field allows the energetic field of the mother to soften and this is why the game is so effective. The child will only release its vigilance if it feels the mother present and settled. When this occurs, the infant can soften and yield into mother's body. Have mother share aloud the birth story and process her emotions. Watch the child's play or the infant's responses and empathically reflect back to them the emotional tragedy of their separation. This is difficult due to the complexity of terror and the end result of relief at being born!

Parents will need a felt-sense of protection in order to help their child. Without this, they have no reference point for relating or parenting from an embodied sense of safety. If parents never knew protection during their childhood, they must be coached and sometimes placed in the role of the protected one during sessions. This gives them a felt-sense of the need for protection relief it provides, and helps them better attune to their child's fears related to C-section.

Use the Protection Game to release any residual terror held in the bodies of father, mother, or infant and to re-establish a shared felt-sense of safety and potency. Doing so allows families to re-bond at a mutually connective level.

The Protection Game is an enactment game with good enough parents, a little one, and a bad guy. In traditional roles, the protective parent (usually Dad) pushes the bad guy out of the room while the "nourishing parent" (usually mother) stays with the little one and keeps him calm. She is trusting Dad to protect them. This helps Mom's nervous system to settle, thus keeping the little one settled, and allows Dad to be powerful and potent rather than feel impotent. It also brings power of connection back into the parental bond and to the family matrix. The movement during the game helps release parental numbness, fear, and mistrust. The parents come back into relationship and integrate the shared difficulty of the birth event.

Phase 1
Therapist modeling with the stuffed animals

Phase 2
Involving the family in the game

Phase 3
Game debrief

The uncompleted birth needs to be sequenced

- Help mother complete her push
- Do physical push exercises so mother has a body-felt sense of power and potency
- Use acupuncture to re-establish correct qui flow on each side of incision
- Help the baby find potency
- Help them learn to take action and move forward
- Reconnect energy from cranium to sacrum
- Find the breath in the skull bones
- Find the integrated spine
- Dismantle the need to push so hard
- Meet and reduce annihilation fear
- Uncouple belief that pressure equals annihilation
- Heal fragmentation and despair

Completing the interrupted birth push for mothers
on land or in warm water pool

Help mothers regain potency by completing the interrupted birth push. Do so on both an emotional and physical level. Mom must be able to vocalize, sound, and really push in order to release cellular inhibitions of her power. Doing so repairs Mom's sense of power and ability to ground through her legs and pelvis, which was interrupted when the incision cut through muscles and the energy of the stomach meridian.*

Mothers complete the interrupted push in office sessions by leaning against the wall and pushing against me. I place their feet on my hips so they can feel contact with my body weight. I encourage them to make noise and to let the body "go for it." Unprocessed emotions release and Moms feel stronger and more connected afterwards. They feel powerful and satisfied upon completing that push.

If available, I treat in a Warm Water Aquatic Therapy pool. I first condense the mother with her legs tucked up against the pool ladder until she feels the impulse to push. I encircle her as she is tucked and give her support to flex into the area of her abdomen that may have remained numb or disconnected. Sometimes she will feel nauseous due to anesthesia memory. I then suggest she squeeze her organs, as if squeezing a sponge. As she releases the toxicity, I encourage her to take deep breaths and stay present.

As her vitality returns I coax her to begin pushing with her feet and extending her legs a bit at a time. We stay connected through this "waking up of power," and when she has regained her sense of energy, the push bursts forth and I am often pushed forcefully backward through the water! Moms feel elated at finding the connection to their legs and pelvis reclaimed. When there is full potency, the body organically pushes. Women emerge with a sense of power and integration through their legs and abdomen. They feel more potent to meet their child's needs when this push is completed.

Once emotions and sensations are re-integrated I suggest Mom visits an acupuncturist if she is comfortable with this method of treatment. Acupuncturists can "needle" the scar incision and re-establish the meridian flow. Mother's who have had this done report a return of power they had long forgotten since the birth!

*The book, *Tracking The Dragon*, by Dr. Janice Walton-Haldock, DAOM, describes the impact on chi flow and how to place the needles in order to re-establish correct flow of chi.

The Cochina is the Native American spirt dancer who walks always backwards. He is known in this tradition as the trickster, the coyote, or the one who sees things with a fresh view. These are the positive ways to experience a breech birth, and mothers have birthed breech babies successfully both in water and on land. It is common with twins for one twin to be in the breech position to accommodate two babies in the womb.

Sometimes a baby can be encouraged to turn during the last weeks of pregnancy. Women have used slant boards, acupuncture, exercise, and meditation to help babies rotate successfully. One mother reported her baby shifted once she explained to her that a breech position is a difficult way to arrive. Occasionally a baby will turn and then turn back.

Why does breech presentation occur?

This question addresses the mystery and uniqueness of birth. We don't really know. If there is prenatal violence, or ambivalence from the parents, the baby may not want to come out. Sometimes the baby is fine while small but while still growing gets in a position it cannot change in time to adjust. Often the baby will let you know why they came breech when allowed to express their prenatal story.

The most useful thing to help an infant or child process a breech birth is to celebrate their successful arrival, name the complications, encourage the push with the head, and help them find a felt sense of the value of moving forward in life. Breech birth produces a dramatic pull on the jaw as baby exits the womb. There can be residual fear, pain, and weakness in the neck and disconnection through the head into the spine. Find professional support to work through these imprints. Tendencies to not complete, not cross thresholds, or be highly anxious at deadlines can be symptoms of breech position.

Methods used to reposition baby

Japanese midwives	Use a long piece of fabric placed under mothers belly. They lift the baby back up out of the pelvis so it can reposition and find a better orientation.
Acupuncture	Both gentle needling and Moxa combustion has been used effectively to help a baby turn.
Slant Board	Mom spends time laying on a board with her feet above her head to help a baby turn.
Doctor assisted pre-birth attempts	Some doctors have been trained to use their hands directly. They use pressure on Mom's abdomen in an attempt to rotate the baby pre-birth.

Modern medical insurance rarely allows breech births in hospitals

They are scheduled as automatic 'C'-sections.

- The hips are not as wide as the head
- There is often great pressure & pull on the head
- Hips can be displaced
- Hands on BMC ligament and Cranial-Sacral sessions are recommended
- Let the baby find its way out
- Provide respectful encouragement
- Intervene only when life-threatening

Support the baby's choice to arrive in this manner

Process emotional components

- not wanting to be here
- fear of completing events
- feeling different

Behavior linked to birth phases

Issues of time, orientation, follow-through and completion

Birth sequence imprints related to timing, planning, pacing, and follow-through are exhausting. Understanding birth phases and dismantling habits reduces self-judgment and provides new options. Use current behavior challenges to determine which phase of a project is troublesome and assess if related to difficulty in birth phases.

Phases of birth

Repetitive patterns of behavior in life can be linked to birth phases. One client sabotaged her college assignments. She was very bright but was plauged with this pattern: She waited too long to start assignments, then focused in a determined panic, and then goofed off due to the pressure, convincing herself she didn't need to work so hard. The night before the paper was due, she would stress and write the paper quickly. However, she would not complete the final part and so couldn't hand her paper in on time. This was a repetition of her birth rhythm due to C-section. She was stuck in the birth canal (too long to get started), zoned out (anesthesia overlay), waited till there was excess pressure and wrote quickly (C-section births are rapid) and failed to complete or hand it in (had no felt-sense of meeting pressure and finding completion). With proper naming of birth phases and somatic work to integrate sensation and release shock, this client was able to change this pattern and successfully enjoy her school assignments.

Interrupted birth phases shows up as patterns in adult life. Assessing birth phases helps one understand and shift behavior. Premature births have no planning stage. Anesthesia imprints interrupt taking action. Forceps interrupt follow through, as do C-sections. Post-birth NICU care, babies placed in the nursery instead of with Mom, or surgery for Mom that interrupts bonding, will interrupt the integration phase. Identifying birth phases demystifies and interrupts self-sabotaging behavior.

Working with birth phases helps life become easier and less limited

How does one currently behave in meeting goals and needs? Are there common places of difficulty? Tease apart behavior to see if it is linked to birth sequence. No matter how long ago birth occurred, the body tissue remembers what happened due to neural imprinting. Help children or clients release emotions from that early sequence and repair the ability to find satisfaction. For parents, I suggest seeking professional help. It will provide great relief in the parenting issues of timeliness and cooperation in their children.

Birth Phases			
Intention	desire	potency	creativity
Preparation	planning	forward thinking	gathering resources
Action	potency	body power	navigation + clarity of direction
Follow-through	completing tasks	using support	taking risks
Integration	celebration	connection with others	rest and recuperation

Look for shock imprints with babies labeled as "indigo" children

The popular "indigo child" syndrome is alarming. Such children are considered especially spiritual. However, I have treated some of these infants, and they are often in a state of shock. As their shock lessened, they became more normal and responded with emotions to stress rather than "bliss out." They were not limited to a sweet dissociative spiritualized self. Supporting a child to be grounded helps them live a functional life. Spirituality develops from an embodied place rather than through dissociation or projection from parents or other adults.

The open-hearted beauty of the "indigo" spirit is seductive. Often I reluctantly remind parents that the body produces an opiate that drives dissociation under stress of a perceived life-threat during birth; this dissociation appears spiritual. Grounded parents appreciate the results when this indigo quality is dismantled and their child becomes more relational and present. However, if the parent retains a spiritualize shock imprint, they are less capable of supporting the integration of their child.

The work of reclaiming a body-sense potency without diminishing the health of the spirit must be done delicately so the spirit is invited into the body rather than in conflict with the body. Parents must be supported to grieve for the loss of the spiritualized "indigo" nature and educated to notice the value of the grounded child. Help parents identify the cost of dissociation for indigo children. Parental love will support their child's authentic open-hearted nature while giving them a chance for an embodied life.

Origination of the term "indigo child" from Wikipedia, 2011

"Indigo children" is a pseudoscientific label given to children who are claimed to possess special, unusual and/or supernatural traits or abilities. The idea is based on New Age concepts developed in the 1970s by Nancy Ann Tappe.

The concept of indigo children gained popular interest with the publication of a series of books in the late 70's and the release of several films in the following decade. A variety of books, conferences and related materials have been created surrounding belief in the idea of indigo children and their nature and abilities. These beliefs range from their being the next stage in human evolution or possessing paranormal abilities such as telepathy to the belief that they are simply more empathic and creative than their peers.

Although there are no scientific studies to give credibility to the existence of any indigo children, or their traits, the phenomenon appeals to some parents whose children have been diagnosed with learning disabilities and parents seeking to believe that their children are special. This is viewed by skeptics as a way for parents to avoid proper (and generally pharmaceutical) pediatric treatment or a psychiatric diagnosis which implies imperfection. (continued in side bar)

The list of traits used to describe the [Indigo] children has also been criticized for being vague enough to be applied to almost anyone, a form of the Forer effect. The phenomenon has been criticized as a means of making money from credulous parents through the sales of related products and services."

Wikipedia, 2011

Thoughts on Modern Birth Practices and Womens' Choice

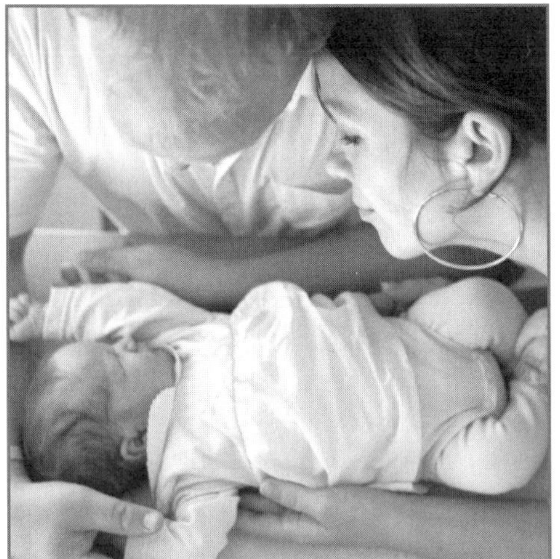

Non-interrupted labor allows a Mom to be present to greet her new infant

The hidden costs of managed labor Unnecessary birth interventions and ignorant procedures contribute to children who are hyperactive, difficult to settle, and have sensory-motor challenges. I see these children daily in my psychotherapy clinic, and observe the suffering of well-intended parents who are overwhelmed through tending to children who have special needs. Fortunately much of this sensory motor activation and challenge is resolved when parents and children go back through early birth stories and integrate their experience. I am treating post-birth shock and resultant behavioral problems daily with a full clinical practice. If birth providers pay attention to oxytocin moments for bonding, children may become more securely attached and better able to meet pressure and transitions in life. Active prevention to eliminate unnecessary interventions and support bonding would bring relief.

The positive intent of the Medical community is to offer helpful services; however power and financial issues come into play. Birth and death cannot be "guaranteed" by technology. Obstetricians are given the extreme power that once was shared with midwifery and fate. The medical financial system assumes responsibility for women's prenatal care, birth education, and birth outcome and this is a big business. (see DVD "The Business of Being Born" available for free from Netflix).

Impacts on Society and a Woman's Psyche Incredulous women have reported their success at non-intervention births. *"This wild moaning and powerful part of me showed up, and we did it!"* (mother's comment post-birth, when a storm necessitated she give birth at home). Society has not examined the long range consequences to a woman's psyche when her birthing experience is interrupted. Interruptive interventions are disempowering to women at a very deep level. Many modern women don't even know what they are missing, since birth has been interrupted by pain medication for generations. The ability to birth is one of the realities of a female body;* yet without this opportunity, a woman loses a certain kind of accomplishment success. The expectation that she can meet pressure and have a successful outcome is weakened, and the sense of needing to be rescued by the doctor (who is often male) is rampant. This sets up a false expectation of the "masculine coming to the rescue." The masculine and feminine archetypal forces become unbalanced. Women who surrender their birthing power unnecessarily may in fact weaken relational exchanges between men and women on a societal level.

Women returned to natural birthing in the '70s; however they weren't prepared for the pain, being falsely expected to "spiritualize" the birth experience. Protocols swung back to birth as pain management, thus interrupting connection to the baby. It is becoming difficult the world over to have non-managed labor, and the required use of C-section is escalating.

The Fear of Death US Western culture is a culture that fears death and so avoids meeting it. Our elderly are pushed out of mainstream society and kept alive through costly technologies that diminish quality of life and meeting the reality of death with grace and connection. The reality of birth is also kept isolated and is feared. It might be better to educate towards more natural birthing, (as well as graceful dying) and use technology to save the lives that need to be saved, rather than as a protocol for life at all costs. Please don't misunderstand my concerns. Supportive life-saving emergency procedures are not what is being questioned. I question the wisdom of pain management protocol, and the loss of female generational support to navigate the task of birthing, where a mother is allowed and supported to remain awake and aware while giving birth, thus staying connected to her infant through this transition threshold.

See DVD, *Unassisted Birth*, mentioned in the resource section. Some women don't realize that women are even capable to deliver unassisted. This knowledge needs to be retained in the female psyche.

Birth as pain management

When addressing birth options with pregnant mothers, please help them consider how to navigate pain and ways to reclaim their natural ability to give birth. Please help birth not be about "pain management" but return to an empowering connective ritual between mother and child.

Due to the loss of cultural wisdom and birth familiarity, women are pre-focused on the pain of birth. Hospitals tend to promote this focus as well. Individuals experience pain through many lenses. Woman might experience labor as a terrifying task, as an opportunity to display strength and heroism, as well-deserved or wholly undeserved punishment, as the normal consequences of a specific and self-limiting condition, as utterly unbearable, or as easily dismissed suffering preceding great reward!

Culture and experience also dictate how pain should be expressed, and that expression-stoic silence, occasional wincing, low moaning, constant complaining, or uncontrolled hysteria, to name only a few examples-can further shape the nature of the physical feeling... in cultures where the custom is to remain silent, women experience the sensations of labor differently than in cultures where screaming is the

expected reaction. Asking and answering the important cultural question, "How am I supposed to behave in this situation?" dictates not only outward behavior but often physical and emotional sensation as well. -Jaqueline H. Wolf, *Deliver Me from Pain*, 2009.

Cultural loss of Birth Wisdom and Opportunities for Repair Consider the generations of impact of medically assisted labor and the imprints carried forward in women. There is a cellular matrix of anaesthetized birth stemming from the late 1800s that has entered the cultural matrix. How does this influence pregnant mother's expectations and experience of birthing? It is common for a woman's first birth to carry the imprinted fear and echo of her own birth experience. If her mother were anesthetized, she would have come into the world unsupported and confused with anesthesia. For this reason, it is recommended that women who are going to give birth receive perinatal sessions to clear their own story prior to giving birth. Many women who have done so report a relief and clarity while giving birth that they felt would not have been available without these preventive sessions.

Prevalence of C-Sections

*Only 15% of pelvic shapes are deemed too small to allow a baby to exit.
This is the optoidal shaped pelvis. A procedural scan for this pelvic shape could reduce the exaggerated use of C-sections.

"Women from Mexican villages are told the date their baby will be "born" at their first check up, and are flocking to hospitals to "deliver." personal commentary, nurse from Mexico City, 2005.

"It is very difficult in Turkey for women to have a natural vaginal birth in hospital." personal commentary, Turkish woman 2012.

Help to Educate Women

The interruption to bonding makes elective C-sections a formidable and reproachable alternative. Please help educate women about possible emotional/development consequences from C-section and chemical interventions. Help stir interest in how best to implement supportive changes in current obstetric procedures.

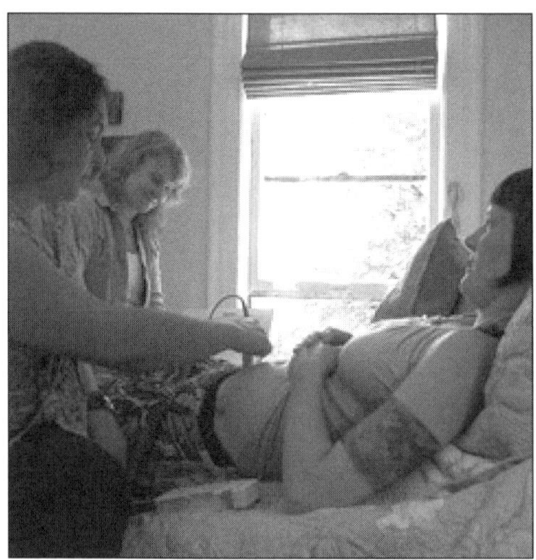

Support for meeting the reality of child-birth

Western medicine can serve most effectively as an emergency back-up for birthing, rather than a front-line choice. It is extremely useful when there are complications or higher risk situations. When western medicine-methods are utilized, please provide treatment and hands on sessions to repair the physical and emotional shock field of the woman and child.

I appeal to women to reclaim birth. However, by demanding again to be in charge of one's birth process, one must also accept the reality of the journey of life and death. We are in a fortunate time where women can bear the risk of hosting life and death in their inner psyche, while still having back up emergency support. They can take charge of birthing and not expect to go through it unaware, numb, or disengaged. Society would need to provide adequate support and liability laws might have to be modified to include accepting the loss of an infant at birth. Prenatal support would include working through fears, surrendering to the mystery of birth, and also to accept the baby's karma. Accepting that the greater mystery of life force is not under one's control appreciates the reality of the mystery of birth.

This type of birthing demands a true surrender. One must open to the mystery, accept being out of control, and stay present to the extreme sensation of birthing. Unfortunately, sometimes babies die. That is an incredible loss, and it takes time to heal this loss, and to accept fate. It is important to release guilt and to grieve. Women I know who have met birth loss in this way have a sense of character that is built only through direct experience with birth, life, and death. One must access an inner courage that has been available to women for centuries prior to the managed labor model.

I do not approach these thoughts on birth lightly or from an idealized position. I know the hardships of meeting death in a number of circumstances; having had two second trimester miscarriages, having my father die when I was a toddler, and my beloved husband pass three months after our marriage. These experiences have demanded me to relate to life with a perspective that includes death. Facing these realities are aspects of life.

For those wanting the Western Medical support, there are birthing clinics and hospitals that provide quality birth support with minimal intervention. Michele Odent highlights an exemplary clinic in Belgium that utilizes water birth methods. Many US hospitals include a Birthing Room option. In these settings the focus is on slower pacing and allowing the couple to stay connected during the birth. Emergency equipment is in the room behind closed cupboards, ready in a moments notice when needed for life-support. Educating couples about how a more organic birth supports their child's future development, and providing them access to alternative medical settings will help such settings become more accessible. With managed medical birthing as a back up process, rather than as the only way to proceed, birth may again be a threshold crossing. It may return as the essential rites of passage teacher that it is. When a woman has the following: educational support for nervous system sensitivity during birth, containment, quiet, support to focus on the birth, and sensitivity to the birth's own pacing, she may again find the shamanic aspects of herself that birth brings to the foreground.

The Loss of the Pelvic Mobility

Another factor relating to birth complications is body flexibility. Keeping the pelvic floor supple and mobile is a larger cultural issue. Squatting occurs daily in many countries, including squatting for defecation. This supports the pelvic floor to be toned and supple throughout life. However, due to the use of the chair, Westerners no longer squat on a regular basis. Chair sitting actually disables pelvic strength and resiliency, and use of the chair has drastically interfered with pelvic, lumbar, and sacrum low back mobility. Western culture has less hip movement in dance forms, and many women suffer from lack of sensuality and sexual pleasure due to pelvic tensions. Women with a strong yoga practice can have difficulty birthing because their muscle strength is layered on top of lack of resiliency due to growing up without squatting. Many fit women have been disappointed when they needed an emergency C-section due to this occurrence.

Encouraging women to squat, dance, and refuse to be placed on their back during labor can help birth be vaginal without interventions. Being on all fours, standing with support, birthing chairs that support upright pelvis, or squatting, rather than mother lying on her back during childbirth, supports ease of birthing. The pelvis can rotate and move with the baby's head when mother is not on her back. Back placement must be removed as standard birth positioning procedure, and positions that allow pelvic mobility encouraged.

A Woman's Choice There is no simple answer to deciding how to birth. Issues are interwoven with deep-seated societal fears and beliefs. Reclaiming birth also means reclaiming death, and fear of death is prevalent in western culture. Using medical assistance for birthing as a back up method, rather than a primary method focused on pain relief, demands that we educate woman about the realities of birthing. The backlash after the '70's when women moved from natural birthing back to hospitals is reportedly due to the oversimplification of telling women birth was a "wonderful" experience, and not educating women to meet and face the physical pain of birthing, due in part to generations of loss of this knowledge.

Decades of drugged mothers and managed labors has diminished the natural cultural support related to birth awareness. However, helping women know there are options around designing a birth plan and choosing how to birth creates an opportunity for non-invasive procedures (unless in emergency) and enhances a woman's depth of presence and personal dignity. Personal empowerment through birthing responsibly may have long-range positive ramifications for our culture in bonding, attached parenting, and a broader experience of the interdependence of life. Taking time to ponder, to become educated, and to face the reality of birth as a threshold makes choosing how to birth an aspect of continued empowerment. Doing so can also support potency for parenting post-birth.

Chapter four addressed birth themes and imprints. The following chapter addresses post-birth impacts on infant behavior and bonding.

Whenever hospitals administer invasive interventions (whether to avoid liability, or save lives), it is imperative to interrupt the effects as early as possible. Ideally, hospitals would make available physical and psychological post-birth care for families. Biodynamic Cranio-Sacral sessions would help, as would BodyMind Centering® sessions, as would perinatal psychological sessions. If this were post-birth protocol, covered by insurance, it would reduce the mental health and educational costs to society.

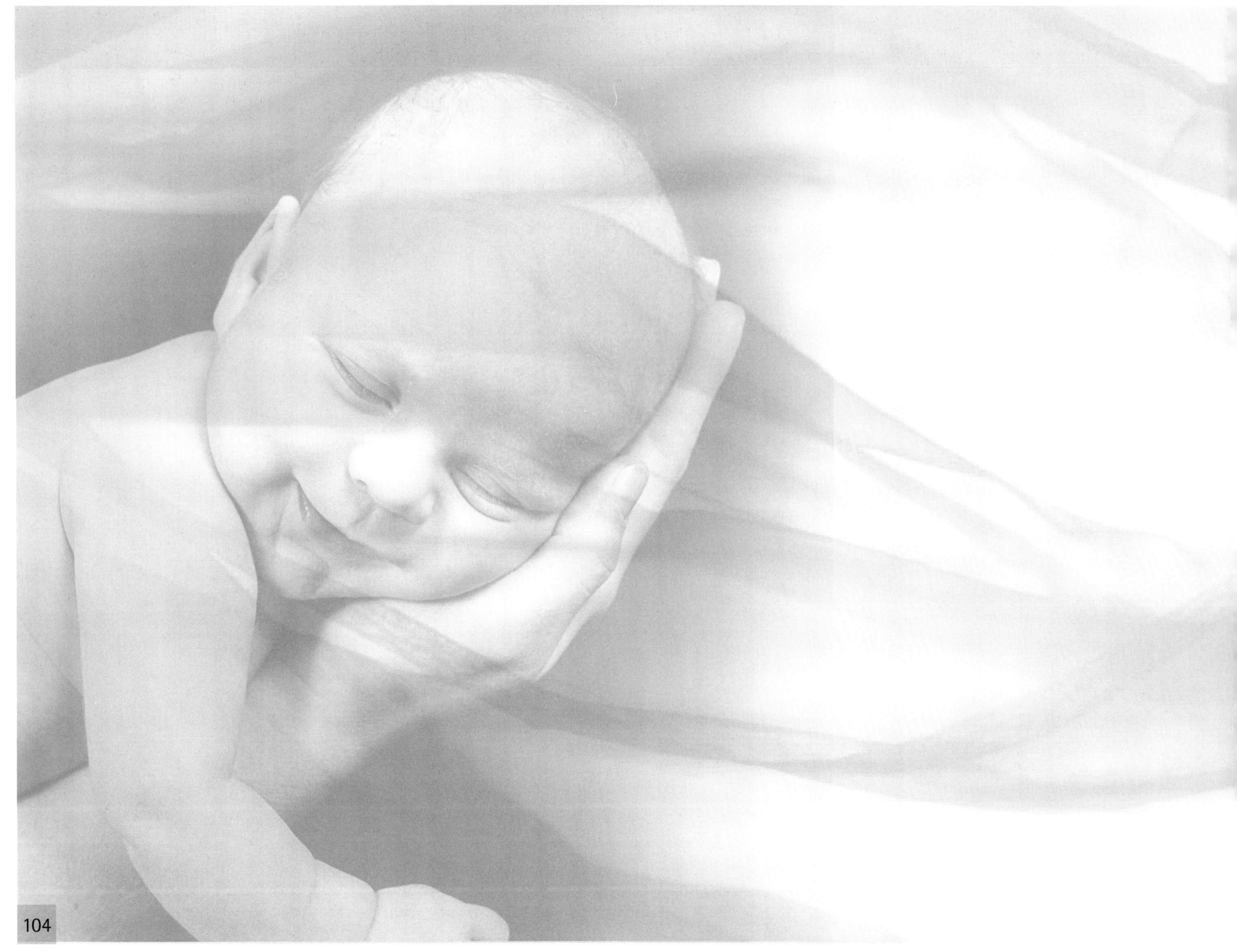

Chapter 4

Post-Birth Themes

Infants do best when placed skin-to-skin with Mom post-birth. This supports healthy bonding, self-attachment, and ensures a healthy self-regulation. Due to ignorance, emergency, or protocol, this bonding time is often disturbed. This chapter highlights themes that interrupt bonding and the subsequent issues that occur.

Bonding is essential and helps the nervous system and social regulation
The ability to bond and connect for mother and infant is a precious moment in time, and worth supporting. Bonding creates a later resource for parenting success and is a tremendous time of new learning and discovery filled with sensory adjustments. Mom is recovering from birth, and baby must orient to the pull of gravity without support of the prenatal waters. Sensory perception is now in direct relationship with sound, light, touch, and pressure. Mother and infant must learn the nursing dance, and often need help. Mothers go through the dramatic shift from carrying a child to tending a child, with the subsequent sleep deprivation, adjustment to being needed at such a huge level, and physically reclaiming their bodies. If oxytocin was not masked at birth due to procedures, mothers received the hormonal body support for these efforts.

Post-birth is the time of psychological attachment. The relationship between mother and child is more tangible and perhaps emotionally vulnerable. Babies need quiet, stillness, calm, and a sense of safety and joy for their natural humor and curiosity to emerge. Mothers need support with household chores and the needs of their other children so they have time to recover, bond, and discover their new baby's unique language.

Repair of interrutped Bonding Interrupted post-birth time sets up mother-child patterns that last well into adult interactions for both parties involved. Beliefs are created and behaviors established in the subconsious relating. Fortunately, these impressions can shift due to the plasticity of the neural system. I treated a 40 year-old "child" and her mother whose bonding had been interrupted due to forceps and anesthesia. The infant was placed in the nursery rather than allowed to nurse with her mother and enjoy the connection of eye gazing and touch. This session re-established the felt-sense of love and connection each had yearned for during and following the birth. This healing occurred 40 years after the birth, and validates the ability of the body-mind to repair the earliest of imprints. I have facilitated a number of such repair sessions and they result in a deeper trust and connection on an instinctual level.

It can be difficult to comprehend the rare sensitivity of a newborn and meet this imprint with empathy. As a clinician, listen to the story from the perspective of a tender and fresh nervous system. Remain empathic and listen to the body expression, un-met needs, arousal, and beliefs. Help clients of all ages to befriend their body, reclaim ability to feel sensation, and to seek and respond to pleasure. Help mothers release guilt or blame and to re-pattern emotional response patterns with their children that were linked to interrupted post-birth experience.

Post-Birth Themes

Early invasion issues	Early cutting and clamping of the umbilical cord resulting in rapid drop in babies blood volume, bulb suctioning of mouth and nose, drops into the eyes, cleaning, weighing, measuring and separation from skin-to-skin contact with the mother. Abrasive or aggressive handling procedures.
Energetic influences	The emotional tone and energy of the delivery room personnel: behavior and emotional attitudes of doctors, nurses, and delivery personnel.
Separation issues	Anything other than skin-to-skin contact with mother post-birth. Separation from mother (or father) for any reason, i.e. nursery time, Neonatal Intensive Care Units (NICU), post-birth surgical procedures for mother that require separation from infant, twin births or multiple births, a twin or multiple's death, mother's illness, infection, or birth recovery needs.
Later invasive procedure	NICU care, circumcision, jaundice lights, infant quarantine.

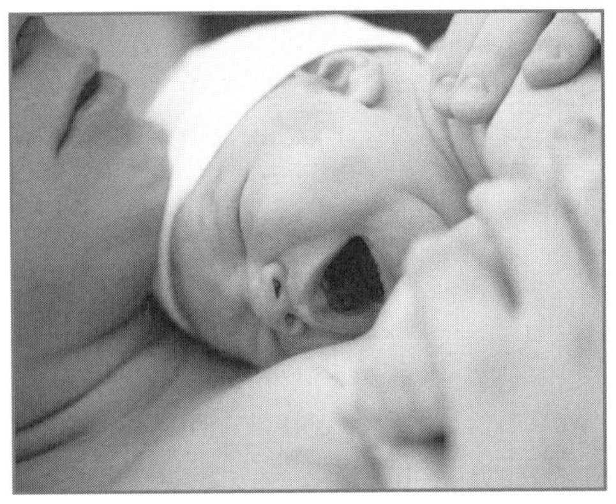

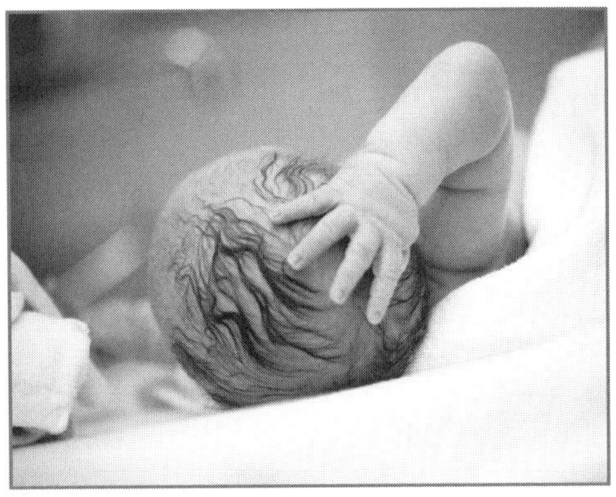

Most post-birth mothers want to hold their babies—and rest!

Mothers are busy bonding, counting toes, gazing in rapture, and settling into the huge transition of life that a birth brings. This is not the time to separate baby and mother. The oxytocin moment is a hormonal infusion that floods mother's and baby's bodies when baby's head descends and presses on a point near mother's bladder. Oxytocin promotes the love needed for the vast amount of care a newborn demands. This hormonal support for motherly love is essential as it prepares Mom to accept the loss of sleep and physical/emotional challenges she must endure while parenting a newborn. This oxytocin moment is relatively short in duration and should not be interrupted nor masked with birth chemicals.

When not limited by shock, a baby also utilizes this natural oxytocin hormone. It falls in love with mother post-birth. However, a baby in shock due to a difficult birth is handicapped and sometimes not ready to bond. This can be disappointing to a mother. She may feel baby's disconnection but not been counseled on how to understand why baby is not able to connect. Often babies need help to clear their nervous system of stress from the birth in order to bond easily. Helping mothers know this relieves their disappointment and fear that they have done something wrong.

Coaching a mother on how to name the difficult moments of birth out loud to her infant helps to repair dissociation and sense of safety for the baby. Imagine the birth events from an infant's perspective. Empathize and name aloud and let the baby respond emotionally. I coached a mother to do this with her week old infant who went through confusion, terror, anger, sadness, and finally forgiveness. He then settled contentedly into his mother's body and was no longer fussy or tense when held. Naming birth events helps baby release emotional feelings of fear, abandonment, anger, and loss. Babies are reassured when mother understands and they more easily settle.

The following pages describe post-birth imprints. Treatment is to support mothers, so I will write this next paragraph as if in counsel with a mother and father.

"Please reconcile any inner turmoil from a birth. Release guilt for misfortunate events, especially if support was inadequate or interrupted. Anger, fear, disappointment, and sadness are all common experiences. Feeling cut off from your spouse due to the hospital taking charge is another common experience. Mothers giving birth are drawn unconsciously into their own experience of being birthed, especially with their first born child. This cellular memory can cloud the current experience of birth and make the birth more difficult. Processing your own birth prior to giving birth clears the space for new experience."

A skilled therapist can help a couple or new family recover from a difficult birth that interrupted the couples bond and brought waves of shock into the family field.

Birth impact on fathers

Unconscious birth memories can interrupt a father's ability to be present or his willingness to be available during a birth. Many cultures do not ask men to be present for birthing, as it is too far out of the archetypal code. In Western culture, it is more common for fathers to want to attend the birth. However, if Dad's own birth issues became activated during the birth of his child, he may have withdrawn or become overly intense and vigilant. If he needed to step back and let the professionals handle it all, he might also have dissociated due to a feeling of disempowerment or fear for his wife's circumstance.

In a complicated birth, fathers can feel they failed on an archetypal level to protect their family. Mom may have felt unprotected by Dad even though he was doing what the doctors asked for. She may carry hidden resentment. Guilt or resentment can cloud connections between Mom and Dad post-birth.

Dads who address their own unconsicous birth memories prior to attending their baby's birth will be most able to stay present and supportive. Father's need to be allowed a position of useful power by midwives and physicians. Under emergency procedures, it is useful to give the Dad a task so he feels capable and useful, even if it is as simple as telling him to hold his partner's hand and send heart energy to her and to their baby.

Repair birth impacts for couples

Unaddressed issues of birth shock can lead to incredible friction, and even lead to divorce post-birth due to unaddressed shock held deep in the subconscious. Support pregnant couples to clear their birth histories prior to giving birth. Help parents to acknowledge, grieve, and repair any interruption in their bond as a couple related to a difficult birth. Held residue from unprocessed birth trauma can interrupt the "sense of team" a couple needs as they step into this next role of parenting.

Proactive birth planning helps to prevent post-birth trauma

Remember to be proactive with birth planning and prevent unnecessary hospital procedures. Support couples to know their rights in delivery requests. Parents can inform hospital staff to keep the cord unclamped until it stops pulsing, and suspend cleaning, weighing and measuring in favor of holding the baby immediately following birth. The baby can be washed in mother's arms in a gentle manner as needed. This attention to the delicate needs of bonding and the critical timing of oxytocin at the bonding moment will establish a life-long connection that supports trust and a feeling of social and relational safety.

Bonding stressors for infants and mothers

Chemicals

- anesthesia
- induction drugs
- residual prenatal drug effects

Interventions

- forceps
- vacuum suction
- breaking of the waters
- C-section
- repositioning of baby

Skin-to-Skin Interruptions

- cleaning baby
- bulb suctioning nose and mouth
- post-birth operations for Mom or baby
- nursery baby care
- NICU care
- circumcision

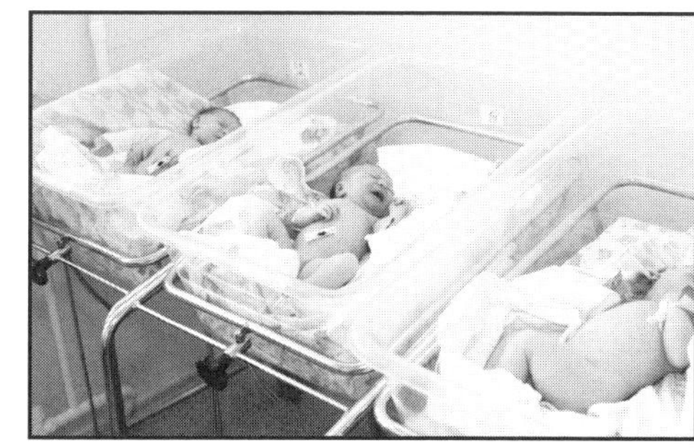

Post-birth Cleaning Impacts and Birth Plans

Post-birth cleaning imprints are the first experience beyond the womb. They are invasive and create separation and overwhelm in the infant nervous system. They often follow the significant shock when the umbilicus was clamped and cut. For suctioning, a plastic nozzle attached to a rubber squeeze bulb is inserted into the baby's nose and mouth. You can see infants pull back in a startle response. Suctioning is accompanied by other procedures where baby is taken from the mother, rubbed down with a towel by strangers, weighed, placed on a cold table, and squirted in the eyes with drops. While intended to prevent infection and make baby "clean and presentable," they significantly traumatize the infant who is then returned to the mother. Many mothers have stated they thought their baby was "clean enough!" When viewed from the infant's perspective such treatments are perceived as inhumane and interrupt bonding.

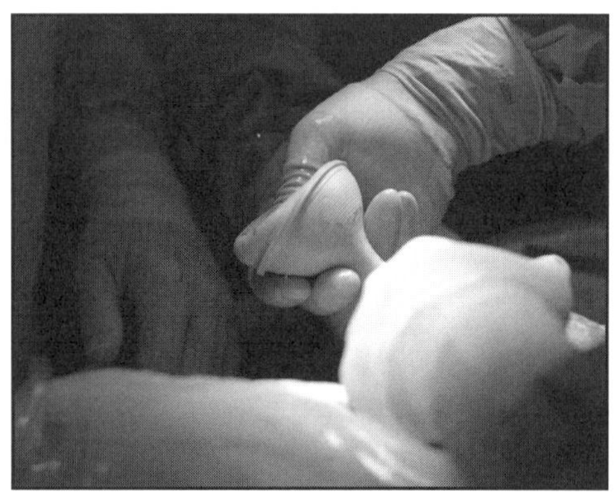

Karen Strange, a certified nurse midwive who teaches neo-natal resuscitation, feels adamantly that suctioning is unnecessary, especially if the umbilical cord is left connected. Babies who have an intact umbilical placenta receive oxygenated blood while they transition to breathing with their lungs. There is not an urgency as they can self-clear airways. If problems, this midwife suggests to show mothers how to use their hands and mouths to help their baby. Suctioning can be employed only as a last resort.

What will it take for this protocol to be modified? We need to prioritize infant bonding and self-attachment by allowing immediate post-birth skin-to-skin contact of mother and infant and support feeding at the breast.

Birth plans

Creating a birth plan helps mothers to take charge of their birth experience. Encourage expectant mothers to consult books, midwives, and friends who have birthed in a less conventional manner. Women often don't know they are "allowed" to ask for methods other than what is told to them.

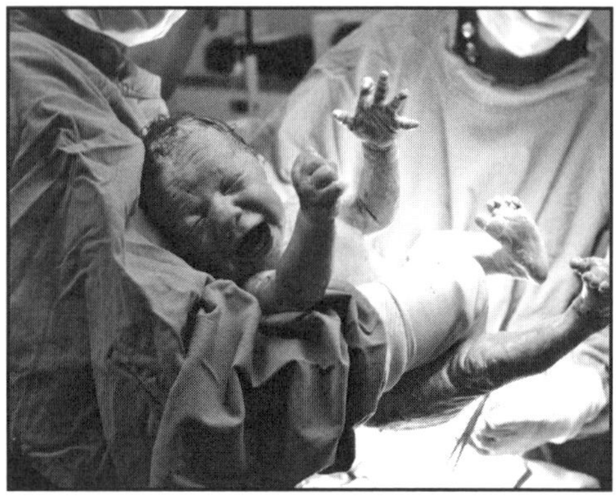

Create a birth plan and make sure you have the support to follow it

Prevention and education are the best resources. Birth has happened since the beginning of human time, and has been successful even when completely unassisted. Mothers want to do what is right, yet only have access to managed labor models as the example. Interrupted bonding is a real factor that contributes to a hyperactive infant or child. It can produce problems later in childhood that are not immediately evident at the birth.

"Mothers, please speak to midwives, even if you are having a hospital birth with an attending physician. Find out what is possible. View the latest birth videos and choose some that are not from hospital as a comparison. Read books about birth plans, write down what you want, and make this known to your birth provider. You are a consumer! Have your husband or a friend be an advocate! Choose what is comfortable for you and your partner and please avoid unnecessary procedures."

Cord clamping and cutting

Placental blood is oxygenated blood and creates a gentle transition to breathing. Imagine the effect on an infantwhen the cord is cut early. Cutting the cord before blood has drained out of the placenta into the baby's body is shocking to a newborn's body and heart. With early clamping and cutting of the cord, your baby loses one quarter of their blood supply immediately following birth! EMTs (emergency medical technicians) will tell you that anyone who loses one quarter of their blood volume goes into extreme shock. Some midwives consider it an amputation.

Early cutting is felt by the body. The baro cells of the heart measure blood pressure and feel the drop when the cord is cut. This is especially detrimental to babies born prematurely because the lungs are the last organs to develop and premies desperately need that oxygenated blood to help them adjust. Placental blood is actually the baby's blood, not the mother's.

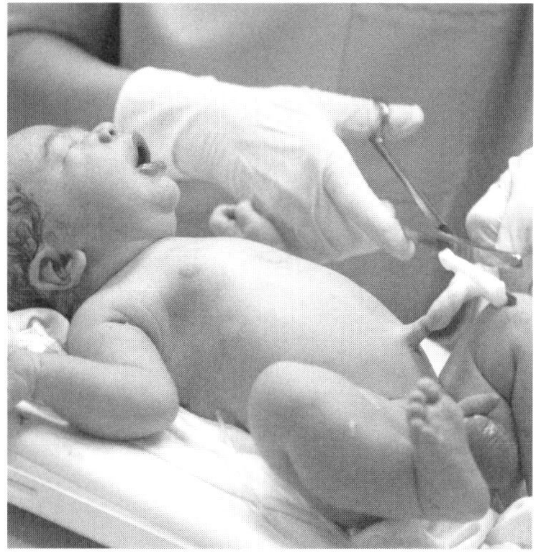

Umbilical cord clamp and cut. Baby loses approximately one quarter of his blood volume if cut before the cord stops pulsing.

Prevent early cord clamping and cutting

It takes approximately 20 minutes for the cord to stop pulsing. This means the blood has successfully arrived into the baby's body. Babies are more supported. Some cultures leave the cord attached longer. They feel the baby needs time for the "soul" to arrive, and that the soul is carried in the placenta. This is called Lotus Birth.

Why is early cord clamping and cutting practiced?

Medical concerns are that the baby would be flooded by the placental blood and be in danger of receiving too much blood. However, the umbilical cord structure is similar to a vein, not an artery. Veins allow blood to flow back and forth while arteries only flow in one direction. Any excess blood is easily able to flow back to the placenta without problems.

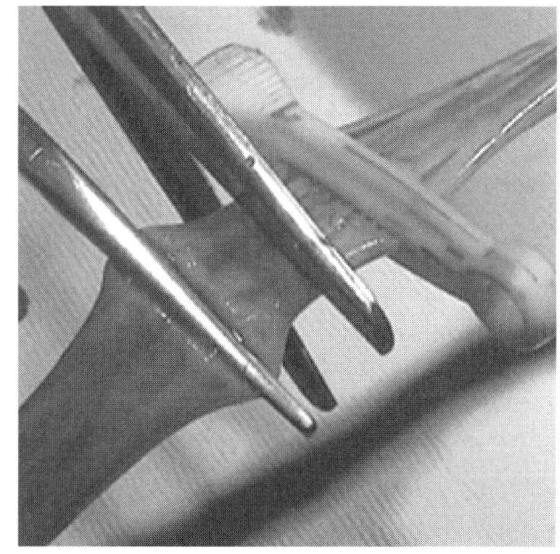

Hospitals are under time and money constraints. Birth would become a longer procedure if physicians waited for the cord to stop pulsing. Placental blood is retained as a resource for blood banks.

Early Cellular memory encodes experiences. When memories surface, they can be integrated and repaired. Cord cut memory will feel more like a "brain state" than a memory. It is full-bodied and pervasive. The following poem written by this author helped integrate the effect of cord cutting and clamping, which was exacerbated by her being born 6 weeks premature.

Poems to take a breath... *(written after recovery of cellular memories of early cord-clamp and cut following premature birth)*

Quiet Heart
by Annie Brook

Barely enough blood to breathe
Yet present now to the sense of this,
Just this...
Life, still-almost nothing
-slow rhythm
All there is
is breath
Inhale... a pause... almost death
Let go the breath
Will it return?

No blood to lift the head
Bones busy and bereft of power
Ignorance abounds
in Doctors who cut away
too quickly
the life blood of the early born
Do they give the still pulsing placenta to bloodbanks,
sell for profit? Where has it gone?

Inhale
Too near death
to name desire for life
Exhale
Too quiet
Quiet heart

Slowly, oh so slowly

Bones make more blood

Life returns

Lotus Birth: Leaving the Placenta Intact

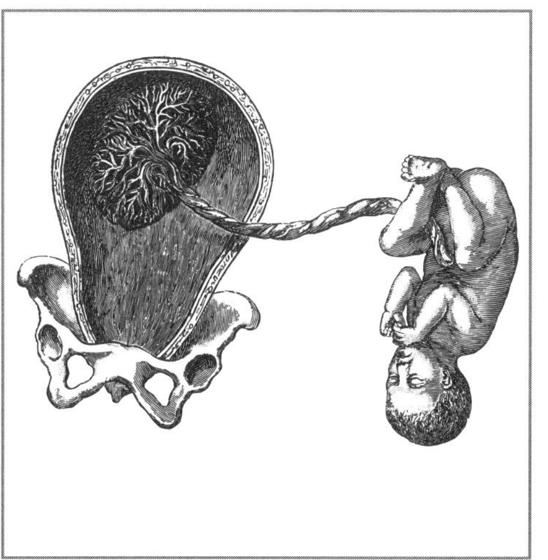

The healthy placenta is rich in blood and filled with nourishment. Visually, it can be compared to the mythic "tree of life." It provides support and containment and is an important part of the early baby's relational life. Other cultures treat the placenta as a significant part of the baby's arrival. They preserve it for a life-time so that it can be buried with the child at the end of life. Some lightly salt the placenta once the blood is drained and keep it until it falls off naturally and is then buried. The Igbos people of Nigeria bury the placenta right after birth and plant a tree over it. In some cultures where malnutrition occurs, the placenta might be cooked and eaten. Various cultures have learned to use the placenta as a gift of nature rather than be offended by it or discard it. (adapted from Wikipedia and added to by this author).

India is the known origin of Lotus Birth as a common practice

Lotus Birth: a gentle approach

- Supports baby's transition from womb to mother's arms.
- The body has a natural breathing timing that is supported through this method
- The baby is learning to mouth and nose-breathe while still getting oxygen from the placental blood

Modern origin of Lotus Births

(paraphrased by this author from Wikipedia notes)

Early American pioneers, in written diaries and letters, reported practicing non-severance of the umbilicus as a preventative measure to protect the infant from an open wound infection.

The practice of lotus birth gained notice in the yoga practitioner community when Jeannine Parvati Baker practiced umbilical non-severance for two of her own births. She is author of Prenatal Yoga & Natural Childbirth, the first book written in the west on prenatal yoga. Jeannine saw lotus birth as a practical application of the yogic value of ahimsa as well as the core yoga sutra teaching inherent in the primal bonding process that "All attachments will fall away of their own accord."

Sarah Buckley, MD, an Australian family physician and noted parenting advisor for Mothering Magazine, published her personal birth stories in the text *Lotus Birth*. Dr. Buckley has produced numerous scholarly publications of her research on the physiological benefits of Passive Management of Third Stage Labor. See sarahjbuckley.com/articles/leaving-well-alone.htm.

Robin Lim ("Ibu Robin") is a midwife and founder of Yayasan Bumi Sehat (Healthy Mother Earth Foundation) health clinics, which offer free prenatal care, birthing services and medical aid to anyone who needs it. She and her team have been working since 2003 to combat Indonesia's high maternal and infant mortality rates, and the Bumi Sehat birth centers serve many at-risk mothers. She was awarded the 2011 CNN Hero of the Year award by the CNN news network for helping thousands of low-income women in Indonesia with healthy pregnancy and birth services.. (from Wikepedia).

Robin was able to resuscitate a still-born baby by leaving the placenta attached and massaging the placental blood back into the newborn. The baby revived. The placenta is nature's way of supporting transition and keeping it attached can be life saving.

On Lotus Birth (from Wikipedia on the web)

In hospitals and global medical centers, common medical training and practice is known as "Active Management" of Third Stage Labor and includes: immediate clamping of the cord once the baby is born, cutting it forthwith, then applying traction to the cord to speed the birth of the placenta rather than leaving the cord-placenta-baby unit intact to provide for a physiologically gentle transition of mother and baby. The cord blood may or may not be harvested for cord blood banking. The baby's umbilical cord and placenta are then disposed of as medical waste or sold to laboratories.

When Umbilical Nonseverance or Lotus Birth is practiced, rarely in hospitals but more common in birth centers and home birth, integrity of the neonate is highly valued, and maternal-neonatal bonding proceeds uninterrupted. While care providers conduct immediate Apgar scoring (measurement of reflexes and vital signs) and provide any needed neonatal suctioning or stimulation, most further procedures are postponed until one hour post-birth. The baby-cord-placenta unit is swaddled by the mother in-arms, or held by a father or nurse during maternal suturing.

In a full lotus birth, excess fluids are wiped off the placenta and it is kept in an open bowl or wrapped in a cloth, in close proximity to the neonate. The cloths used to wrap the placenta or bowl holding it must allow air to pass through so that the placenta can begin to dry out. Sea salt may be applied to the placenta to help this process. Essential oils, such as lavender, along with powdered herbs such as golden seal and neem are applied for their additional antibacterial properties. If drying applications are not used the well-aired placenta will have a distinct, musky scent that can be halted by directly planting it or by refrigerated storage after the first postpartum week. However the placenta will become rotten and extremely malodorous if covered in plastic or air-tight storage. Proper treatment will allow a comfortable lotus birth free of discomfort.

As opposed to "vanishing twin" which occurs prior to implantation, "death of a twin" theme occurs later in the pregnancy or during birth. Death of a twin is experienced as the full loss of a brother or sister, not just loss of a "soul mate." If the twin dies in utero, the living twin must endure the presence of their dead sibling in the womb. There can be a sense of horror, disgust, guilt, self-blame, an identity that one caused the death, and is therefore "bad," and tremendous grief and rage. If the twin dies during birth, there can be a sense of survivor's guilt or a belief that one's power annihilates others. Resulting behavior is to minimize ones' needs to atone for the death of the sibling. Mother's emotions can be split; she may not fully welcome the surviving baby, or may cling to it with confused grief.

Attendants at such a birth are confused as well. Infant death is out of the natural order of life and difficult to accept. Hospital staff may be both horrified and numb when a baby dies or is still-born. The surviving twin will feel this confusion of emotions and may personalize this energy.

Case Study Example

See Case Study #9 that explores issues of identity, shame, survivors guilt, and bonding with a grieving mother due to death of a twin at birth.

Twin loss complications of identity

- Fear that "if I am powerful you will die... or my strength = your death."
- Mother's confusion of how to bond to the living twin while in grief.
- Baby's interpretation of Mother's grief. "Do I make mother sad?"
- Baby's need to grieve when there is "life-threatening sadness" in the mother.
- Basic shock. Living with a secret of the dead twin if this happens *in utero.*
- Baby's excessive fear of abandonment, either through grief or death.
- Shock of the field. Delivery assistants and doctor, extended family and community.
- Basic feeling for baby of being somehow "wrong, or dangerous to others."

Death of a Twin Loss can aggravate a sense of connection with others

Death of a twin imprints cellular consciousness. Identity is confused. One believes they are dangerous to others, and they are unrealistic about their power and afraid to have basic needs. Common client expressions state that, "I would unconsciously hurt someone, something bad would happen! I am too much for people, I need to hold myself back because I am dangerous to others but I don't know how. I just remember what happened before!" This is a dramatic imprint, and living a life of fear of self, while trying to minimize one's impact, is exhausting and confuses others. Such identity beliefs resolve when the story is named and the early shock witnessed and treated.

Death of a Twin Themes

- Survivors Guilt
- If I am powerful others are hurt
- My needs are deadly
- I dare not succeed or I will lose my greatest intimate connections
- Loss of the Beloved
- There will "never be another you... "
- Seeking the perfect mate
- Deep and chronic depression
- Unrealistic demands of a partner
- Unwillingness to show up in practical ways
- Connecting too easily with strangers
- Creating false intimacies
- Overly available to others
- Oblivious to others needs for boundaries
- Inability to feel self unless through another
- Bound to drama
- Enmeshed to shamanic forces
- Life is always intense
- Sense of self identifies with emotional intensity
- Plays into intensity of others while limiting self-expression

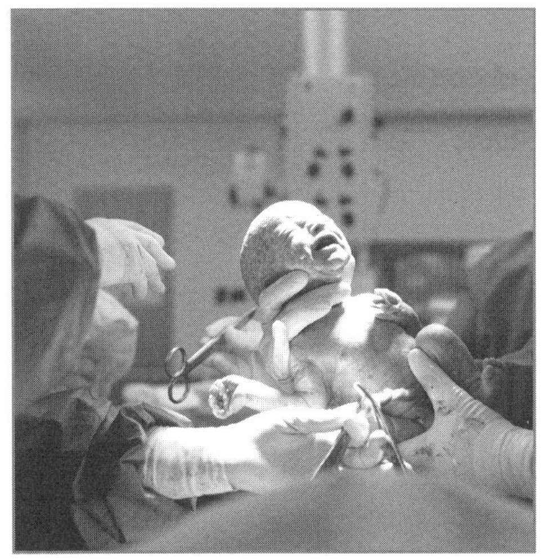

Post-birth bonding following a C-section

A C-section is one of the more frightening births. Doctors wear masks and gloves, mother is numbed from the waist down, and time is urgent. Out of necessity, baby is sought for, grabbed, and pulled out of mother, often with extreme pressure on the neck. Baby is then lifted into bright light intensity in an unknown fast and urgent world. The rapid transition from the fluid world of the womb where baby is connected to mother quickly transforms to a meeting with aliens and alien forces.

Emotions (based on client stories and expression)

The worst part of C-sections is that the baby feels dis-empowered. People report feeling disoriented, shocked during transition, and sad at missing the natural pressure of the birth canal. A vaginal birth squeezes baby's joints, muscles, organs, glands, bones, and tissues. The natural design of birth helps to quicken the healthy life force, transitions one to gravity, and provides familiarity in response to pressure.

Rotating out through the birth canal gives baby a sense of finding its' way through difficulty, and meeting forces successfully. I have witnessed adults born caesarean who have trouble graduating, completing homework, or being the 'point person' in work teams. In mother-daughter treatment sessions, mother's of adult children born C-section lament that their child, as an infant, "was always in charge, not letting me protect them or come to me for comfort when stressed." Meanwhile, the adult daughter is angry at the Mom for not taking charge and protecting them.

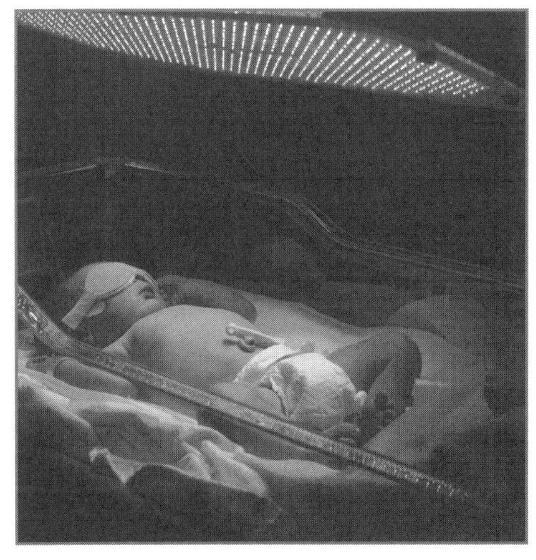

Jaundice lights

Neonatal jaundice is a yellowing of the skin and other tissues of a newborn infant caused by the accumulation of indirect unconjugated bilirubin. Psychological jaundice, which is usually harmless, is often seen in infants around the second day after birth. This usually lasts until day 8 in normal birth; in premature birth, it could last until day 14. It's resolved once the enzyme has been produced in sufficient quantities to allow conjugation and excretion of bilirubin as bile salts. All jaundice should be medically evaluated before treatment can be given. (Wikipedia)

I have treated clients jaundiced as infants, who were numb or tactile defensive in social settings. A standard question I ask children in treatment is if "babies have feelings?" The one child in all my years of interviewing who didn't think so was a ten year old who had been placed under jaundice lights. He came for treatment due to social difficulties at school. At birth he was immediately isolated and placed in jaundice lights for seven days. I used the "Bone Levering" treatment mentioned in my book, *Contact Improvisation and BodyMind Centering*, to awaken this boy's internal sense of proprioception. His face expressed amazement as he began to have awareness of sensation inside his body for the first time! By coming into a felt relationship with himself, he could then feel and respond to others. This book also has exercises to support proprioception and sensation integration. See the body resources section, Volume Two.

Impact of Interruptions in Skin-to-Skin Contact Post-Birth

Skin-to-skin post-birth is the best treatment protocol for healthy self-regulation.

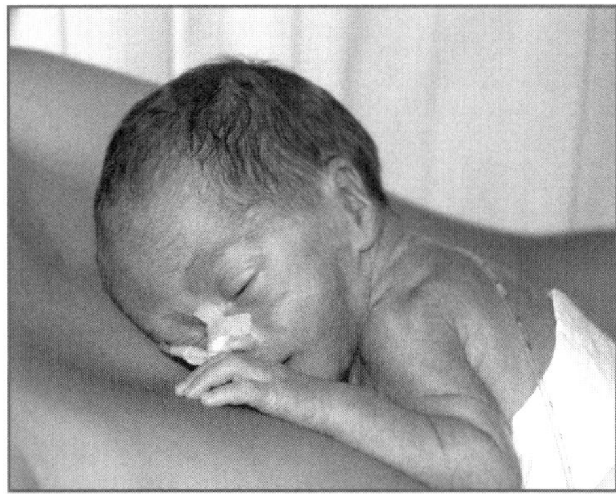

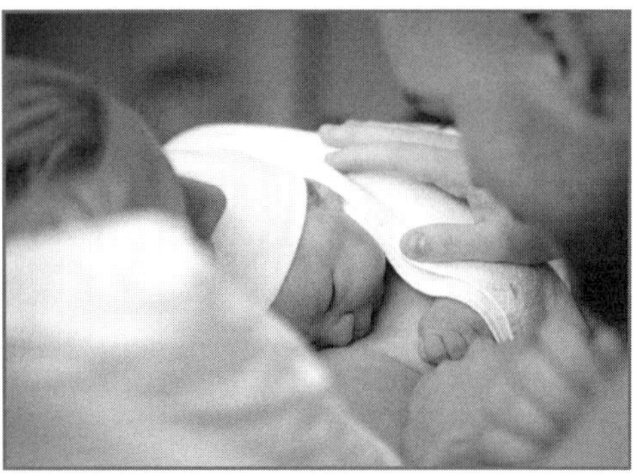

Whenever baby is taken away from mother there is an impact on the mother/infant nervous system. Life-saving interventions are absolutely the correct choice. However, keeping baby in contact with mother whenever possible greatly improves the baby and mothers attachment health. Many mothers are depressed or tentative to engage with their baby's following NICU unit care.

Social Emotional Impacts for later Development Unfortunately, technologically managed births may be due to protocol rather than necessary as life-saving circumstance. Perinatal sessions must evaluate the implications on the social and emotional relationship; both the baby's emotional sense of safety and trust, and the mother and father's sense of being able to protect their child. Whatever the reason for interruption, methods to help repair the mother/infant and family nervous system would greatly support bonding and attachment.

Isolation shock is an emotional and body-based response to the heartbreak of losing connection with Mom. Newborns don't know they exist separate from the mother; they become emotionally traumatized and lost in an "empty abyss." Babies dissociate under such stress. It is the body's protective mechanism that helps their survival; they go numb because it is too terrifying to regulate the invasive and isolating NICU experience without mother's comfort. This internalized terror creates a deep seated freeze in the brain stem and a numbing response that remains in the tissue until addressed with hands on body work and emotional repair. Often it goes unrecognized but displays as struggles with self-regulation.

Repair Trauma with Perinatal and Skilled Bodywork Sessions

Skin-to-skin contact between mother and child and father and child is the straightforward method to help premature infants and repair interruptions to bonding. Once an infant is stable, post NICU unit perinatal sessions are highly recommended. Babies need support to come out of isolation shock, and skilled help to complete the startle reflex and regain sensory motor abilities. Use of primitive reflexes repairs sensory motor response in the limbs, trunk, and brain stem. This rebalances the infant's nervous system and allows for self-regulation.

Bodymind Centering practitioners, or skilled Occupational Therapists use primitive reflexes to help the nervous system and brain stem. Be sure to ask for that support if you have a child who went through NICU care. (see Nancy Goddard's book, *Primitive Reflexes*, as well as my book, *From Conception to Crawling).* Post-intervention bodywork and psychological support will lessen healthcare and education costs; a well-bonded infant who has a sense of social safety will do better in family, social, and school settings.

NeoNatal Intensive Care (NICU)

NICU (units) are designed to save lives and at times they are the appropriate choice for post-birth care. However, their value may be overstated and overused; see DVD Kangaroo Care for medical research on stress and alternative options). Side effects are highly detrimental to the nervous system balance and sense of social safety. NICU units isolate mothers and infants, and the care an infant receives is invasive, even in the best of circumstances. Babies often have feeding tubes, IV drips, or bandages over the eyes. They may have been in an oxygen tent in earlier hospital protocol. Their skin is pricked for IVs and blood drawn through heel pricks. Numerous heel pricks/day for many days/care translates to torture for an infant. Their natural primitive reflex responses of protective flexor withdrawal and extensor thrust are overidden. This can pattern a deep seated rigidity in the ankles and legs which can lead to joint problems in the knees or hips later in life.

NICU babies seek yet fear touch. This makes them susceptible to ambivalent attachment issues. In addition they are bound within a perimeter of glass. The sense of "being enclosed in a bubble" and not aware of relational needs is common in adults imprinted with these conditions. Babies were often placed on their backs looking up at lights that were too bright. Fortunately eye masks are now used. Back lying forces the baby to go into extension, rather than the flexed pattern that allows the baby to curl in and self-regulate. The Morro startle reflex becomes ingrained and these babies are often need contact yet won't allow it due to actile defensiveness. This author's personal experience with prematurity and NICU care helped develop the understanding of how to repattern the social-emotional senses and phsycial body. This emotional and psychological repair is essential when there has been NICU care involved in any post-birth setting.

Any Interruption Of Contact Has Repercussions		
Feeding schedule		
baby overrides its natural rhythm and becomes anxious around food	lack of self-trust, ignoring one's needs	no ability to pace needs
Change of caregivers		
Who is here? Where is my Mom?	abandonment issues	dissociation
Dispair and poor self image		
I can't do anything to change this	I must have done something wrong	I am a bad person; self attacking thoughts

Back lying is sometimes necessary but more difficult on the baby than the sidelying position used below. Fortunately Kangaroo Care methods are being proven highly effective with premature infants and are replacing incubator use in some countries. See Resources Section for more information.

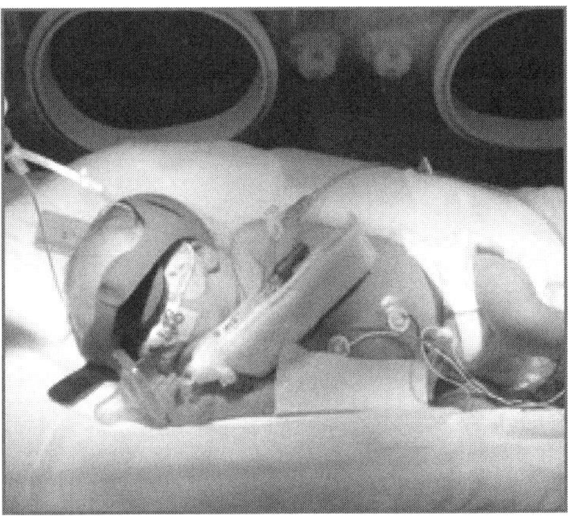

Above photo courtesy of Emma Sayge and her parents (age 6 when repairing her birth story).

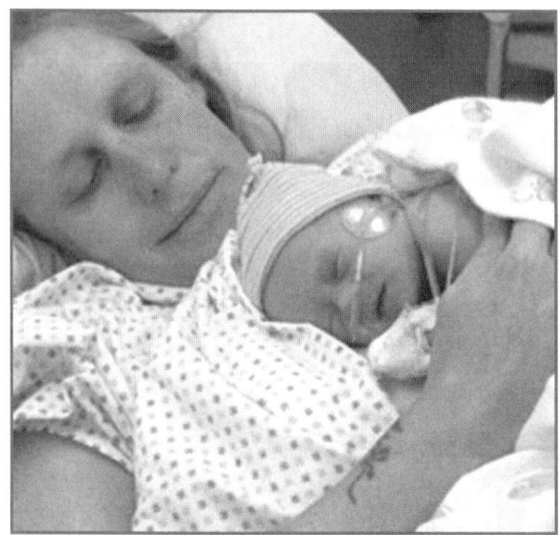

Emma Sayge and Mom skin-to-skin. Mom had to insist on this with hospital staff. Smart Mom!

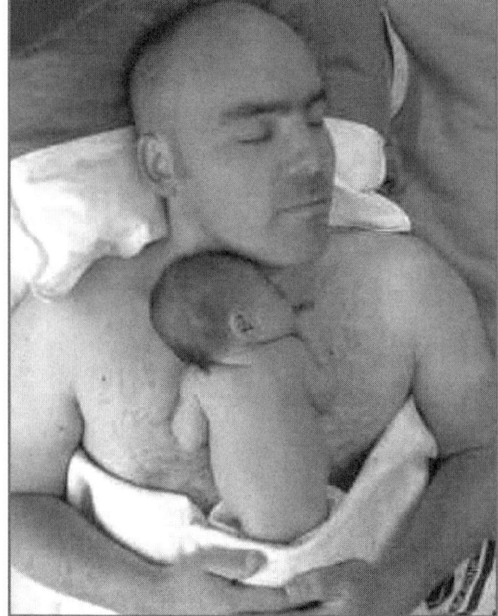

http://www.kangaroomothercare.com/galleries.aspx

Skin-to-skin contact versus isolation

A premature infant does not necessarily demand incubation. Dr. Nils Bergman, a South African MD, used Western medicine research methods to evaluate premature babies and measured stress levels in the early born in South Africa. Dr. Bergman found that incubators delay infant weight gain, increase infant stress, and interrupt bonding. Dr. Bergman conducted research to see if these expensive incubators were needed. Research showed they were not!

Bergman followed indigenous cultural custom and placed infants on the chest of the mother for immediate and consistent skin-to-skin contact. Babies were tied to mother with a cloth wrapper so her hands were free to go about her daily tasks. Babies rested into the mother's sleep rhythms and thrived with better weight gain, less release of stress hormone, and better temperature regulation. This was in high contrast to the control measurements of infants in isolated NICU care. Skin-to-skin on mother's chest gives the infant the best chance of survival.

NICU babies suffer from high stress hormones and elevated cortisol levels. They enage in despair crying due to isolation, and cycle through arousal, anger, sadness, fear, and despair. Their nervous system can be programmed to believe they always need help, or that the world is not safe and no one is there. Dr. Bergman's research shows that skin-to-skin babies thrive in comparison to infants placed in NICU care! Baby's sleep when mother sleeps, their breathing regulates, and temperature is supported since mother's or father's temperature modifies as much as four degrees up or down to help baby adjust. Infants develop well in a cocoon setting known as Kangaroo Care. Dr. Berman's method is less expensive than NICU care and far more effective than isolation in a sterile environment. My firm belief is that we overuse technology in western birthing practices that involve managed labor, and Dr. Bergman's data supports this.

- Incubators: first marketed at the Worlds' Fair as a great advancement in technology
- May not be as effective as originally thought
- Highly Technological Managed hospital care has pervaded the American birth model
- America has only 1% home birth rate to date
- 1950s and 60s: mothers not allowed to touch the infants or enter the NICU room.
- Had to watch their baby through glass.
- Interrupted bonding the norm in NICU circumstances

Summary

Events at birth engage questions of life and death, and the preamble oath for Western physicians says they must support life at all costs. NICU care creates strong defensive imprints, high emotional costs, and long-term societal costs in terms of special needs resources in education and health care. To help dispel these costs, immediate Kangaroo Care should be available as a choice for mothers. Post NICU care insurance might save money by requiring cranial or Body-Mind Centering sessions. One must imagine how an infant perceived NICU care and what response patterns to stimuli were created. Otherwise, the child may develop reactive attachment disorders or carry the imprint of invasive care throughout life. School, social play, and adult intimacy can be damaged or impeded by unresolved terror deep within the nervous system. One is grateful for life-support when needed. Identifying and repairing stress and terror imprints will make that life so much more enjoyable.

In-hospital nursery time

Babies taken from the mother and placed in the nursery following birth lose skin-to-skin contact, are put on a feeding schedule, and often in a room with many unhappy babies. Nursery care imprints the nervous system with unfortunate patterns relating to a sense of safety in the world, of trust, and of nourishment. Infants in such care become dissociated, vigilant, or a combination of the two. Best possible care is skin-to-skin contact with the mother immediately following birth and maintained as consistently as possible.

Emotional and primary imprints with NICU care		
Isolates under stress		
Inability to seek help	difficulty self regulating	compensated high tone
Vision through bubble		
does not fully "see" under stress	light and sound sensitivity	dissociates rather than looks
Baby seeks yet avoids contact with other		
distorted facial recognition	tactile and sensation "sensitive"	may be "triggered" by blank television screens

Summary of Support for Parents Parents may experience guilt when reading about perinatal psychology. Guilt is natural but interferes with repair of attachment wounds and imprints. The unfortunate experiences of a difficult birth are real, impactful, and need processing. Denial, minimizing the impact, or not talking about these events impedes their healing. Parents can also become dis-empowered with post-birth stress and never regain their footing as a couple. Residual resentment or fear interrupts trust. Please seek professional support to reclaim connection. Parents need each other as teammates in order to parent well. Reconnecting emotionally with yourself, your spouse, and your new infant, and celebrating life brings fulfillment.

The most useful thing to integrate difficult births is to acknowledge out loud what happened, feel emotions, and process them through journaling, art, dance, movement, grieving, and if possible, with a skilled therapist. It is completely alarming when a baby is taken away. Know that a child will have feelings about this; sharing and resolving these feelings repairs connection. Parental feelings are often masked by the need to care for an infant.

Summary Notes to parents on Emotions: Please process your feelings as well as support your child to process theirs. Doing so integrates the birth experience and builds resiliency. Allow the child to express fear, sadness, and rage at what they perceived as abandonment due to isolation. Watch for signs of the birth story in toddler behavior and play. Support the story to be told and interact with the child during this play. Create a "baby book" with pictures of drawings of their birth to help the child address the story.

Summary Notes on infant development: If an infant is born premature, get early developmental intervention from Body-Mind Centering infant development practitioners, or trained Occupational Therapists. Early assessment and intervention supports brain integration, joint alignment, body ease, reducing the not so easily noticed problems during the crawling phases of development that lead to late difficulties with learning and sensory processing. Premature babies do not experience the muscle loading of compression that a full term baby experiences and lack the flexion support of the deep muscles of the psoas. A skilled BMC practitioner can help to address the following: primitive reflexes to reduce residual startle and regain flexor withdrawal and extensor thrust through the legs; muscle touch support to help the psoas current and fire properly; tactile repair of sensitized skin; touch compression and rotation of the organs to rebalance parasympathetic tone in movement; and nervous system perception work for ease in visual and auditory processing.

Summary note to therapists Training in perinatal psychology supports families to realign following traumatic separations post-birth, and to deal with the unexpected transition into the hospital environment and back home. Get proper training and employ this skill set to be a highly effective therapist. Doing so helps re-stabilize clients age infant to adult.

Scheduled feeding themes

Hunger is a new sensation for a post-birth baby. In a healthy enough pregnancy, the infant had enough food. Being regulated to a feeding schedule sets up power dynamics of struggle, override of body sensations, need to resort to will to combat unmanageable hunger arousal, and adaptive survival responses that aren't supportive for ian infant's nervous system development. In my clinical practice I have seen many adult and teen eating disorders related to early feeding interruption of baby's natural feeding rhythm.

Meeting basic needs

The sense of satisfaction during feeding sets a good example for a sense that one can succeed in life. Early nursing allows sucking movements and develops the palate, the brain stem, and the digestive tube. Sucking also activates the parasympathetic nervous system. When hunger and sucking needs are not met the infant becomes fraught with anxiety. An infant does not track time passage and cannot know food will arrive on schedule. Babies dysregulate during prolonged hunger and learn to go numb, which often masks an inner panic. This is especially true if there were complications during the birth already imprinted around needs and support.

The Value of Nursing

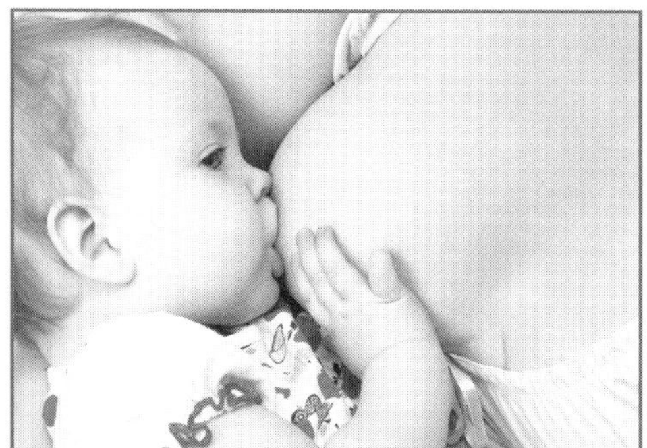

Nursing is a primary event in an infants life and provides the building blocks for a body felt-sense of satisfaction and contentment. It is a comparatively short time in a child's life and such an important baseline that one need not worry whether the infant is controlling the mother with its need. Nursing allows the mother and baby to bond in a simple way, and is ideally done with skin-to-skin contact. Please use a lactation consultant to help with any complications. They are skilled and can help mothers to find ease.

Allowing the baby to nurse is important physically as well as emotionally. A baby who is nursed experiences equal head rotation and turning of the neck since it suckles from one breast and then the other, whereas bottle fed infants are often held only on one side. A bottle nipple is not long enough to reach the soft palette so the sucking pattern does not sequence deeply enough into the mouth and root of the infant tongue. In addition, bottles often let too much milk into the baby's system. The infant will create extra tension in the throat as it attempts to reduce the incoming milk stream while still needing to suck. This is only partially successful and infants often consume too much milk. In addition, formulas contain unnatural sugars, smell differently than mothers' breast milk, and are often much harder to digest. Some clinicians think forumla may influence later obesity issues in children.

Treat interupted Nursing experiences Interrupted nursing creates emotional and phsyical implications. Nursing can be interrupted due to a mom returning to work, her milk drying up, or having difficulty with pain. As with any interruption, find the beliefs encoded related to interrupted nursing and follow the body sensations of tension. Support mothers to release guilt or anger from this experience. Help clients release the imprint of feeling abandoned, or digestive problems related to inability to eat formula, and find a way back to ease in the bodymind. Struggles with nursing can set a power dynamic psychology that hijacks simplicity. Food issues can originate in nursing issues. Such issues release when the origin is named and the body re-patterned.

The value of smelling and nursing

Smell registers in the most primitive part of the brain known as the olfactory area. This is called Cranial Nerve !; however this "nerve" is an actual extension of the brain, rather than a nerve development. If the unfortunate first experience of an infant is cutting the umbilicus followed by nose and mouth suction there will be shock in the tender tissue of the nose and mouth. This can interrupt the ease of rooting with the nose and the ability to orient under pressure. A nursing infant measures the distance from mouth to breast with it's nose and is establishing a sense of spatial identity. This is an essential orienting skill useful under stress.

The role of smelling

Not only eye gazing, but smelling is an essential part of nursing.

The sperm smells its way to the egg.

The zygote may partially smell its way to implantation.

The newborn smells its way to the breast and measures spatial distance with its nose.

Smell provides an orienting function for the infant

Check the Frenulum for nursing problems

The frenulum is the skin attaching the tongue to the floor of the mouth. If this tissue is too short, an infant will have trouble sucking.

Historically midwives used their fingernail to slice through this tissue in order to help the baby nurse. This was a life-saving intervention and necessary for the baby to develop a strong enough sucking impulse.

Some doctors do not know to check for this problem, and it can wreak havoc on a mother's sense of capability. Tongue movements help pattern speech, and spine and head rotations. Crawling can be adaptive due to a non-free tongue.

One mother I know had 6 weeks of terrible stress before the frenulum connection was noticed and corrected. Think of the emotional issues that could have been avoided due to that unnecessary stress.

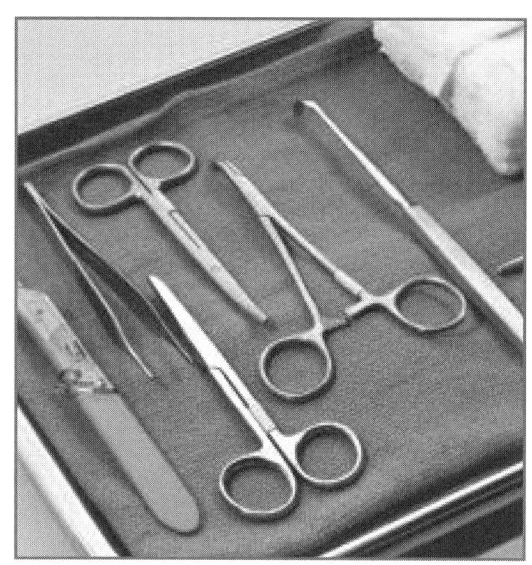

Circumcision

Circumcision is the removal of the male foreskin of the penis. There are many myths related to this procedure, including myths about rampant infection or even masturbation. Infection is rarely true when a child is taught to wash properly, and circumcision itself can cause horrible infection. People of Jewish heritage have a cultural/spiritual loyalty to the practice, yet the original Jewish practice took a small nick out of the foreskin rather than remove it, and was a way to identify fellow Jews. Most Western babies of non-Jewish heritage are circumcised in hospital See the excellent article by Mirriam Pollack: *Circumcision: Identity, Gender And Power, Miriam Pollack, Huffington Post, Feb. 28, 2012.*

Prior to 1981 many western hospitals acted under the assumption that babies did not feel pain. Hospitals used no anesthesia during circumcision. Nurses were usually required to perform circumcisions. In 1978 nurses in Santa Fe, NM, refused to perform this operation. They saw pain responses in the infants and walked off the job rather than inflict such pain to newborn babies. They put their jobs at risk and helped start a national outcry and educational movement against the routine practice of circumcision. (personal commentary, David Sawyer). As people are educated about the actual method of circumcision, many are questioning why male infants are exposed to such an early and shocking practice. Research on circumcision as part of religious values shows an interesting variance on past and current methods.

Facts of Circumcision Practice

www.NOCIRC.org or www.circumcision.org

- The penis looses approximately 15 square inches of skin
- The foreskin contains 3 to 4 feet of blood vessels, 240 feet of nerves and between 10,000 and 20,000 specialized nerve endings.
- Circumcision permanently diminishes the sexual feelings for both the male and female.
- No national health organization in the world, including the American Academy of Pediatrics (AAP) and the American Medical Association (AMA) recommend circumcision for healthy male infants.
- Approximately 90-85% of the world's male population has intact genitals. The current circumcision rate in the U.S. is about 50%.
- Many studies show circumcision is unnecessary.

Social conformity, ignorance about anatomy, and misconception of religious practice are all reasons circumcision is still practiced. Fortunately, with research, facts are coming forward.

In Jewish culture, the penis was circumcised to mark loyalty to God. In ancient times this early circumcision did not remove the entire foreskin, but was a distinguishable nicking of the tissue. A return to this type of circumcision would still protect the penis, maintain religious values, and reduce infant shock in the genitals (personal commentary by Miriam Pollack).

- Infection is rare as the glans is a self-cleaning organ
- Foreskins are often utilized to repair 3rd degree burns at hospital burn units
- Early shock to an infant's genitals has unacknowledged repercussions on adult sexuality

Notes on current circumcision practice

It is difficult to acknowledge one's ignorance and to make smart changes without feeling defensive or guilty. This is certainly true of circumcision. Cultural and sexual issues related to circumcision practice are loaded with fear, resentment, and ignorance.

It Takes Courage to Change

Fathers must become instrumental in protecting their male sons. Mothers must help educate themselves and their husbands. Fathers often say, "I want my son to be like me," or "I don't want him to be teased in gym class." A mother succumbs to father's view in support of the family. This puts the mother in a double bind; she notices most directly the change in her infant before and after the surgery. She may feel guilty for not protecting him but didn't want to go against her husband's wishes. Babies return from circumcision in a state of shock, with a noticeable change in trust and responsiveness after the circumcision operation. Numbness minimizes a sense of the inmpacts. There are risks of infection and even a need to repeat the procedure in some cases. This further traumatizes an infant, all for an unnecessary practice.

Scores of adult male clients have gone back and explored their circumcision experiences. Fathers and business men with strong family values have admitted to a sense of outrage and fury at not having been protected. Emotions vary from terror to sadness to a rage at women if female nurses performed the procedure. Cellular memories of sensitivity and pain are identified and released. Sexual clarity and pleasure is enhanced when one clears traumatic emotional imprints related to the genitals. When shock is released, the body no longer over-rides numbing memory and allows more pure sensation and movement.

Identify the coping responses

Self soothing

- overly content or numb
- lip sucking
- rocking
- isolated play

Baby is still angry

- dysregulated
- fussy
- unable to soothe

Avoidant behavior

- looks away from contact
- will not engage

Anxious behavior

- escalates easily
- vigilant tracking of parent/environment
- hard to settle
- anxiety
- panic arousal

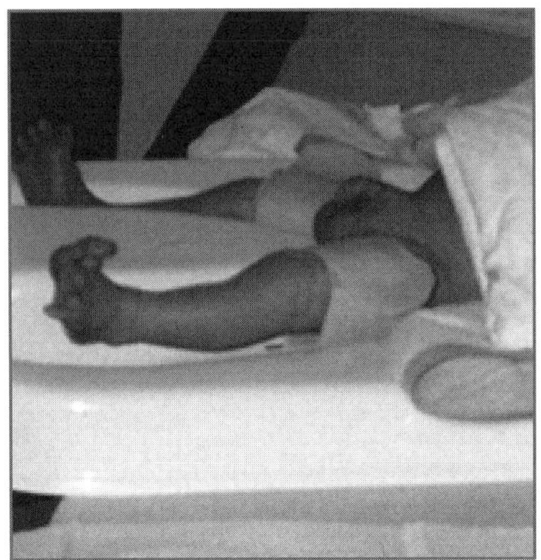

A baby strapped into a hospital circumcision board. Prior to 1981 it was thought babies didn't "feel" pain. This procedure was often done without anaesthesia.

If you are a prospective parent, please discuss the practice of circumcision and these mentioned effects. Take the time to become educated, even if the subject is uncomfortable. Research on the internet. Talk to parents who left their babies intact. Find support groups for dialog so that all your questions can be answered.

To personally heal the emotional imprint of past circumcision, or to help a child heal, find a body-centered therapist. For best results, choose a somatic therapist trained in pre and perinatal work and early shock and trauma.

Finally, if you are so moved, please help spread the word to other men and prospective fathers. It is an uncomfortable subject to speak about and highly necessary if this practice is to be discontinued. Current methods of circumcision will only end when enough men step forward and insist their son's genitals be left intact.

A Personal Decision		
Emotional repercussions		
can influence baby's trust	can interrupt bonding	can interrupt grounding through legs
Physical considerations		
not deemed medically necessary	reduces lubrication of glans	studies show adult sex less pleasurable
Not a health need		
does not reduce infection	the glans is a self-cleansing organ	men must protect their sons

The writing that follows was generously offered by a forty-five year old male uncovering his cellular memory of circumcision. He shared his thoughts to help others understand that young infants do remember, and that an adult can be influenced by these early events.

M's story healing circumcision imprints

(authors note): This story is included to give a first hand experience from a man uncovering early imprints related to circumcision. Most men who go back through this emotional territory end up enraged for a time and then more integrated and powerful. Integration and power appear once the influence of circumcision-related trauma on early identity beliefs are resolved. Remember that an infant will make things their fault in order to have a locus of control in an uncontrollably dangerous situation. Working with circumcision imprint is a courageous and necessary work that enhances male dignity. It must be done for this practice to be stopped. When rage can turn toward healthy political and social activism, social change can occur. The following journey is not finished, but shows the process of exploring this imprint.

M's story...

"Years ago when I was involved in re-evaluation counseling, I read about men doing emotional process work around having been circumcised. This was the first time I took in information on the physiological and emotional implication of this procedure. I was fascinated by the idea of being able to process this violation but had no context for how to travel back and explore something that happened so long before I had conscious memory.

Recently, my back went into spasm. For many years I have had episodes of my back seizing up. It usually happens when I get stressed and the stress is related to doing new things around new people. I end up frightened and shy and have a feeling of being overwhelmed. My pattern has revealed itself over the years very similarly: I get fearful and don't feel these feelings, and then my back will go into painful lockdown.

The last time it happened I was in Moab, Utah for a contact improv dance gathering. My back went into spasm again, and it quickly became clear that this back problem was emotionally initiated. Since I couldn't dance, I spent the day by myself searching for the meaning of this event; digging for the feelings, being with myself, discharging in various ways.

I had recently been exposed to new information relating to early imprints, and I spent time exploring my birth. It was the first time I had ever done that, and I had some vague but powerful images and feelings arise. I noticed I did not want to come out of my Mom at birth, and that it didn't feel safe to me to arrive. That evening my friend Annie and I talked and she asked if I had ever explored my circumcision.

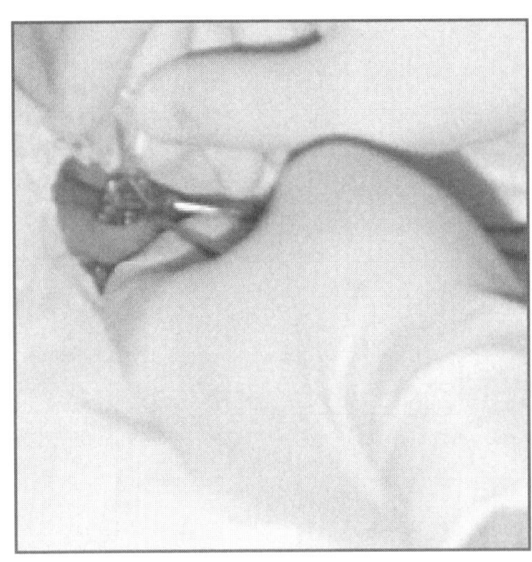

I said, "No, but I have always been curious about that." She described how most hospital circumcisions are performed. She explained that the little boys are strapped to a board to hold their limbs down while the procedure is performed. That image created a deeply disparaging sinking feeling in my gut. I had imagined that one person held me, and the doctor had a little scalpel and he just quickly did a little slice around my penis. But now, hearing that there is actually a specially designed board with straps to anchor us down and hold us in place is infuriating. As I write this, the symbology of that enrages me further.

Several days later I found myself having a mental argument with my father about something. I got really angry and said to myself, "What the hell am I so angry at my Dad for?" And the answer rained down on me. It was as if someone else was speaking inside my head: "He didn't protect you! It was his job to protect you."

It was clearly implied that the circumcision was what I needed protection from. So I engaged in the conversation, "But my Mom could have...". "NO!" the other voice cut me off, "IT WAS NOT HER RESPONSIBILITY!" Whoa! That gave me pause. I really got it, I have been so pissed at my Dad all these years because he didn't do his job and protect me when he was supposed to. And as much as I believe in equal gender rights and responsibilities, somehow I knew without a doubt that this was true, it was absolutely his responsibility to protect me.

A week or two later I had a bodywork session from a dear woman that I implicitly trust. What enfolded in that session was a very deep emotional catharsis... deep crying and wailing. More information "dropped." First was the message that my circumcision had imprinted into my being the idea that "there is something very wrong with you, because it is imperative that we strap you down to this board, and chop off this piece of your penis which is the most highly innervated skin in your entire body." Whoa... that deep feeling that I have been aware of for sooooooo long, that something is inherently wrong with me at the most profound of levels, at the deepest layer of my core being.

I guess I had crossed it off to the guilt and shame of being raised Catholic, or some remnant of original sin interpretation or the like. But there it was, three days old and they had to do this thing to me where they cut off a piece of me.

Then came the anger... it came in waves and waves of angry tears and wailing. How could this doctor mutilate his brother? Anger at my father for not protecting me from him. My father who is intact, how could he let this happen to me? It is a violent storm of emotion that I still have so much work to do around. I feel how strongly I am still suppressing as I write this. My God, have I only uncovered the tip of the iceberg? Is this why I have an inherent distrust of men? When you are only three days old and totally unable to protect yourself they strap you down and rob you of part of your sacred manhood... how absolutely disgusting, revolting, perverted, despicable, unfathomable, vicious and cruel. I say these words with only limited ability to feel them, I am still numb to them, there is still a lot of work to do. Several weeks after this unravelling, I learned that it is often the nurses who perform the circumcisions in the hospitals. Oh my god! Another layer. Was I betrayed by the women too? I had just begun digesting the idea that my father had betrayed me and now I am being presented with the idea that women might have betrayed me also! Another round of the sickening feeling in my gut. Fuck! This is sick! Why are they doing this? And they justified it then saying that the little boys couldn't feel it, even though they would be wailing during the procedure. And why do I keep protecting them by calling it "the procedure!" It is mutilation, genital mutilation plain and simple! I have so deeply programmed myself to protect everyone around me from my anger.

I asked my mother about my birth again shortly after this. I am glad she doesn't tire of this. I wasn't sure when I was actually circumcised; was it in the hospital, or 3 months later? I had never asked. She explained that she went into the hospital on a Thursday afternoon and had me that evening. She left the hospital on Monday morning, so probably some time on Saturday or Sunday is what she figures. "And when they brought you back to me after you were circumcised you were fine, you weren't crying or fussing at all."

The very first thought I had when she told me this was "Sure, I probably wasn't even in my body. I had gone far, far away." Whoa... 2 or 3 days old, and I get whisked away from my Mom, she is not there, my Dad is not there and I get a piece of my penis chopped off. Who knows, maybe I didn't cry, maybe I just shut down inside. That would fit my experience for the most part. Then I get brought back to her and everything is fine. I am not crying so everything must be fine. I can feel that rage that is trapped inside of me as I write that. "Can't she tell that everything is not fine. Can't she tell that I had to shut down and go away. Can't she tell that the message I was just given is that there is something so wrong with your body, with your penis that they have to strap me down, take a sharp knife and try to cut it out of me. Can't she tell that I have just been traumatized? Violated? Mutilated?" But I am not crying so everything is just fine.

And still I keep these feelings in check. I feel them but not fully. It is so fucked up. In some way I am protecting all of them from my rage. Why? Why is it not ok to rage at them?"

...End of M's Personal Reflection...

Authors' note

The processing of emotions relating to circumcision is crucial for reclaiming a sense of power and balance. Emotional processing frees the nervous system and clears associative memory as experiences are digested and integrated. This allows a fully embodied energy to return to the legs, pelvic floor, and genitals. Addressing circumcision does not mean that one should remain caught in blame or anger. Sequencing emotions allows them to reclaim a stance of power rather than victim; adult feelings of dignity, protection of personal rights, and the ability to protect others leads to integration.

Circumcision is a personal wound that is also relational; sometimes an un-named rage at women is acted out in sexuality with a need for sexual force and violence. The head of the penis is less sensitive without the glans and often needs greater stimulation. This interrupts the sensuality of sexual contact and brings it too quickly into a sympathetic drive rather than an organic flow into orgasm. Releasing circumcision imprint can help men return to an open sense of contact during intimate sexual relating with a renewed sense of intimate pleasure that is emotionally healthy.

Men who are doing this inner work might want to work within a men's group processing circumcision material or with a male therapist who can help unravel identity issues and body shock imprints related to circumcision. I have sponsored male therapists trained in Bodymind Somanautics to begin and lead a men's group that addresses current issues of the masculine, including early prenatal, birth and circumcision memory as it arises. Facilitators Riun Ashlie and Damian Leuthold are successfully supporting men to access and heal early perinatal shock imprints. As men release emotions and integrate early experience, they become more available to their partners and families and more able to receive love and support. Facilitators offer local workshops, individual skype sessions, and will travel to your area if there is enough interest. For more information go to http://beastdragon.com.

Information and education are key to support expecting parents. When expecting mothers and fathers investigate the practice of circumcision and explore their feelings about this practice, as well as consider the impact upon their infant, they can make informed decisions for their baby. Education and emotional connection can dispel father's myths or fears related to circumcising the baby. Even faith-based parents are re-considering alternative procedures and rituals to value the cultural aspects and eliminate the shock to the infant's body. Personal awareness of the procedure of circumcision and it's effect is the stepping-stone toward cultural change.

The capacity to heal and integrate life events is phenomenal. We are blessed with bodies and minds that can re-calibrate and find ease. Applied Neuroplasticity Methods® repair the most ingrained and earliest of traumas. Such work requires diligent effort. Best results occur with the support of a capable trauma therapist who understands neural imprinting and has done their personal work. Early wounds are relational, and repair best in a skillful relational setting. Skilled Bodymind Somanautic therapists and psychotherapists know how to treat early shock and to re-pattern the body imprints as well.

Summary Notes Perinatal healing takes patience. Give yourself the time you need to reflect, digest, process, and await new behavior. Your nervous system learns to heal from the bottom up rather than manage experience. This is the true gift of working at this early level. The primitive brain releases vigilance and guardedness, and new behavior emerges. This occurs through gaining the skills to stay present with sensation and shock waves as they arise. Learning to meet them, name what is happening rather than get activated, and to let them pass repairs self-attachment necessary for successful adult relating and intimacy. One discovers that gently, over time, sustained changes are in place. Complicated behavior transforms when one is not driven by unconscious cellular memory and fear. Relationships deepen, people relax at a sustained level, and life becomes good enough without a desperate need for change, excitement, or activation. Practice good self care and good relational care. Utilize perinatal awareness as support for your spouse or children; doing so produces effective rather than reactive response. Find professional support as needed. At the very least, find a friend willing to explore these themes consciously.

Become good enough Release of perfectionism and finding balance between pleasure and stress in life is the task at hand. For some people, this mean letting go of drama, learning to relax, and allowing the mundane to be OK. For others, allowing excitement, developing a sense of adventure, and taking simple risks brings pleasure and balance to life. Each person will discover areas for growth. Learning how to grow, how to pace a healthy nervous system engagement, and to treat oneself with compassion is key to this phase. Unwind the trauma through naming, reflecting, receiving accurate mirroring and empathy, and shifting behavior so you no longer recreate trauma. One can then enjoy the phase of re-discovering who you are and what you like. Although this may take some time, doing so produces simple and long lasting rewards!

Learn to be a good enough parent, good enough spouse, good enough lover, and good enough friend. Release pressure and orient toward satisfaction. Pick up your inner "little one" so you no longer self-abandon and lose yourself under stress or in relationship.

This chapter addressed post-birth experience and concludes the information on Perinatal Themes. The next chapter shows application of perinatal psychotherapy through 10 case studies. *Birth's Hidden Legacy: Volume Two* has more in-depth theory on early attachment issues and intervention methods.

Proactive prevention

There is a wealth of informative resources available on the internet about healthy birth and bonding. Organizations APPPAH and ISPPM offer resources and hold conferences for educational purposes. Numerous videos support awareness of infants and show natural assisted and unassisted labor. These resources can give expecting parents a sense of possibility for alternative birthing success. The Kangaroo Care DVD shows supportive post-birth care.

On-line articles inform about circumcision, vaccines, and nursing. Baby carriers and slings are available to enhance flexion, safety, and bonding post-birth. Explore these resources, and ask your friends and colleagues for suggestions.

Chapter 5

Perinatal Case Studies

This section contains 10 case studies. They show application of perinatal awareness and use of themes in clinical treatment. Perinatal treatment methods are effective with all ages, infants through adults.

Introduction

Listening to hundreds of "early stories" has given me great respect for the resiliency and cleverness of humanity. The desire to survive and the adaptations we all make in beliefs, identity, and behavior in order to have an inner sense of social safety and support for needs is astounding. Thousands of clinical hours spent listening and working with clients has given me insight to the success of repair when one treats at the level of early impressions and dismantles the inaccurate meaning making and body responses based on these experiences.

The ten case studies selected cover a range of perinatal themes and show work with children and adults. They were chosen to give the reader a sense of how treatment progresses over time. They include prenatal, birth, and post-birth themes.

Clinical work helps perinatal themes unfold and integrate. It is always a mystery to see what will arise in treatment, and to follow the clients instinct of health. I am grateful to have the experience of studying in-depth how the bodymind encodes experience and to have been synthesized methods that truly allow access to the brain's neuro-plasticity for repair. The unique encoding on the body's instincts and the pre-cognitive meaning making based on "interpretation" of life events can shift and change many years later. I have been exposed to numerous plays of humanity through my clinical work, and am in awe of the intelligence of the client in leading me step by step to what they are next ready to share.

Personal stories should be respected and met with a healthy blend of listening, potency, creativity, and willingness to engage by the therapist, client, and parent. It is in the telling and sharing of these stories that shock in the body tissue releases. Witnessing and listening help clients and children process overwhelming events. Doing so creates more room in the bodymind for happiness and ease. Children have less behavioral problems, and are more contented. Adults find greater satisfaction, are less stressed, and establish more intimacy with family. The following case studies show how pre-cognitive stories appear when one knows how to "listen."

Chapter Overview

Case studies that follow detail a session-by-session progression, or are summaries of many sessions. Each highlights a specific treatment of a perinatal theme. Individual session themes are underlined in the text, and reflect the content of that one session within a block of sessions. First names are represented by a capital letter, and all names and letters are changed to protect confidentiality.

It is essential when treating children to engage in an age appropriate manner using this information. This means parents or clinicians must be versatile and skilled in dipping into and back out of the story to engage in play. Doing so helps the story settle, normalize, and resolve. Additionally, it is extremely useful to know body re-patterning skills. There is a return to health as the nervous system creates new behavior pathways. The story fades in significance and is not carried as a trauma of identity linked to a disruptive sense of social safety. Physical re-patterning with accurate emotional reflection and support allow for true behavioral change to occur.

Originally this book was one volume. However, due to length and ease of understanding, I separated this work into two volumes. For further skills and tips for treatment, be sure to purchase *Birth's Hidden Legacy: Volume Two.* This will give the reader advanced protocols, props, body-based interventions, and theory to evoke and engage perinatal material. It is the "tools of the trade" manual for working with pre and perinatal healing and includes all that I use to support children and adults working through their early stories.

Love after Love

The time will come
when, with elation
you will greet yourself arriving
at your own door, in your own mirror
and each will smile at the other's welcome,
and say, sit here. Eat.

You will love again the stranger who was your self.
Give wine. Give bread.
Give back your heart to itself, to the
stranger who has loved you all your life,
whom you ignored for another,
who knows you by heart.

Take down the love letters from the bookshelf,
the photographs, the desperate notes,
peel your own image from the mirror.
Sit. Feast on your life.

— Derek Walcott

Clinical Themes

Vanishing twin

Forceps

Anesthesia

Magical thinking

Baby rescue

Parasympathetic dissociation

Basic existence: character styles of oral and schizoid.

The following case study tracks sessions-by-session progression of an adult male working with intimacy issues in his marriage. It is the longest of the case studies and highlights clinical thinking. It demonstrates the impact of anesthesia and forceps on behavior. I give an overview of how to use this work with adults, and include client history, theory, and interventions used.

Since this case study highlights birth issues related to forceps and anesthesia imprints, the reader will not find in this case study description of the partner in this couple, even though her work was addressed as part of treatment. In couples work, it is very useful to explore perinatal and attachment patterns for each person; and to examine how they interact and counterpoint in the couple dynamic. I have used the phrase "Little John" to describe this adult client in order to keep the perspective of the infant experience in view.

Overview of perinatal therapeutic treatment

The following story examines the behavior, belief systems, and attachment responses that underlie adult behavior. The client is a 49-year-old male who has been married for twenty five years and is the father of three young children.

John entered therapy at the request of his wife due to marital dissatisfaction. John's perinatal history included anesthesia, forceps, and post-birth nursery care. I saw both John and his wife for a period of two and a half years. Treatment also included a series of warm water pool sessions with John and his two sons to support their father-son bond.

Adult John had trouble empathizing with others and most of his needs revolved around himself. John was intensely pursuing enlightenment even though he had chosen the householder path of marriage, career, family. Prior to this therapeutic relationship, he had explored Shamanic work in the desert, intense meditation work including many weekends of group work, and attended numerous corporate growth trainings and personal growth seminars. He put intense pressure upon his wife to join him in these existential pursuits.

Client history

According to John's wife, John's father was narcissistic in personality. John was the youngest of three boys and had a sister five years younger. John expressed that he felt left out with his brothers, and that the family was often playfully critical and demeaning of family members. He reported his mother was overwhelmed raising five children. His parents divorced when John was fifteen, with the father's self-centeredness as the given reason. John went to live with his father.

During the first sessions John presented as a lively, engaging person. He was a successful businessman and team leader. However, John often sped up in conversations, was quick, friendly, creative, and related very much from his mental body. His wife complained of being constantly criticized at home. Under stress John created emotional drama, was critical of the children, punitive in his conversations, and unable to engage in the partnership of raising the children and managing the household. His wife felt she had been under constant siege for 20 + years. She had been in numerous years of therapy and attempted couples therapy. However, when issues heated up John left couples treatment and sought shamanic and meditative work. John and his wife met in their early twenties during college.

John was reluctant to have children and it was the wife's insistence that finally supported the couple to become pregnant later in life. They utilized medical support due to low sperm count and both children were conceived with the father's sperm using artificial reproduction methods.

John's wife felt John's punitive behavior emerge as soon as their first child was born. The arrival of the children came at a time of intense self-imposed pressure in John's work life. John's stress turned into punitive criticism of his wife which was a reason for entering therapy.

At this time, John had started a new project against the objections of his wife. She begged him to stay closer to home to be with the children. Due to successful business efforts, John was semi-retired in his late forties. John chose to use his spare time in pursuit of awakening and through insistence of his wife, entered therapy.

The couple had a wonderful sense of humor when they relaxed together. Unfortunately that was overshadowed by John's punitive behavior and subsequent strategies by his wife to avoid being attacked. She developed a freeze response that made it difficult for John to feel connected to her. She also maintained a vigilance that exhausted her but felt necessary to fend off the punitive behavior. She felt under siege while defending herself and the children from attack and lost the ability for good self-care.

John was a thin man with strong impressions on each side of his cranium. These increased in visibility when John was animated and activated. John tended to engage on a mental level that was brisk and lively. In dialog, he appeared to look inward at his thoughts rather than stay in eye contact and connection. John's face appeared vacant and his eyes were glassy when he reflected inward. He could not feel himself very well or shift his attention from self to other and back. John reported constant digestive difficulties.

Entry points for treatment

There were a number of entry points for treatment based on John's birth history intake and the expressed complaints of he and his wife. Areas of intervention options included: attachment dynamics, response to invasive birth procedures, physical response in the cranium to intense pressure, and issues of life-death survival that might underlie behavioral choices.

Imprints of attachment wounds and fears present themselves in adults in the dynamics of intimate relating. The containment of a committed partner appears to bring these wounds into expression and is often the underlying cause of marital confusion and dissatisfaction.

John presented well. He was easy to like and to engage in conversation. I learned to trust the wife's descriptions of his home behavior in order to work with John's intimacy issues. She willingly worked on her part in therapy. Seeing them independently as well as together allowed me to see her ability to connect and his ability to dissociate and how this dynamic played out in their partnership. It was not until later in the treatment that John's punitive aggression appeared with me. It was then that his resistance to coming into contact became evident. I needed to look beneath the anger to sense the fear that was driving the aggression.

Attachment dynamics

Based on John's later presentation and his wife's disclosures I assessed John as having a controlling punitive attachment style. His fear was managed by controlling others through the use of verbal aggression and criticism. I was curious of the impact of anesthesia on his attachment since it produces both disorganization and disorientation, which are common to a punitive controlling behavior.

Based on a history of forceps, it was likely for John to have somatic imprints related to life-threatening pressure. Abandonment fears and disorientation would likely stem from the effect of anesthesia felt in his mother's body during birth. The sense of contact with mother is lost during anesthesia and she does not protect him during the invasion of forceps. John may have bonded with the doctor as savior rather than with his mother.

With so much stress at birth, it is likely that Little John both dissociated and fragmented. Muscle tone, facia, and fluids would brace against forceps. An unsuccessful and overwhelmed sympathetic fight response turns to freeze. With pressure of forceps, this freeze becomes fragmentation. Anaesthesia also produces low tone in the organs and a collapse. This appears as parasympathetic shock, and leads to dissociation. This often leads to catatonia and a return to the world of spirit.

Assessed client strengths

The work of therapy was to bring John into the realm of the emotional body and into relational pressure. John would first need to enter an embodied relationship with himself in a feeling manner in order to come into relationship with his wife and children. John's saving grace was his commitment to awareness work, his humor, and his dedication to his family "waking up!" John had no idea about the headaches and body sensations that were to follow his unfolding development.

Supporting body-based theory for treatment

The autonomic nervous system has two known components at the time of this writing. They are in order of most primitive to more advanced brain development and include the primitive parasympathetic branch, the more advanced sympathetic branch, and an aspect of the sympathetic considered to be most advanced as in mammals. This is a social function of the autonomic nervous system via the vagus nerve. It is helpful to speak of this as a triune autonomic nervous system, although there are truly only two branches.

The parasympathetic branch governs healthy digestion, the ability to go inward for balance, and sensual pleasure and arousal. Under stress, a parasympathetic response is to faint, become immobile, and dissociate. This leads to catatonia and eventually death, therefore is a more dangerous form of stress response.

The sympathetic branch supports healthy recreation, mobility, sexual climax, and orientation to life. In stress, the fight-flight is attempted but when blocked transforms into a freeze response. The social function of the nervous system in health supports love transactions, community interaction, and awareness of energy in the field. Under stress this function defaults to the sympathetic fight, flight, or freeze. If this function becomes overwhelmed, the nervous system defaults to parasympathetic catatonia coupled with dissociation. Thus we go from the most advanced support of seeking social engagement down to the most primitive, which is the withdrawal response of the parasympathetic.

Pre-cognitive life events that register in the nervous system are called imprints. These often register in a non-linear fashion and may be coupled with successful behavior response to early threat. This response is recorded in the cells and reused as a life saving skill under stress. I have written the following case study description using long sentences to help the reader gain a sense of the consecutive intensity of imprints that occurred for Little John's body, soul, and psyche. I refer to the client as "Little John" to clarify the time of imprinting. While reading one might ask what beliefs about the world Little John might have fashioned in order to survive. Remember the key questions of trust and attachment: "Is the world safe, will I survive, and will I survive in relationship?"

Advice for the reader

The following case study demonstrates how the nervous system can become overwhelmed and create early shock in the body that leads to fragmentation and dissociation in infancy. The following birth history may be difficult to read as it describes impact of a difficult birth on body tissues, emotions, and sensations. I write in a manner that energizes the complexity through long sentences, and reflects in parenthesis on the infants experience from an empathic perspective in order to give the reader a felt sense of perinatal experience based on client expression. I encourage the reader to use good self-care while reading. Please remember to read slowly, to pause, to breathe, and to keep clinical rather than personal perspective if you become activated.

Birth history

When I focused on the immediate events of birth and post birth and the baby that was Little John arriving into the world, I imagined the following: a soul that was connected to spirit in a good enough manner during prenatal time that suddenly lost connection with mother due to anesthesia (I am abandoned. Do I exist? It is my fault!), lost connection with his own world because he could no longer feel his movement and movement and vibration is the baby's first language *in utero*, therefore loss of movement meant loss of power and potency, which meant loss of self (where am I, do I exist? I will go back to spirit to find connection!).

Little John was stuck in the birth canal which could feel life threatening, especially when followed by invasion (no one can help me, mother is gone, I really need help!), was invaded by the entry of forceps into the birthing environment (aliens are attacking!), experienced unexplainable horrible skull crushing pressure (why are they trying to kill me? Where is mother, I must fight back, I am going to die!), felt his spine pulled from above which interrupted his own spinal pushing that was already compromised due to anesthesia (my neck is being pulled off, I am going to die, where am I; I must fight even more!), felt the relief of pressure when the head passed through the birth canal (I needed saving, I could not make it out alone, someone knows better than me, they must be more powerful than I, and able to save others) setting a possible root for the desire for a spiritual teacher.

Once born, Little John was then invaded by the insertion of the suctioning bulb in the nose and mouth immediately following birth, (they are attacking me again, I am overwhelmed, this is really too much!), lost approximately one quarter of his blood when the umbilicus was cut as the placental blood is actually baby's blood and loss of one quarter blood is considered a life crisis shock to the body by emergency medical technicians, (they are trying to kill me, I have no energy left, I am going to die!), was perhaps given to the mother if she were awake but this is unlikely given the date of John's birth, (I must attach to the doctor, mother is no where to be found, where am I; I needed help and you saved me!) but soon taken away for cleaning, weighing, measuring, and possibly drops in the eyes, (I am certain they are trying to kill me, my head hurts, I am dead) and then was taken back to the mother if she were somehow now awake from a full bodied anesthesia or, more likely, taken into nursery care waiting for mother to awaken. (I am lost, abandoned, near dead, and surrounded by unhappy babies. We all must get out of here! Let's go back to spirit! I can connect to everyone back there!).

In nursery care Little John would have been attempting recovery from the nightmare of physical sensation without the safety and protection of mother (was she awake yet?). He would have been surrounded by other traumatized, lonely, and in-pain babies, possibly in a pain cycle due to the residual forceps pressure on his skull, and would have also been placed on a feeding schedule. (I am dying from internal sensations, my head hurts, all the other babies around me are in danger, sad and frightened! I have never known hunger, I cry and no one comes, I will scream but no one comes, I will despair and go away, what is this infant formula? I want my Mom! I am hungry and must suck as I put everything in my mouth to help soothe me. My digestion system doesn't like this!) Little John is startled out of a dissociated sleep to be fed, glad to have company, and then re-startled when he realizes it is not his mother, (I was OK in heaven, don't make me come back, when I come back I feel pain, the world is not safe, my mother abandoned me again, I am going numb but ready to fight, I am angry and unprotected and terrified!). Infant circumcision was performed without anesthesia and was invasive, painful, terrifying, and placed Little John even further into shock.

Imaging Little John's experiences was overwhelming for adult John. We moved slowly in treatment to digest one part at a time. It was as if Little John entered the gravity-oriented world of post-birth through the threshold of pain, isolation, life-threatening procedures, and a total lack of safety and protection. All these factors in Little John's experience went unnoticed. In the adult world, the doctors and mother were happy to have a new baby boy!

Notes about post-birth isolation

Babies should not be isolated following birth according to Dr. Nils Bergman, a South African physician. Dr. Bergman measured the stress hormones of early born infants. He compared infants placed in neonatal intensive care units to infants placed immediately on their mother's chest and tied there for continuous skin-to-skin contact. Babies with skin-to-skin contact post-birth dropped in stress hormone levels, slept in a cycle with the mothers sleep rhythm, matched the mothers breathing rhythm, and began to self-regulate and stabilize their nervous system. Infants with no contact with mother held elevated cortisol levels, lower body weight, and generally showed greater signs of stress response and failure to thrive. Dr. Bergman's study validated the effectiveness of skin-to-skin contact post-birth, especially for babies under the stress of being born prematurely. Babies who received skin-to-skin contact emerged as stronger babies with a greater ability to thrive. Post-birth nursery care is isolating, interrupts the bonding opportunity, and can contribute to further hopelessness and despair in infants.

Mis-attunement and attachment

The dichotomy of experience between birthing room physicians and attendants, birthing mothers, and the birthed baby creates disharmony in the social function of the nervous system of the newborn. He feels the mis-attunement of the mother, which is a key component in creating an insecure attachment. The mother who was unavailable to protect him during labor but is now happy to see him and oblivious to his pain and difficulties feels incongruent. It is likely that this baby is in extreme physical pain. Yet everyone around him is celebrating his safe arrival! No one has accurately reflected to him his recent experience so he can integrate it and move on. This mis-attunement could cause him to feel completely misunderstood and confused. He is in a state of shock, which means he is not ready to bond.

A clinician cannot "know" what an infant experiences. However, treating older children and adults who can name their sensations and perinatal memories as they become conscious of them allows theorists to surmise the impact on the nervous system and psyche. This is especially true when one witnesses the cellular discharge of emotions in adults and older children revisiting these early times. Infants also respond emotionally and discharge these emotions when their experience is accurately mirrored and named by the mother or therapist. Infants can quickly cycle through fear, anger, sadness, resentment, and forgiveness in order to bond. They are quite capable of showing their emotions through facial expressions and sound.

Bonding

The birth process is designed to foster mother-infant bonding. A natural birth hormone of oxytocin mixed with adrenaline is released when the baby's head descends and reaches a point near the mother's bladder. This hormone supports mother and baby to have the strength to finish the birth and to bond and fall in love. It is the same hormone present during adult orgasm. Only during and immediately following birth is oxytocin present at its highest levels. This makes the bonding moment a critical time for the self-regulation of the infant-mother dyad. However, this hormone effect is compromised when labor drugs are introduced into the mothers blood stream.

Impacts of anesthesia and birth position

Little John's mother was completely anesthetized during birth. In addition, her birth position was on her back. This was common procedure in many hospitals of that era, and is still in practice to this day. When a mother is on her back, the sacral promontory is like a hill the baby must climb over. The natural expansive ability of the mothers' sacro-illiac joints and the softened pubic symphysis in the pelvis is meant to shift and open as the baby progresses. This natural joint motion is compromised when the mother is on her back and the weight of the baby is pressing on her sacrum and blood vessels. Use of labor drugs and birth positioning can complicate the birth and lead to more and more interventions, such as forceps or vacuum suction or even caesarean surgery. Mothers should be supported to squat, be on all fours, and give birth in a position that allows full range of movement through the pelvic joints.

Anesthesia intended for the mother enters the baby's body through the blood stream and the umbilicus. Hospitals choose a dosage amount based on the mother's body weight that is far too much for an infant. Thus Little John was drugged prenatally; of course he could not get out! His consciousness was distorted prior to exiting the womb. His natural potency was immobilized. Without the movement support of his mother, he became stuck in the birth canal and forceps were used to pull him out. His natural spinal push pattern was interrupted and became a spinal pull from the outside. Spinal integrity of his body was interrupted and Little John was then taken to the nursery until mother awoke.

Note on imprints of nursing, colic, and sense of safety

If Little John were nursed, at least his body might have begun to self-regulate through contact with the mother and the deep movement of the tongue, mouth, and esophagus into the gut. However, as a bottle-fed infant, that internal rhythm and massage did not occur. The bottle nipple is made of synthetic material foreign to the baby, and is too short for an infant to establish the deep reach and pull of the sucking rhythm. The formula used can be quite dissatisfying for infants and the combination of formula and bottle nipples often produces colic.

Given his first impressions of the world based on a traumatic birth, Little John may not have thought of the world as safe. During feeding he may have actually avoided contact with the mother even when in her arms. He may have been a fussy crying baby as he was in a pain cycle and carrying an unresolved pain imprint. His nervous system might have made an association that self-attention means intense pain, therefore better to not feel. Alternately, Little John could have been highly dissociated and presented as an overly contented baby. This dissociation stems from going numb in response to intense body pain. Perhaps he had never come fully into his body.

Post-birth repair and brain imprints

Had Little John been given a Biodynamic Cranio-Sacral session or a Body-Mind Centering® session immediately post-birth, he might have been able to come out of the shock of dissociation due to pain from forceps. Cranial-Sacral hands-on treatment sessions support the integration of the spinal chord, the fluid rhythms of the body, and supports the skull plates to regain their mobility and natural position. Little John could have received a Body-Mind Centering session that took pressure out of his bones, reconnected his organs, and sequenced the stiffness of anesthesia out of his joints. Thus his natural resiliency would have returned.

Both prior mentioned treatment methods are gentle and noninvasive. Such treatments would have allowed Little John to regain an internal rhythmic support of his nervous system. His natural desire for mother and his ability to attach could repair. However, Little John was not given such treatments as his post- birth care was not addressed from an infant perspective.

Progression of clinical work

Because of the extent of time in treatment, I did not detail each session but chose rather to highlight the themes that emerged, the methods used, and results of that work. The sessions occurred over a two-year timeframe and included land sessions and warm water pool sessions.

John's goals for treatment

The primary goal for John was to develop a felt sense of how to relate to others; especially the ability to empathize and connect from an embodied level. He sought behavior change from a controlling punitive attachment style that expressed as criticism and passive-aggressive displays with his wife and children. He wanted embodied skills that helped him re-direct anger in a healthy manner that did not displace that energy onto others. He needed support to repair bonding with his two children and longed for a deeper connection with his wife. A first step would be to help John actually feel the impact of his behavior on the family. Ultimately John needed to develop a sense of his own needs and learn to get them met in the context of intimate family relating.

Methods of treatment

The presence of a therapist trained to recognize perinatal themes is critical to the repair of early pre-cognitive shock. When they accurately name, reflect, empathize with, and mirror the client's experience, the nervous system repairs early brain states of overwhelm and defense. What was initially traumatic as a pre-cognitive cellular memory is brought to consciousness and sequenced through the body without re-traumatization. Surfaced early memory witnessed by an attuned therapist allows a human participation and empathy that supports clients to integrate via emotional processing, ownership of the experience, and resolution of the shock pattern contained in the initial situation. Teaching a client to "surf their shock," helps them become empowered in directing their own behavior change. In addition, any adaptive strengths developed by the client in response to such early obstacles can be recognized and highlighted.

Initial work and subsequent sessions

Treatment began with a number of warm water pool sessions. This supported John to bond with his children as a playful, interactive and embodied father. The water environment allows children to be energetic and is especially useful as it is sensory-motor focused. Water sessions were followed with office sessions that involved sand tray, play therapy, and developmental movement work to support embodiment and connection.

Short descriptions of treatment sessions follow. They are expressed from the client's emotional viewpoint and the session title expresses the main content. The reader can see that sessions overlap in theme and are linked to physical and emotional imprints of John's birth story. The courage John showed in meeting these early imprints was touching. His dedication supported the work to evolve.

"I need pressure in order to feel myself!"

In numerous sessions it appeared that John sought intensity. It was as if John needed this intensity in order to feel himself. He organized relating in the sagittal plane, which is a frontal facing plane, and moves along a continuum for forward and back. This can feel aggressive, and felt very pressured to this therapist. John was missing the ease and comfort of horizontal engagement. This is a typical response of forceps birth; it is a very sagittal force of pull that interrupts the baby's natural birth rotation. Doctors can sometimes see so little of the baby's head when they apply forceps that they inadvertently pull the baby in the opposite direction of the natural birth rotation. This is disastrous for spinal integration in terms of ligaments and fascia planes. Pulled out in they wrong direction complicates a baby's felt-sense of knowing and orientation that stems from body integration. A baby is making a rotational choice by the time the head crowns during birth. To be pulled in the 'wrong' direction can set up a deep mistrust of one's own choices in life.

In this session we examined that need for pressure in relationship dynamics, the intensity involved, and the impact such pressure would have on a normal adult partner. We explored how tiring this orientation and seeking of pressure might be for John and for others. We also identified how the pressure of forceps contributed to this need to have pressure in interactions as an adult. John was continually relating to his children and wife through pressure that pushed them away due to the intensity.

"Why bother?"

This session revolved around an inner hopelessness that was debilitating and influenced a sense of feeling disconnected in marriage. Hopelessness is a common theme when there is anesthesia during the birth. Naming and identifying that it did feel hopeless at birth and the connection with mother was lost at that time helped to contextualize the feeling and differentiate this from normal adult difficulties.

"Yuck, I am being poisoned!"

This session brought out the sensations of nausea and discomfort that were left in the tissue imprints of anesthesia. Anesthesia memory comes out of the tissue when working somatically. One can smell it and often the client feels a sense of metallic taste. Clients will have a numbed look in the face, and sometimes a greenish discoloration around the mouth. Teaching a client to squeeze their organs, similar to squeezing a sponge, can help them to discharge the nauseous sensation and have room for more oxygen and inner support. It is not actual anesthesia but anesthesia imprint that remains and influences the tissue. It is helpful to clear anesthesia imprints early on during somatic work so that the client has more energy available for tracking and sensing emotions.

"I would rather go away than connect to Mom"

This session was explored in a sand tray using small toys in sand to show the stories of the psyche. During this John put himself beside his wife. He then made a big circle in the sand linked to his spiritual teacher and that teacher's assistant. He described this circle as full of love. John wanted to go toward the teacher for support and connection. I suggested putting John's mother into the story; he did so by placing her upside down with her head buried in the sand. John's sense of pleasure was to move toward the teacher, rather than his family. He sought connection spirituality, not so much with his wife, and not at all with his mother. This session helped me to really see the depth of avoidance that was present in John.

"Shields are up!"

In this session John identified the habit of bracing in his musculature and speeding up in his thoughts, speech, and actions. This behavior prevented intimate contact and was a manner of maintaining control and safety in his adult life. Bracing and speeding up is a common response in the nervous system as a survival strategy to avoid being crushed by forceps. It creates a high tone in the musculature and often masks a low tone in the organs. We worked to bring breath into the bones of the skull and help the tissue to soften through movement, awareness, and touch. John began to take ownership of his muscle pattern and began to yield to a more balanced tone.

"I will leave you before you leave me!"

This is a common attachment strategy to overcome inconsolable sadness and loss. Here we dealt with the loss of contact with mother during a birth with anesthesia. The entire prenatal time is spent in a moving dialog. Movement and sound is the world of the prenate; they become familiar to feeling a response in the fluids and tissues of the mother. This allows the prenate to feel connected and in relationship with mother. When the mother's tissues go numb during birth, the prenate will experience the panic of abandonment because previously responsive tissue is no longer active and available. The prenate will become fearful and will also have a harder time getting out of the birth canal. They may speed up and miss the somatic cues that help through its skull to navigate the necessary twists, flexions, and turns that occur during the birth through the bony pelvis. This deep seated fear and high tone in the nervous system makes it difficult to follow softer cues in adult relating.

"I am afraid to connect with you but I want to!"

Hold your pinky finger in the line of sight of a client doing perinatal work; this serves to somatically invite attachment at that instinctual attachment level. This session navigated Little John's resistance to contact. He was able to work with this and find his feeling of "first impulse" to reach out and grasp when he made contact with my little finger. This impulse is often filled with potency and can be a quick grab of the finger.

"I am so mad and cannot move my body"

When the body cannot move, the emotional energy goes into thinking. This is a fight response that moved into the mental body, and is often a sympathetic self-attack or a mean projection onto others. *"I will criticize others in order to feel alive! I can move my voice and my thoughts and I am angry at being abandoned and interrupted."* This session explored how the mind races when there is limited movement in the body, and how thought energy is solidified when the body cannot move. Here birth movement potency was transformed into emotional anger and finally to criticism. When the expression of movement is limited it can transfer to the emotional body as anger, which without opportunity to sequence, becomes transferred into the mental body as thought. This energy expresses as criticism of others and of self. This session explored the neural pathways of limited anger, its movement into thought, and how it resulted in criticism. John was able to witness the impact of this habit, both on himself and his family when he responded to them through his critical mental body.

"No one is there, it hurts too much!"

This session brought to awareness the pain body and the seduction of pain. When an infant (or an adult) is in pain it is very difficult to have any available attention for others. The client can appear quite narcissistic because everything revolves around them. However, they are attempting to relieve intense pain. Little John had linked the pain body with self- contact and contact with others. In order to come into relationship, he would need to go back into this pain. This was terrifying and accelerated his sympathetic activation and his avoidance of contact.

"If I connect to my wife I will die'"

In this session it became clear how much John was actually avoiding his wife in a similar manner as he had avoided contact with his mother after she had "abandoned" him during birth. Because intense experience can become coupled in the nervous system, my hunch was that any seeking of contact was sympathetically loaded as dangerous, and would lead back to the internalized pain. John was able to take ownership of this tendency and to explore releasing that internalized fear.

"Better to be existential than to feel my emotions"

John had a tendency to respond with existential comments rather than relational comments when confronted about day to day issues. These comments were laced with a passive aggressive tonality. John was unaware of this behavior; however his wife was entirely frustrated by his responses. The passive aggressive tone caught her by surprise and the mental "globalization" of the issue at hand, rather than addressing the points presented, served to distract her from the issues she was trying to resolve. Globalizing strategies are reminiscent of the induced existential nature of consciousness under anesthesia. This point of naming the existential response needed to be highlighted a number of times before John could see how "globalizing" was a way he avoided relationship.

"I will not come into relationship"

In this session I needed to continuously challenge John to connect with me emotionally and somatically. It took some hands-on tissue pressing and somatic tracking until he could feel the anger and rage underneath the avoidant tendencies. This was a very useful session because the potency for contact was held in the anger. We had to ignore the avoidance, which often masked as a spiritual directive and allowed John to perpetuate staying unattached.

"Lean into the fight"

This session was a continuation of the prior one. I invited John to unmask his anger about inviting him to relate, and applauded his ability to stay present while angry. John engaged me with a substantial amount of anger. He was quite mad at me for insisting he come into contact. Allowing this anger to surface built the muscle for true potency rather than passive.

"If I let go of spiritual seeking I will go unconscious!"

This session met the point in John's experience where the anesthesia entered his nervous system. John could feel the fear of going unconscious and the imperative not to do that at all costs. This was reminiscent of the birth anesthesia where he lost his own ability to move and lost connection with his mother. This imprint becomes set in place when high sympathetic arousal is subsequently overridden with a drug- induced second-hand anaesthesia. This is exactly what happens to an infant who is subjected to second hand anesthesia. They are forced to go unconscious against their will. Meeting this moment will mean meeting the fear around the loss of control that anesthesia produces. I knew at this point we were closer to the fear but not yet ready to meet it. The need to avoid the fear also explained the huge draw to spirit and escape, and is another factor common in the anesthesia birth imprint.

"If I go unconscious I will die"

Meeting fear on a brain state level is essential for its release. Clients need to know that they can meet and release the "life-threat" now even though the fear was overwhelming to the infant self. Dissociation was a good response during the initial event. However, the adult body is bigger and has more cells to uptake and process the overwhelmed experience of the past. It takes skillful navigation here. The clinician does not want to re-traumatize but to teach the client how to surf his or her own shock response. This is empowering and helps the shock field to lessen.

"I will get all the information from my "guru"

and become better than he" (beat the doctor who took away my power). A baby seeking its way through the birth canal is loaded with potency. Use of forceps robs the infant of its sense of effective life force. Their potency is channeled into protection and an adult or child with forceps experience often picks fights or is argumentative. Ironically, forceps also provide salvation and save the infants life. They may have been absolutely necessary at the time of delivery. However, the relief at the salvation from pressure is tinged with the anger at being rescued and interrupted. "I wanted to do it myself!" is a common expression during this time in the therapy. In order to feel potent again, the infant must reclaim its power that was taken by the doctor.

It is essential to work with the spinal ligaments and reintegrate spinal integrity. People with forceps experience often have a hyper sensitivity or weakness in the neck area. Their spinal pushing force was interrupted and became a pull from the outside. I use hands on pressure down through the top of the head and into the spine to help reclaim the sense of personal power and potency. I highlight the developmental Body-Mind Centering® head to tail pattern. I also explore the psychological implications. With John the force of his ambition to become enlightened felt coupled with his loss of power. The intensity of spinal fear served to pressure his intensity toward salvation that was also projected onto his family.

"I will become a spiritual teacher too!"

By this time in treatment there has been significant work on returning to the body and awakening tissue sensation. Now it was imperative to bring the cognitive pieces clearly into view. For this I used stuffed animals as this helps to externalize and make tangible "ideas" of behavior. We set up a scenario with a mother and baby, and a spiritual teacher and spiritual "buddies." I enacted John's scenario showing his tendency to move away from attaching to his spouse and family and back to the comfort of the spiritual group. I then asked John to directly sense in his body the energy he felt when watching the scenario.

John admitted that he could feel an inner whoosh or rush that took his consciousness into a global or wide perspective. This is often the sensation of an early anesthesia imprint. People speak about feeling larger than life, or smaller, or going back and forth in size, or having a vast consciousness.

I next asked John if there were any spiritual ambition driving him. He said it had lessened with his current teacher. However, there remained a strong drive of ambition that was definitely sensate based. John felt highly unwilling to release the idea that he would survive without spiritual effort. My clinical hunch was that there was terror at the core of the ambition. I also sensed John's interest to regain the potency and power that was lost due to an interrupted birth where he was "rescued" by the doctor with forceps.

Addressing spirituality is very important in development. One must come to terms with ones values around the question of spirituality. Yet spirituality was not the direct issue in these circumstances. Seeking was masking the early imprint. This effort allowed Little John to remain dissociated in the existential realm rather than address the body felt terror around anesthesia, loss of safety, and loss of self. Integrating this imprint would allow a mature inquiry into spiritual matters rather than seek the felt sense of existentialism encoded at that time.

I left John with the homework to explore his discomfort at the thought of suspending his work with this spiritual teacher for another 6 months. This teacher had often "tuned in" and helped to clear energy that was uncomfortable or blocking for John. I encouraged him to consider not having someone else clear his energy. I preferred to see him develop the capacity to meet the fear directly. This is the empowering step of working with ones shock imprints. When the mature adult can actually stay in relationship with the early terror, the imprint wound can heal. It is as if the adult self is able to stabilize whereas the early infant could not. This also sends a message to the psyche that the dissociated younger self is no longer in charge and that there is a conscious healthy adult present. When this becomes a trusted inner relationship the split off self can integrate. In adult intimacy, it is essential for each partner to pick up the undeveloped younger parts of themselves rather than asking their partner to do this for them.

At this point the therapist is helping the client to build a strong enough psychic container. The goal is for the client to have the ability to hold their own psyche intact while releasing somatic sensations and imprints of disempowerment and fear. This is complicated but essential work in the reclaiming of an integrated adult self.

"I cannot move, no matter what I do, I am resigned"

This is the point of awareness when the infant realizes mother is gone, he is stuck in the birth canal, and he cannot get out. This moment of awareness is very useful for healing if the client can stay present. It is where defeat and terror meet, and includes anticipation of sensations of anaesthesia heaviness and emotional overwhelm. It is the "just before" moment prior to being drugged and having the crushing pain of forceps that encoded a pain cycle. If John can retain sober free attention, he can release more of the core terror.

Here the therapist must slow things down, insist on a connection and bear witness. It takes courage on the part of the client, and I watched as John tracked the impulse to go toward anaesthesia or toward the pain cycle, and held his ground against those forces. By doing so, John allowed a different sensation to enter his awareness; he sensed a very uncomfortable heaviness approaching. He became aware of the felt-sense heaviness in his body due to anaesthesia. John would have experienced this through his mother's tissue and then his own. Based on client descriptions, it is a terrifying sensation due to the immobilization and subsequent sense of the void created by anaesthesia. By staying present with the sensations, John had more sensory information and more chance of reclaiming cellular presence. Doing so sets a possibility for adult intimacy and reduces reactivity under stress.

"I can't feel my legs contacting the ground!"

This session was focused on potency and grounding. Through exploration of sensation, I discovered that John's birth trauma had been coupled with a later trauma of circumcision. This is common, and an un-named force that can de-masculate a man's natural power. It may also contribute to emotions that block sexual potency. Bringing energy into the legs opened the awareness of the effects of circumcision terror that were coupled to the birth imprint. We used BodyMind Psychotherapy methods of awareness, expression, and energy sequencing to help John bring energy down through the genitals and into the legs. John was able to find power in his connection to the earth which allowed him to express anger from an embodied place and find his potency for adult relating.

Closure Notes

John has demonstrated great courage and tenacity to unlock and repair relational dynamics with his family. John's capacity for relational presence is new and needs to be practiced. His unquenched desire to move forward with his spiritual teacher is not yet resolved and can take him away from connection with his family. My concern is that the need to be rescued (forceps is a baby rescue theme) is being projected along with dissociation onto the spiritual seeking. As of this writing, John is diligently working toward meeting his imprints and keeping his eye on my question.

As John resolves any need to escape, he can then do the work of intimacy that adult relating and parenting require. My clinical recommmendation was that John suspend for another 6 months his spiritual seeking and work instead on relational issues with his wife. As of this writing, John has agreed to limit his seeking to one month and then re- evaluate. His wife has born the effects of John's relational imprinting for many years and is beginning to lose her resiliency.

As a clinician I must offer support for the couple , and make it clear to John how his choices impact his relationship. The most effective next steps are for John to actually meet his fear and feel how former fear-based behavior impacted his family. Once he is able to do that, he can repair family relating. His spiritual path could become integrated rather than interruptive of family life. For couples therapeutic work, each partner must work on relational dynamics that occur due to each of their attachment and birth imprints, or any later events that contain shock. The above sessions only describe the individual work related to John's imprints. For full functionality of the couple it would be important for John's wife to unwind any residual imprinted shock in her field.

Conclusion

The above case study was presented in detail to inform the clinician as to the effects of birth imprints on behavior. This was specifically related to relational dynamics that presented in an adult male, age 49. Birth history included a birth process where the birth mother received anaesthesia, followed by the use of forceps on the client during delivery, circumcision, and post- birth placement in nursery care that interrupted bonding. This study highlights the complexity of relational dynamics and survival fears that become imprinted in the infant nervous system and influence adult behavior. As a clinician, I have experienced many variations of this forceps/anaesthesia theme with a diversity of clients. Birth imprints are a very real influence on the earliest imprinting of the nervous system. They underlie behavioral response choices that express many years later in adults and children when under stress.

Clinical Themes

Auditory startle speech rhythm

Use of spatial planes in treatment

Use of satisfaction cycle in treatment

Young children have a high risk of ear infections, because their eustachian (say "you-STAY-shee-un") tubes are shorter and more easily blocked than the tubes in older children and adults. The eustachian tubes connect the middle ears to the back of the throat. The tubes help the ears drain fluid. They also keep air pressure in the ears at the right level. When you swallow or yawn, the tubes open briefly to let air in to make the pressure in the middle ears equal to the pressure outside of the ears.

Sometimes fluid or negative pressure gets stuck in the middle ear, leading to infection. The eustachian tube carries fluid from the middle ear to the throat. Sometimes during a cold, the eustachian tube becomes swollen and fluid is trapped in the middle ear. Bacteria or viruses can grow in this fluid and form an ear infection.

Most ear infections form in the middle ear. The pressure outside the ear gets too high. This causes ear pain and sometimes trouble hearing. To bring relief, the doctor makes a small cut in the eardrum to drain fluid and to make the pressure the same inside and outside the ear. Sometimes the doctor will put a small tube in the eardrum. The tube will fall out over time.
edited from (www.webmed.com)

The special sense of the head and neck: perception

The special senses of the head include auditory, taste, smell, vestibular (balance and weight shifting in relationship to gravity) and vision. Vestibular is the most primary as the vestibular nerve is the first nerve to myelinate (myelin is the functional fatty coating for transmission of nerve impulses). A baby hears *in utero*. It also feels vibrations transmitted through the fluids of the womb space.

Paying attention to auditory invasion and auditory startle response in clients can help support deep healing as clients open neural pathways that may have been guarded or blocked. Reaching to feel movement with the small muscles of the ears is useful for children who had any form of ear or eustachian tube surgery. Reaching with the ears is useful to interrupt the deep seated freeze response in the brain stem that may have resulted from trauma due to blocked airways, throat issues, or bracing against the presence of forceps at birth.

Client assessment

With Somatic Psychotherapy, one can treat without knowing the birth history by tracking the body. If a client is in for a few sessions, I work with the body directly and layer in the prenatal if supportive. Wendy's speech had a noticeable stop-start in its rhythm. It was jarring to be in conversation with her. I became curious how her speech showed interruption of the Satisfaction Cycle (see article by this author at www. bodymindsomanautics.com). Wendy's vocal pattern went from a push to a reach but did not follow through to take hold, pull, and then yield. It was as if her voice were caught in a push to reach with no yield or follow through. In terms of spatial planes and support, I became curious about the unfulfilled forward and back movement of the sagittal plane. If she could not move fully back or forward she would not be able to receive contact or reach fully to another.

Treatment

I used the "Reach with the Ears" Body-Mind Centering exercise to help Wendy open her awareness to her own sounds and to open the possibility for shifting her internal sense of reach deep within the brain stem. I stood behind her and made sounds. I asked her to reach with her ears as she reached back in space to locate my sound. I then asked her to feel the connection with me and use it to move forward in space. Once she had the motion, I asked her to repeat moving backward, transition to forward movement, and then to add making a sound as she moved forward. I wanted her to generate new sensations in her perceptions via movement and sound. I worked to assist her to move back through her brain stem into homologous push, and sequence next into reaching with her voice. Use of sound vibrates body tissues and awakens the glandular system. Newborns use of glandular support is superb and fresh, and the sounds of infants are filled with vitality. This repeated practice with Wendy opened her to new sensations and awareness. She was able to shift out of her stop-start speaking rhythm and to engage with more enjoyable vocal communication.

Case Study #3 Related to Auditory Processing

Clinical Themes

Forceps impact on auditory perception

Staying present to sensation rather than bracing in the ears

"Reach with the ears" in treatment

Client assessment

Gail had forceps at birth and the ensuing internalized body bracing and taught tissue tone. Gail's birth procedures followed standard protocol of the times. This meant Gail's mother was completely anesthetized without medical need and that her birth position was back lying. This position drastically limited mobility in the sacral iliac joints of the pelvis, put extra weight on mother's vena cava vein and was a contribution that slowed birth. Anesthesia was administered as a "cocktail," which not only included anesthesia which dulls pain, but scopalomine, which interrupts memory. Birth positions and medications used resulted in Gail being stuck and being born via the use of forceps.

Gail was a psychologist and interested in resolving her deeply seated nervous system patterns. I noticed a tremor in her neck, as if the head were confused about its placement on the neck. I became curious about issues of self-worth, doubt, and follow through. These are common themes when forceps imprint exists. I wanted Gail to be able to follow through in a direction without equivocating.

Treatment

I used movement explorations to see if Gail could reach with her ears and find the "back space." This is the area we use when we listen to things coming from behind us; the backward reach allows us to travel down the spine to the lower limbs and to rotate the spine more easily and fully. Gail had difficulty and found that learning to reach with the ears produced tears and a softening in her nature.

As she reached, I asked her to stay present rather than reach and then go away. Gail slowly learned to tolerate the discomfort. Rather than go away from sensation, she added cellular breath and learned to explore the sensations contained within discomfort. Gail found she could reach with her left ear more than her right. Doing this brought into awareness a sense of confusion about which way she wanted to turn her head. Together we wondered if she might have been pulled out in the direction opposite to the way her body was positioned for birth.

Eventually, through the practice of staying present to sensation rather than going away, the right rotational pathway opened as an option for turning. Gail found an entirely new dimension in her orientation to life. She was able to release bracing deep inside her neck and brain stem.

B was 4 years old. He was considered "twice-gifted," both exceptionally bright and hyper- active. B was a smiley kid who would escalate when he did not get what he wanted. He struck out at children when they playfully touched him or came too close to him in the school line. B's hypersensitivity made it difficult for him to relate to normal social conditions with pre-school playmates.

Both parents were supportive of B's needs and constantly looking for behavior and sensory-motor support for him. Problems escalated when B was 3 and his younger brother was born. B had almost died at birth and had the complication of the umbilical cord around his neck, which forced the mother to choose a cesarian birth. B was born the day after 9/11, a day of cultural shock for US citizens due to the attack on the Twin Towers in NYC. B was born with an Apgar score of 1, and was revived by nurses using CPR immediately after the Caesarian operation. (Apgar is a vital signs test given immediately after birth).

"I am bad. I am a bad person." B muttered this constantly under his breath when he had an emotional meltdown. He struggled with transition, whether it was the transition of ending a therapy session, shifting from reading to art in school, or getting into or out of the car.

Sessions included times with B and one or both parents. Methods included role play of his birth story using the stuffed animals to represent family members and hospital staff, sand tray, sensory-motor play, and games he created. The healing of B's nervous system happened by bringing to life the events of his early birth and pre-birth history.

Larger field impact relating to fear

Early infant perceptions include what occurs in the surrounding birth environment. B was born the day after the 9/11 bombing of the World Trade Center in New York City. The bombing resulted in tremendous cultural fear, and this fear would have been present in the hospital and in all those attending B's birth. One learns to listen for complications due to social influences.

Intake followed by Protection Game

I used the Protection Game with B and his parents early in treatment (see props in Therapy Skills chapter). B was very much wanting to fight the Bad Guy and it took a few times before B was able to relax behind his parents. As the parents became more potent by protecting B in the game, B was able to settle more into his body. This began to reduce his inner anxiety and reactivity under stress.

Umbilical cord wrap theme "meeting the snake."

In this session we explored the impact on Little B of the umbilical cord around his neck during birth. The umbilical cord actually impeded his birth and was life-threatening. Each contraction pushed B and tightened the cord around his neck so he was effectively being choked. Cord wrap is very common;

Clinical Themes

Haunted womb

Near death

Umbilical cord wrap

Field impact of traumatized culture

Note to the reader
I have worked with many gifted children who have had difficult births and wondered if early shock and dissociation seems to increase perceptual abilities, producing both a gifted ability and make it harder for a child to self- regulate. A renowned specialist with gifted children, Dr. Linda Silverman noted that 85% of the gifted children she was worked with clinically have had pitosin administered during birth. (public lecture, Boulder, Colorado 2008).

many physicians say it has no "choking" effect. However, adults who accessed body-felt memory of birth with cord wrap have claimed they felt a sense of blacking out during contractions. This may be a felt sense or actual sense due to partial constriction of oxygenated blood. Cord wrap does carry a fear-based imprint in clients and affects the throat area and/or the carotid glands in the neck which measure oxygen in the blood. This somatic imprint is significant, since no one can accurately attune to the baby's hidden struggle. It becomes a "secret theme" issue as no one on the outside perceives the amount of struggle, fear, or despair the infant is negotiating.

Cord wrap can result in conflicts with Mom, as it appears to the infant that she did not protect her child from this danger. In fact baby's often associate Mom with this distress because the cord was linked to Mom's body. This can result in false and irrational blame of Mom. It is very helpful to address cord wrap and explain how no one knew, and it was not Mom's fault or baby's fault. I let B know that maybe he was playing with his cord, like a dolphin plays in the water with toys. It wasn't a real problem until the birth began. With cord wrap, the goal of treatment is for the child to come into relationship with the experience and reduce residual tension in the throat that often remains braced and activated under stress. The cloth snake is a useful toy to reduce cord wrap impressions. B was immediately drawn to this snake when he walked into my office. Based on years of clinical experience, I recognize that look of both attention and alarm. To work with this, I showed the story of B's birth using the cloth doll, pelvis, placenta and umbilical cord. These are midwife practice tools I have in my office and find essential for processing early birth stories.

I showed the doll coming through the pelvis and getting caught. 'Ouch, that hurts! I can't breathe!' Then I unwrapped the cord from the doll's neck. "That's better!" Little B spent the next several sessions playing with the cloth snake. He made cages for it, making sure it could not get out, and wrapped it around my neck and pulled me around. I made sure this was done in a safe manner and not repeated outside my office with others playmates. As B would "pull me around" I would say, "ouch, that hurts. Somebody help me!" Then B would rush up and unwrap the cord and we would clap and celebrate.

Work with the snake brought B into relationship with his own story and made it tangible. He could then express the anger and terror of not being able to move along during birth. After several sessions with the snake, B was finished with this part of the story play.

Educative touch to the neck
In this series of sessions I introduced gentle educative touch to the neck. First I touched my own neck and rubbed it, making pleasure sounds and letting my neck "say" how good that felt! Then I placed my hands on B's neck and asked B to touch my hands using his neck. This is a sensory motor technique where the overly

sensitized child is motoring with the tissue of his neck, bringing himself into relationship through touching me. Motoring is a connective and "push into reach" activity rather than a withdrawing activity, and helps one to better inhabit the tissue. Motoring releases freeze responses and cellular imprints that carry a sense of threat related to touch or pressure.

My goal was to engage the tissue in movement so B would explore his environment using his neck and would reduce the chronic internal bracing. With cord wrap it is common for the neck to brace as a way to defend from the life-threatening pressure of the umbilicus during birth. This habit continues under stress. Usually there is extreme terror beneath the bracing. Terror can drive aggressive responses in a child seeking protection. B was at first reluctant to explore touch. With slow gentle guidance and practice he began to enjoy how "smart" his neck was, and how he could feel things with his skin and throat.

Working with the neck tissue has many beneficial and sustainable results. The neck area houses many cranial nerves that govern sense of balance, hearing, sight, and sound. Cranial nerve X, known as the Vagus nerve, is very important for social emotional behavior as it governs excitability and relaxation of the organs of the body.

Another tissue to relax is the carotid body. It is on each side of the throat and measures the amount of oxygen in the blood. If cord wrap is constrictive, there may be surges of oxygenated blood. Massaging and releasing this area is helpful. Finally, letting the neck turn rather than brace is supportive for bilateral scanning which supports reading. Scanning is also used to check for danger or safety, and allows one to assess whether things are actually life threatening. Turning the head crosses the mid-line of the brain and brings about better integration of body support for reading, thinking and coordination.

Working with death themes at birth

"I almost died!" This session was with B and his father. B's color at birth was gray, which was alarming to all. Immediately the nurses worked to revive him. Dad was right beside them and reached out to B with his little finger, saying, "Where's my baby boy?" B responded and grasped Dad's hand. This moment of contact with Dad was the first reassurance B had registered in his cells following the trauma of his birth.

During this session Dad told that story to B. We spoke slowly so Dad could feel his emotions from that time, which were filled with terror and relief. B could sense the intensity of Dad's fear and relaxed and settled as Dad processed it. This allowed B to meet his own fear and realize that his birth was scary and that he made it! B laughed and clapped, and we celebrated that he woke up when he heard Dad's voice!

The next sessions involved working with the imprint of death. I have a large print on my office wall by visual artist Rance Hood. It shows a Native American Indian on horseback. There are three shadow riders on each side and an owl overhead. In Hood's culture, the simplified interpretation of an owl is that it symbolizes death's presence. In our next session, B spontaneously stood up on the chair to reach the print, and began pointing to all the death figures and then to the living one. He was speaking about himself, "almost dying", and celebrating that he made it. We went through the success of the story again with Dad, while B celebrated the feeling of surviving. Coming to grips with almost dying at birth helped to release shock and fear held deep within B's body tissue. It is common to see the return of vitality to body tissue when someone remembers their near-death experience and integrates that memory. This was true as B released his look of panic and fear.

Haunted womb theme "baby despair."

The following sessions dealt with events in Mom's life prior to B's pregnancy. In perinatal work, one is trained to notice if an infant picked up energy from prior events that occurred in Mom's womb tissue before they implanted. Processing this material can help energies release and help with differentiation of sensation for a child. These sessions clearly brought haunted womb themes to the light and helped resolved more layers of B's anxiety.

Many years prior to B's conception Mom (at age eighteen) had been raped, become pregnant, and had an abortion. This story was filled with violence and grief. Mom was distraught about whether to have an abortion. Abortion was against her heart feelings and values; however she was haunted by violent associations the rape. She wondered if she that would interrupt her ability to bond with her child. Finally she painfully chose abortion realizing she could not reconcile the violence and that was not a good way to welcome a new baby. These are the difficult real life choices; rape is a terrifying experience and this mother made the difficult "best choice" based on her emotional availability at that time.

B was conceived 12 years after this event and had no knowledge of it. I was quite curious about why B's birth had been so difficult. I invited Mom to an individual session without B; here she could finally process the story of the rape and abortion. When it had resolved enough in her body, I suggested we find an age-appropriate way to share the early story with B. Doing so would help clear cellular impressions he would have received based on womb tissue memory.

Mom and I discussed treatment prior to the session with B.I suggested to Mom we use stuffed animals to help show this story to B, and that we find a name to call the little one who was aborted. She suggested "Baby Despair." In B's session, we did not mention the words "rape" or "abortion." We talked about a bad man who hurt Mommy. We talked about "Baby Despair," who would have been an older sister or brother to B. In the session Mommy said goodbye to "Baby Despair" and grieved. She told B that she chose to say goodbye and not give birth since "Baby Despair" had such a painful beginning.

Little B watched Mom's face intently during this story. He settled into Mom's lap with a huge sigh of relief when it was completed. It was the most settled I had seen him during the entire course of treatment and he was finally able to rest fully into his mother's body. Sessions were concluded shortly thereafter due to successful behavior changes with less sensory activation in social settings. Little B had worked hard, and sequenced so much of the shock through his nervous system. He had more room to be a settled and engaging child without huge escalations when activated. His parental support was exceptional, and the family was happy with the results.

Rape is such a sensitive topic and parents are often afraid this knowledge will hurt the child. I have only seen positive results in naming such secrets. Cells appear to know the events anyway, and respond through tension, fear, struggle or shock. Naming them allows the story to settle and tissue to yield. With haunted womb issues it is essential that violent and shocking events are named in an age-appropriate play therapy manner in order to be successful.

Note about cellular memory

Scientists, parents, and clinicians have learned that memory exists in the cells long before cognition develops in the brain. These imprints are implicit, and accessible when there is recognition and support in the environment. Children show them through play. The shock energy is resolved in the body and nervous system when implicit cellular memory is brought to the surface, witnessed, and interacted with. This takes it from the implicit level to the explicit, and then the participatory. I was skeptical of the degree to which one could "remember" pre-cognitive events until I saw the expressions of children in clinical sessions. I have seen four-year-olds remember Mom being beaten while they were in the womb by expressing an uncalled for violence with their peers and in sessions. I have seen adults startle in the surprise of cellular memory as it became conscious. Best of all, I have seen clients bodies relax when "secrets" are named, and with children this can be done in an age-appropriate manner.

With haunted womb issues it is essential that violent and shocking events are named in an age-appropriate play therapy manner in order to be successful. In B's sessions, we did not mention the words "rape" or "abortion." We talked about a bad man who hurt Mommy. We talked about Baby Despair, and that B would have had an older sister or brother. We talked about how sad Mommy was and that she chose to say goodbye to Baby Despair and not give birth, since baby despair had such a painful beginning.

Clinical Themes

C-section imprint and repair

Annihilative terror

Auditory startle

Abandonment

"Sneaky Power" power dynamics

This case study involved a year of sessions with "P" and her mother and father to repair the imprint of a scheduled C-section birth. It was a very supportive family; mother was present for all sessions and father able to attend for a few as needed. P was three and a half at the start of treatment. I learned much from her and it was a delight to support her to integrate and heal the internal terror lodged in her nervous system due to C-section birth.

Current events

P began having emotional melt-downs at preschool and at home just prior to Halloween. These were the first symptoms that alerted her parents that there was some internal struggle. P came from an emotionally well resourced family comprised of her parents plus two older siblings age 6 and 8. Her parents sought treatment for P due to social behavioral changes at school and sudden onset of emotional outbursts. P appeared frightened in ways unfamiliar to her mother. She became demanding and controlling of play peers at preschool and would barricade herself and a friend inside the play space.

Prenatal and birth history

Dad and Mom were nicely involved with the pregnancy and happy to be pregnant again. Their two earlier babies were born via successful vaginal births. Mom discovered during the first third of pregnancy that the placenta was blocking the cervix. This unfortunate news meant it was impossible for P to arrive vaginally.

Mom was alarmed by this news and both worried and sad. Her past pregnancies and been carefree and she enjoyed the connection with her babies during the birthing process. Mom described birth as empowering and connective for herself and her babies. This news clouded her ease with the pregnancy. In addition, Dad was only able to be home on weekends during the pregnancy. They had recently relocated just after becoming pregnant and Dad was flying back and forth to another state for work. This strained Mom's ability to relax as she was alone during the weekdays while pregnant and raising two young toddlers.

In addition to the emotional strain, Mom had excessive pressure on her diaphragm from the pregnancy. She was not getting rest because she could not lie down to sleep. She was sometimes startled awake and out of breath; she sat upright at night in order to catch her breath. This developed a stress response in Mom's breathing rhythm and anxiety about the birth. Although Mom cognitively understood her emotional needs, her body stress levels elevated during pregnancy. This was a natural consequence of the added stressors of loss of consistent physical contact support with her husband, living in a new area, and being alone with two young children while pregnant.

Birth experience

P was born through a planned caesarean. Normal C-section surgery includes use of anesthesia, a rapid birth, and a brightly lit and cold delivery room. There are physician attendants in the room as well as the surgeon, and in this case according to Mom, an extra amount of activity and many professionals in observation in the delivery room. With all this excitement, a nurse dropped a metal tray just as P was being lifted from the womb. The sound was very loud according to Dad and P went into a body startle response. Dad was impacted by this event and during the intake he mentioned how loud it was and P's response. P was then separated from Mom and held by Dad while Mom was stitched up post surgery.

The family was then placed in a hospital room post-birth for the remainder of the day that was located in a very busy and noisy area. Finally, due to Mom's insistence, they were moved to a quieter area in the evening. Mom said she and P were then able to bond and relax.

Assessment

There were a number of factors that caught my attention during the intake, such as: late October timing of recent symptoms related to Dad's travels in late October during pregnancy, P's auditory startle when the nurse dropped the metal tray at delivery, the high level of hospital activity near the recovery room post-birth, and the impact on Mom's and P's nervous system based on C-section protocol and intensity. These would all relate to first attachment and that "moment of meeting."

Late October was an "anniversary month" of Mom's prenatal stress time; however I had to rule out normal social activation during Halloween. Mother said her other children didn't have such emotional overwhelm at Halloween and she recounted how stressful P's pregnancy was for her.

Retained auditory startle in the nervous system has a significant impact as it interrupts the ease of integrating sensory information. It can produce a freeze response in the tissues in the brain stem, increase vigilance and protective responses, inhibit ease of crossing midline in the body, and interrupt integration and sequencing of information through the brain stem. The combination of auditory startle and the rapidity and coldness of a C-section birth will often produce a tactile defensiveness, a need to control, and hypersensitivity to touch.

Treatment plans

The main goal was to assist P to tell her story through play in order to help her release stored trauma. Doing so would support both she and her parents to sequence any remaining emotions from P's birth. On the physical level, I wished to support P's nervous system integration and the ability to regulate stress. I wished to see a decrease in her high tone, her need to control others in play, and her auditory and tactile sensitivity. I wished to support a relaxed bonding with Mom and release of her un-named fears.

Sessions

Intake

The first intake was with Mom and Dad. They were present, supportive, and curious as to how to help their daughter. They were open to the concept of early imprinting on the nervous system and willing to move forward with treatment. I find it essential to have a structured intake prior to working with the child. Doing so fleshes out the level of support available in the family. It also allows time to educate parents toward the ideas of nervous system overwhelm related to behavioral response in children.

During the session I include how prenatal and birth events contribute to fear and control issues. Intake with the parents allows the clinician to determine what residual emotions remain for the parents from the birth or prenatal time. I explore this with them and address the importance of allowing their emotional integration to happen in private sessions and also sometimes during sessions when the child is present. It is common during a difficult or disempowering birth for the couple to lose their connection with each other. Repairing this allows a stronger parental team for helping the child. The above details of the birth information were gathered during the intake session.

Working with auditory startle imprint

Too Loud! Danger! ...oh, no! The next session was with P and both parents. Having both parents present is an asset for at least the first session, as the child feels more secure when parents are aware of the connection to their birth story. I introduced the session using stuffed animals to model birthing and inquired about the specifics of the child's birth.

Due to symptoms of hyperactivity and control, we used the Protection Game as part of treatment (see chapter on Therapist tools). Dad was very successful at protecting the family and pushing the bad guy out of the treatment room. He also remembered and named the nurse dropping the metal tray and how that sent P into a startle response just when she was born. This was a significant witnessing and provided the context that helped P to deal with her auditory startle.

For the game, P picked a bad guy from the selection of animals and definitely wanted to be the one to confront him. After we had played the game a few times she was able to relinquish the protector role to her father and allowed herself to be protected. Mom became more engaged with the story as well when she witnessed her daughter's responses.

The following sessions were just with Mom and P as Dad was working. Mom progressively became more interested and engaged with helping P to process the birth imprint. She shared more of her experiences with P and allowed herself to feel emotions that she had not had time to process during this difficult experience. Supporting parents to integrate left over emotions is a key aspect of this therapy. It creates a much deeper layer of support and interaction between mother and child during the playing out of the birth story. Such emotional processing promotes bonding, resolution of difficulties that occurred during the birth, and helps mother be able to meet challenges in behavior with cooperation and understanding of why her child has been dysregulated.

Reducing internalized fear projection by "making friends with the bad guy"

This theme involved several sessions and was the work of taking an ungrounded fear and making it concrete and related to experience. The reason for doing so allows a child to sequence the fear from nameless to real and to find capable ways to deal with the aggressor. Once that occurs they can integrate their experience, come to grips with fear, and transform fear into power and knowing.

P picked her "Bad Guy" fear representative during the protection game, and then asked for it during each session that followed. She chose Mr. Talking Head, a stuffed toy head with a scowling face that has a little voice box in it. When you bounce or throw it, as she was wont to do, it says things like "you knuckle head!" I am always intrigued how each child will pick the representation that serves them the best.

We spent many sessions throwing the bad guy out of the room so P felt safe. Next she was able to have the bad guy in the room as long as he was inside a rope circle boundary and the big stuffed dog was guarding him. We then were able to reach a session where I said I thought maybe the bad guy was really the doctor (who performed the C-section). Maybe he was not a bad person but was simply too rough. I voiced this following play that was representing P's sense of being in danger and worried about someone getting her. I wanted to both begin to reduce defenseless terror and give it a ground, seeing it as part of her real experience that she could name and begin to integrate.

Next followed a number of sessions with the bad guy being in the room and guarded by the big dog while P played in the tent and tunnel I have as therapy props. Eventually I was able to "teach the bad guy some manners" so he could be supportive with Little P during the C section. I knew we had reached a major integration when she asked to take him home to play with her other animals and learn some manners from them!

Meeting the loud noise!

In order to address the auditory startle, I asked Mom again about it. She described the event, and I then demonstrated what it would be like to be surprised by a big sound by hitting one of my gymnastic balls with a stick. P was intrigued and delighted. She growled at the loud sound and wanted to make it herself. I let her pound the ball with the stick. This was repeated at her request in a number of sessions until P had integrated that portion of sensory overwhelm. I chose a motoring activity to interrupt the freeze response which so often occurs when there is a loud startle.

Supporting Little P's parents

As Mom recognized that P was "telling her birth story" in session, she felt relief and that things would turn out well for her daughter. I helped Mom to learn to recognize and interact with the play through modeling and naming what I saw out loud. This also helped Mom to see how hard Little P was working in order to heal birth imprints and express early infant needs. Mom learned to meet these early un-met needs with both compassion and clear boundary setting guidelines which allowed P to feel safe.

In sessions I encouraged Mom and Dad to identify and express their own feelings as they emerged. Switching attention from child to parent is done to process what is most activated in the moment during sessions. Doing so invites parents to stay connected with me and allows the wisdom innate in the child's process to continue to surface. Processing emotions for parents and child allows the emotional interactive field between them to become congruent. Little P relaxed when her parents processed their emotions skillfully, as she could feel the burden of unprocessed emotions in their field. Children can always feel this tension, even if they don't know what it is about. Clarifying it helps them to relax!

As the field became clear emotionally, Little P released her fear and felt seen and understood. This gave her mastery over the difficult birth event. When Mom expressed her sadness at not being able to have a vaginal birth, and that she chose this, Little P stopped the quality of self-blame that appeared in earlier sessions.

Therapists must teach the parents and child to recognize when things are speeding up. This is known as pacing; speeding up is a sympathetic activation and increases the fight/flight response. It also interrupts healthy digestion of a difficult event. Fast talking and jumping from topic to topic are examples of speeding up. Experiences become integrated and resolved when therapists help the parents with pacing; teach them to slow down when listening to an activated child, to breathe and to pause, and to help their child do so. Ironically, as I teach this, it is often the child that reminds the parent to breath at home! Breathing and pacing support emotional self-regulation for all.

Sometimes a faster pace is necessary to meet the rapid energy that the child wishes to express and their sense of danger. This liveliness allows a child to find the healthy motoring against danger when there might have been a forced impotence (due to anesthesia or circumstance). However, I pace here as well. I name the danger and actually make sure the motoring is balanced with the ability to stay relational rather than go back into the shock response. This skillful navigation of pacing contributes to the sense of healthy resiliency and success at digesting difficult experiences, allowing them to settle, and refinding the "good enough" recovery in order to take in nourishment and be relational with self and others.

Reflecting the truth of what occurred in any event, reframing interpretations the child may have made of the experience, and enlisting the parents potency are the most supportive things a therapist can provide.

With Little P, Mom was able to align with her necessary choice to have a C-section rather than with the disappointment and inability to protect Little P from the intervention. It really was a matter of making a life-saving choice. Once Mom emotionally integrated her choice, she was able to hold integrity for that. This gave Little P a stronger sense of Mom in order to orient to Mom's presence amidst the confusion of C-section intervention.

We need a curtain!

At one point in treatment P demanded a curtain. I thought immediately of the curtains used during C-sections to prohibit the birthing mother from seeing the operation as she might go into shock. I have a large red flannel sheet in my office and moveable office chairs. I also have ropes I use as circles on the floor for boundary indicators. I tied my rope between the arms of two chairs and hung the red sheet over the rope. P insisted Mom climb under the curtain with her. Mom spoke about her sadness at not seeing P when she first arrived. Much play with the curtain followed in subsequent sessions. Often a child will bring the mother under the curtain with them in order to repair the sense of safe and secure connection with Mom that was interrupted. Sometimes P insisted I join them and sometimes she insisted I "stay out!"

Which way to go?

I have a collapsible red cloth tunnel that children crawl through. I pull it out so the child knows it is there during one of the early sessions. Then I let them ask for it in future sessions. The tunnel is used repeatedly. Some children will set it up without an exit possibility. It seems to simulate experiences for the child, and I have found it helpful to make physical contact through the walls of the tunnel. When P entered the tunnel and touched it with her hands, I touched her back. She then put her head and face against the fabric and I gently rubbed her face and head. Tunnels seem to create some sense of being in the womb and being seen. At one point P insisted her Mom sit at one end of the tunnel. P entered the tunnel and then became very confused about whether to come out the tunnel or to reverse direction and go back toward her Mom. It was quite emotional for P and it took her a number of attempts to figure out how best to reach her mother. This tunnel session simulated the attempt to stay with Mom rather than be pulled out by the doctor and the resulting confusion of separation. The resolution of her confusion showed apparent integration of being pulled out and then carried back to Mom. I frequently use probing questions in order to determine how to accurately reflect what the child is doing so her narrative becomes coherent.

Identifying with power and being sneaky!

P helped me to understand how children identify with the power figure and yet have to have even more power than the doctor. P taught me how essential it was to feel powerful by showing me her sneaky side. P took a small toy and put it behind her back. She asked me to pick which hand held the toy. No matter which hand I picked the answer was a triumphant NO! As this behavior emerged, P became obviously sneaky. There was a look that came over her face and through her eyes. Her mother and I commented on it and agreed that it had a manipulative and "magical thinking" feel to it. (note that this has a different look and feel than the age-appropriate imaginative play). We began to identify and to differentiate good power from sneaky power. Mom was excellent in interrupting sneaky power and pushing it out the room. Her powerful presence in meeting the sneaky behavior helped P to regulate and to identify her good power. It helped her turn to Mom for support rather than have to make herself more "powerful" than she actually was during the C-section.

One of my therapeutic goals was for P to be able to surrender rather than fight the C-section experience and see the doctor and mother as a supportive team on her behalf, since that was the true reality of a necessary C-section.

Little P really helped clarify for me one of the major dilemmas of power struggles in perinatal experience. If one cannot have direct power, they must assume covert power in order to survive. My hunch in this matter is that being sneaky, dissociated, and unavailable for contact is a brilliant strategy for a C-section delivered child used in order to get away from the doctor (as the invasive alien tearing her away from mother)

Such children cling to Mom in terror and attempt to fight the strange doctor whose hands are seeking to pull them away. These doctors are bedecked in protective glasses, a cap, gloves, and a mouth mask! The infant cannot avoid this rapid invasion of the womb by the "alien" figure and the subsequent separation from safety. There are strong body responses as well. Infants will physically brace in their internal muscles in an attempt to avoid being lifted out of Mom's body. This can result in a braced tone, without the resiliency of the nice squishing through the joints that a vaginal birth provides. It can result in an inability to fully integrate sensory input, brace against it, and behaviorally appear as a need to "be in charge!" Their nervous system under stress reverts to this activated state and controls rather than become overwhelmed. Little P demonstrated this in her 4 year old behavior in preschool where she demanded a friend join her in her barricaded play space and was "in charge," not only of her friend, but of the safety and protection needed!

A high sympathetic arousal causes fragmentation that provides a sense of alternative escape. Although the infant cannot fight or flee, they can "sneak away!" in their own psyche. Such fragmentation often produces behaviors that are rapid, highly creative, and covertly or overtly defensive in nature. Children seem determined to remain escalated when aroused rather than feel the terror and trap that led to ultimate submission.

The internalized fear in the nervous system sets a baseline need to control and be self- reliant. P was able to reduce this arousal state as she repeated through play the nuances and details of her birth story, and as her mother and I recognized and reflected back the events that happened at her birth.

Working With C-Section Incision Imprint

In one session P managed to find her way behind a Japanese folding screen in a corner of my office. I could barely see her through the slim vertical spaces between the panels that allow the screen to fold. P removed the duct tape that was supporting sound proofing from the office next door, and began taping the cracks in the Japanese screen so no one could see her. I asked what she was doing and she shouted, "very important work!"

I reflected on the invasive incision to mothers uterus that the infant experiences. This cut is followed by a loss of fluids, increasing baby's body sense of alarm, and then the Doctors hands must tear open the tissue (based on current medical protocol that tissue heals more naturally through tearing than a straight surgical cut). P was taping the crack, and repeated this for a number of sessions. As play would start she returned behind the screen, asked for tape, and retaped the cracks. She then asked her mother to come back with her and insisted that I be on the outside. Sometimes she was aggressive toward me and other times welcoming, especially if she had identified a toy as the "bad guy!," which allowed me to be more supportive rather than cast in that role.

During this confusion between safety and good and bad, it is important for the therapist not to take a child's aggression personally. Rather than see it as "bad behavior" therapists do best to work with aggression consciously to redirect, reframe and ultimately hold limits and safety. They must interact in a manner that allows one to be supportive and still maintain the therapeutic repair inherent in the play of the story.

Often I will say, "OK, I will stay out here and watch for bad guys" so that I am part of the story and not cast in the aggressor role. This allows me to be effective while empathizing, and remain both as witness and protector. I am also available to support Mom's deeper understanding of aggressive behavior when it arises, and how to work skillfully to support healing expression and necessary limit setting.

Meeting annihilative fear

This point in the treatment progression is difficult. Usually the child will show the amount of internalized terror. One can see the panic and dissociation. It is real terror and difficult for the mother to witness. The therapist's job is to make sure the child does not become re-traumatized at this moment but sequences the activated fear. Such fear can be mobilized into energy that is available for the child's sense of health. Some clinicians do not work at this level for fear of re-traumatization. I have found that it is often unavoidable as the child tells their story, and so must be witnessed and digested to release and repair nervous system stability.

When annihilative fear emerges, it is important to inquire if the child felt they might die. Often the child brings this to the surface verbally when I ask "what are you afraid of?" I often hear, "I might die!" I have heard this from children I had previously thought were too young to think about dying. Little P said these exact words and Mom burst into tears. Her empathy for the amount of terror her daughter felt as an infant was dramatically increased. This knowledge allowed Mom to accurately reflect, name, and then help P meet and regulate the fear. It is common for aggressive behavior to mask underlying fear.

Therapists must meet this level of terror for the child both verbally and in an embodied way so the child feels accurately understood. This is sometimes difficult if a therapist has not processed their own annihilation terror from the inside out. Often the child or client has shame for being afraid. It is important to move through that emotion. I remind a child that they survived and it was definitely very scary. I remind them it was not their fault. I reflect the terror accurately and tell them there was nothing they did wrong or mother or the doctor. I add that mother and the doctor made a choice that they wanted this baby to live.

This helps normalize the decision for a C-section and empowers the mother's choice for the operation. P's Mom made it very clear that she wanted a live baby and made that choice knowing P would be scared. She was sorry it was hard but affirmed she wanted a live baby and a C-section was necessary because the placenta was in the way and it was impossible for P to get out.

When annihilative fear appears it is important to pause, breathe, and slow things down. I help a child to kick their legs in order to motor the energy, use sensory brushing for calming, and have mothers hold and comfort their child. Often the mothers cry when they see such expression of terror. I inquire if the mother also felt afraid at the birth. Sometimes this question surprises the mother since she was numb due to anesthesia. However, she often finds and releases fear she had no opportunity to process during the birth. When Mother releases her fear, the child settles more easily.

Addressing closure of treatment: "No, you can't play!"

Parents often ask how to know when the child is finished with treatment. My experience is that the child will let you know. Little P began to push me out of the play naturally after many, many sessions. She was less eager to come to sessions and by this time, had already taken the "doctor" home to play with her stuffed animals. Ideally there is the luxury to let treatment closure be a natural expression of the child over a number of sessions. Taking time for closure is helpful as doing so re-patterns the ability to meet transitions; especially as in a C-section when the birth transition was so incredibly rapid and intense.

When I sense closure approaching, I reflect on issues from other sessions with children who experienced similar circumstances to see if we missed any pieces of the story. I speak to Mom about these things and measure the resiliency and needs of the family around treatment ending as well.

When moving toward closure, the child will sometimes attempt to re-introduce danger that was already processed. This can be an "upper limits" fear as health returns to the system. When I see this occurring, I interrupt such behavior and reiterate the good work and completion that has already happened. As with any behavior change, reverting back to old habits and behaviors is seductive for a child as well as an adult. Reminding the child that they are safe and protected and can find their way is reaffirming and sets the tone for their transition away from treatment.

Sometimes parents have to end treatment even if we are not finished. Under these circumstances I look for a named resolution and highlight the intelligence and resources the child has discovered. Part of treatment is to support parents to have healthy parenting skills, and i I often recommend parenting classes when parents do not know how to work as a team. Classes can be a helpful transition for parents who can no longer bring the child for treatment.

When there is the luxury to pace completion, I assess the repair and integration of perinatal events for the child and address this with Mom, making sure she has a clear sense of behavior changes. When that seems secure, I will begin to end the treatment. Often I will speak aloud, "maybe we are done with this story!" and see how the child responds. I look for and name closure. This begins the process.

As mentioned, healthy closure can take a number of sessions. I watch for indications from the child that the story has completed. I also work to wean the child off coming to play with me. I highlight pleasures with the family and what they might do when we are not playing in therapy. If the moment arises where I feel completion, I may end a session in the middle of the hour and use the rest of the session time to transition in leaving the office.

This allows me the time to have a nice walk out to the car with the mother and child. Sometimes I give the child a transitional toy that was significant in their work, or a soft cuddle blanket as a protective nourishing reminder of their good work.

Completion indicates that fear and activation have settled. During the last sessions we interact more by having play "tea time," and healthy social interactions rather than fighting dragons. During this time, I might look around and say "wow, the bad guy is learning manners, and you let your Mom know how complicated and confusing this silly birth was for you! What a good job, and Mom knows now how to keep you safe." These little affirmations help to anchor in the closure and the progress the child has made.

P's work significantly showed me how energy and identity attach to power, and one's body-based need to survive at all costs. I also saw how cleverly control masks fear in a child. There were many more details I learned but have omitted due to the length of this case study. However, in my treatment with other children born with C-section, I have come to recognize repetitive themes related to the confusion of this birthing. I am continually grateful for the learning that both P and her mother allowed me to explore with them as they integrated the difficulty of this birth event.

A further note on how to support parents

Most often parents bring children for treatment. However, if the parent has residual trauma from the child's birth, they are less able to support the child. For this reason it is extremely helpful to build good relations with the parents and encourage them to pause in session when they feel any emotions. It is sometimes useful for the parent to do some individual sessions prior to working with the child. Taking time to track what occurs in the parent's emotional field will help the child to settle and feel safe.

Based on what I see reflected, I will suggest the couple or parent attend a session without the child in order to clear what occurred for them during birth. I look for this if the child becomes too activated when Mom and Dad are working the birth experience during sessions. Often a parent's own unresolved shock from their birth gets activated during the birth of their child, especially with the first born or if the circumstances are similar.

Dad often feels disempowered and helpless. It is difficult for him as he has no way to "motor" the experience of the birth and has to sometimes witness his wife in agony. For this reason, in some cultures Dads were asked to hold space in the "outer circle" with other men, rather than waiting alone outside the delivery room. I also know that some Dads have taken charge in a very powerful way and repaired earlier experiences of impotency. Be sensitive to what is occurring for the parents as part of treatment.

Often a parent is sad and frightened during a C-section. Both parents might have been exhausted after the birth, especially Mom if she attempted for many hours to birth vaginally. She may have been hungry. Or simply done! She might have been checked out due to overwhelm or anesthesia and not have been able to be at all sensitive to what occurred for her child. Mom usually needs to finish pushing through her legs and pelvic floor to regain the potency and grounded power so necessary in parenting.

Parents may feel guilty for something beyond their control. Take the time to let the circumstances be felt emotionally and processed, especially if they felt overwhelmed by events and too vulnerable. Following individual session repair, it is very helpful for the child to witness that parents have come to terms with birth events and are present. Treating the entire family system during birth integration guarantees the most successful outcome for resolving behavior problems for the child. Include support for the parents to return to a felt sense of empowerment, parenting teamwork, reclaim their own affection that is not "triangulated" by the child, and settle for a "good enough" birth experience.

Background

M was 53 years of age, mother of four grown children. Her presenting problem was a feeling of low energy, and struggle in things she attempted. She had normal health and plenty of support from her husband. Yet her inner feeling was one of low esteem.

In response to events, M felt she was never good enough. M had a successful life with a satisfying career and loving family. Yet inside she felt inadequate, and this feeling gnawed at her. She did many sessions on gaining her potency, finding her voice, and speaking out. However nothing touched this deep-seated sense of inadequacy.

Finally, her work led her to cellular imprints at the moment of birth. She remembered the stories told to her about the birth; how the doctor was a friend of her father's and had remarked, at the moment of her birth, "oh, another girl. Again!" Her father had been quite disappointed.

M was unable to unravel this low self-esteem until the moment she remembered that cellular imprint. She remembered feeling powerful having arrived through the birth canal. Upon hearing those words she described going into shame and withdrawal that led to an immediate collapse of her potency. Remembering this moment through her tissue allowed her to interrupt the habitual collapse.

"Oh, another girl. Again!" said at the powerful moment of meeting post-birth produces a shock effect. From an adult perspective such comments might seem insignificant. However, this mistaken gender theme appears in many instances of treatment. Being welcomed with disappointment becomes coupled in the nervous system with identity, and a belief that 'no matter what I do I am a disappointment!' One can spend a life proving this is not true, or carry an internalized collapse. Such believes are a double bind and must be unraveled to release the energy for health.

Unkind remarks are damaging at a core level because an infant is wide open and receptive. There was a pattern set during this moment of arrival for M. She felt the power of beginning, followed by dismay and disruption, and finalized with the feeling of being outcast. This pattern expressed repeatedly in M's life. It was not until she slowed down her physical sensations and tracked the subsequent thoughts and responses that she could break the cycle.

Sequence a shame imprint into an energy imprint

Subsequent sessions helped M to meet the sensations produced by shame, which were intense. As she could stay present to sensation and let it cycle through, M was able to shift from the belief in shame as an indicator of personal fault to shame as an indication of something wrong with the environment, not with her. We worked to transform shame into energy. M found the anger beneath the shame, and

Clinical Themes

Mistaken Gender

Low self esteem

Shame

Secrecy

Mis-attunement

then the potency within the anger. The next step was to bring this potency into quality self-talk, self-care and healthy boundary setting. M worked with her tendency to seek approval from others, an outer referencing that felt out of place. Such behavior was actually a form of self-abandonment and put peers in a compromised situation, as the underlying need was palpable and impossible for others to fulfill. The actual abandonment in the environment was from both the doctor and the father who missed greeting M as a beautiful arriving baby girl.

With abandonment present in the field, the double bind linked potency with abandonment, and played out in M's life that she abandoned her potent instincts and sought affirmation from others. The order of healing was first for M to notice the sensations she felt related to abandonment, to digest that the energy of abandonment came from the field, and to realize those sensations were no longer necessary for her survival.

Then M had to identify the sensations that were a precursor to abandonment; notice when they occurred, and interrupt the entire neural pathway rather than follow the seduction of old habit and sensation. Doing so allowed M to stay oriented in time and place. She refrained from going into an internal shock wobble that caused her to orient toward others views and opinions. When M stayed present, she could release the need for affirmation from others in order to feel internally secure. Physically M worked to develop a healthy and pleasurable sense of push, which gave her new affirming sensations, and supported healthy boundary setting in social interactions.

Summary

Babies long to feel welcomed. Their nervous systems become easily overwhelmed when negative parental response or surrounding circumstances follow a birth. Without training and support in how to listen from an infant perspective, adults rarely understand the fragility and impressionability of newborns. We do want healthy and resilient children that are not overly sensitive. However, contrary to some beliefs, early reassurance and quality contact does not spoil a child but will enhance the opportunity for a child to develop secure attachment and a healthy sense of self in the world. Parents who allow a child to explore, to develop, and to feel valued support the child's sense of security and self-worth.

Case Study #7 Incarnation Shock

Clinical Themes

Existential delicacy

Pacing

Contact boundary

Power dynamics

Incarnation shock occurs very early in one's consciousness and is more diffuse, less tangible, and more deeply buried in the psyche. This can make incarnation shock difficult to work with as it is so dissociative. The following case study describes useful interventions when working with this theme.

H was a successful business woman, and single mother of three. She had a deep connection to spirit, a very intense personality, and a valor aimed toward life having deep meaning, purpose, and fulfilled expression. She was quite artistic in her profession.

H's incarnation shock surfaced when dealing with repeated instances in her professional work where students challenged her in unkind ways. H felt students targeted her, became disappointed in her, and tried to turn others against her. For H, these student behaviors triggered a deep feeling of betrayal, and she felt the need to defend herself and push back against their behavior. This student behavior felt deeply threatening to her, and was emotionally exhausting.

Overview of clinical treatment

One must work with very slow pacing in order to process existential themes. Existential imprints appear as strong sensation coupled with dissociation and quickly activate to a global body sensation due to their existential time of imprint. Incarnation shock is highly overwhelming and dangerous because the entire field activates without a sense of self for reference.

Slow pacing allows this global activation to decompress and interrupts the cycle of fragmentation and dissociation. Pacing 6 to 10 times slower than normal is required. This allows the body to transition a shock pattern of activation and escape into the ability to stay present while withstanding the sensations of terror. However, going slowly is felt as dangerous, so it takes a fortitude on the part of the therapist to insist on this pacing and to teach the client to work with it. This can happen only if there is an attuned trust developed where the therapist (teacher or parent) holds a grounded presence and the containment of social connection thus interrupting dissociation.

The therapist is the outside witness, and the client learns to become the inside witness. Learning to do so interrupts any enmeshment and supports the client to stay present with intense feelings until they settle. Tracking sensation white maintaining contact utilizes the vagus nerve in a manner that retains enough safety to allow self-witness. The sensations can be felt as energy that is no longer life threatening.

When incarnation shock appears in client work, it can be useful to consider that there was shock during the transition from soul to body, at the time of conception. The existential nature of the distress is another clue that it may be incarnation shock.

Ask a client to reflect on their conception from stories they have heard or a felt-sense in their body. They can imagine what time of year, the location, surrounding environment, and the type of connection between their parents. Was there a sense of love and conscious presence, or violence, inebriation, or boredom. During this exploration, imagine aloud how their conception might have felt to an arriving soul, coming from the protection and safety of spirit, and assess how it might be shocking to one's very nature. Naming aloud the imagined transition from soul to body helps clients to titrate the sense of annihilation that occurs at this time. I ask the client to dip into the sensation and then reorient out to the room by looking around, and to widen their view. I encourage them to breath deeply and interrupt any tendency to speed up in thought or action.

Resolving incarnation shock helps to release deep-seated terror. Together client and therapist are looking for the "bottom" of the fear. Clients describe this type of fear as "fear in the bones, an inability to settle, an un-named uneasiness." When incarnation and annihilation shock release, clients unravel deeply held tension. They begin to trust the state of relaxed attention rather than vigilance.

Supporting clients to address incarnation shock is best accomplished by a therapist who has already processed their own annihilative shock or witnessed others doing so in training. It takes skilled facilitation to meet this pacing. I think it is difficult to hold presence while another navigates existential terror until one has met and survived it in one's own tissue. I highly recommend skilled supervision if this issue arises in clients.

When there is protection and safety in the environment, the little one does not have to push back against the threat of annihilation shock. It can simply arrive into a field of safety. Protected souls don't need to defend, just to arrive. This invites an inherent sense of potency rather than an earned sense of potency. There is no need to feel potency by "fighting the unseen danger" and to push back because the right to arrive and be welcomed is trusted and established.

When that sense of welcome is missing, either due to alcohol, violence, or simply lack of presence and connection between conceiving parents, the nervous system responds. It activates both "sympathetic- and parasympathetic-like" responses within the fluid sensations of the body and creates a body sensation of flooding or overwhelm.

Alarm and intensity similar to sympathetic vigilance becomes coupled with catatonia, similar to parasympathetic dissociation. The "conceptus" is so close to the existential world that its arriving consciousness can take early experience into global dimensions. During adult interactions people with incarnation shock can have grand vision and dynamism yet bring cellular intensity that may be overwhelming when relating to others due to lack of early protection. The body responses of a client will guide the therapist to what treatment is needed. Often it is a mix of spaciousness and containment. I often imagine myself going to the "edge of the universe" to hold a soft circle of containment. This allows the existential shock to settle and gives the client the space needed to begin to settle into the body.

Exploration of incarnation shock

I began to explore incarnation shock with H after many sessions that built rapport and allowed both she and I to meet this next layer of work. I was drawn to this theme for a number of reasons. First, there were repeated incidences of attack and betrayal. Second was the intensity of expression in H when speaking of these incidences and her tendency to perceive danger in a global manner. In addition, body cues supported the impression that betrayal and aloneness occurred early in cellular development of the fluids rather than later in tissues of muscles and bones. The key to unravelling incarnation shock is pacing and verbal contact by the therapist. I supported H to go slowly enough to digest her sensation, and wondered aloud if abandonment occurred not only at birth but also at conception. This inquiry led H to find a deeper breath and sense of settling. I reminded her that an arriving consciousness notices whether it is safe, even at conception. H identified with existential distress.

Sequencing incarnation shock

H and I sat side by side rather than across from each other. Doing so offered a horizontal turning of the head for connection; this promotes rotation through the cranial nerves and crossing of the midline which automatically reduces stress. It also set us up to be "on the same team" rather than sitting across from each other. We were connected spatially, but had no touch contact. Touch would have been overwhelming when working at the existential level.

Next I supported H to feel her sensations, and to stay connected through presence and awareness of sensation responses both internally and in relation to me. We established the right spatial distance between us based on her ability to track internal sensation and to feel supported by me at the same time. This is known as "contact boundary" work and demands a delicacy of awareness. I wanted to be at the edge of H's contact boundary without invading her space. (see contact boundary and spatial proximity in Body Resources chapter).

The therapeutic goal was to support H to find the bottom of her fear without activating the sense of annihilation. To do so, H would need to stay in contact with her young inner self and with me. The ability to maintain connection when there are triggered sensations of perceived danger is a vital part of this theme. Often a client will drift off to an isolated frozen loneliness or become enmeshed in a shamanic and energetic vortex. Self- connection at this time interrupts self-abandonment, enmeshment with other, or cold isolation. H's pattern was enmeshed and finding the right contact boundary while allowing connection allowed H to digest the sensations of terror.

Naming and sequencing

I named aloud impressions of conception H had shared with me in prior sessions. This reflection helped her to feel seen and to exist inside a global activation. She was able to find a balance between activation and withdrawal, and with practice to apply the sense of safety when she felt activated outside of sessions.

Reclaiming sense of self-presence in relation to incarnation allowed H to let go of the impulse to enmesh with others projections and become triggered. Sitting with her own energy allowed her to step out of the way of these projections and to differentiate them as "not about her" and that she did not need to "heal them for the planet." An existential need to heal energies in groups is an indicator that one is working with incarnation shock, which highlights the existential nature of this imprint theme.

Working with incarnation shock supports healthy embodiment. People become more grounded and present. They feel less overwhelmed by their perceptions of others energies.

Chemical imprinting through Mom

Both emotional energy from mother and chemicals she ingested during birth or prenatal time can enter the infant through the umbilical area, or through the "energetic field" during birth. Two brief case studies highlight this theme.

Clinical Themes

Chemical imprinting

Ancestral genocide

Tissue tone and sensation

Nourishment

Contact boundary

Case A

Background

D was an adult male aged 34, who had chronic pain that was reviewed by medical professionals and deemed to be psychosomatic. The pain was a nervous system inflammation that affected D's joints and a feeling of irritation below the skin.

There were two influences of chemical imprints. One was due to allergy medication Mom needed during the pregnancy. It is common for clients whose mothers received medications while pregnant to exhibit a level of sensory integration difficulty or tactile sensitivity. The second imprint was a spike in stress corticoids due to emotional abuse. D's mother was under constant emotional attack and criticism from her husband, which caused an increase in stress corticoids via the hormonal stress response. D had these chemical impressions and affect in his early developmental field.

One presenting issue in treatment was that D desperately sought contact from his partner, including sexual contact. This helped him to regulate the intensity underneath his own skin. However, his partner felt the desperation and pulled back from it. The desperation was off-putting to pleasure and she felt pressured to respond rather than invited. The energy of orgasm provided relief from the physical pain. This was a set-up for tension as D projected a desperate neediness onto his partner to provide pain relief through sexual engagement.

Sensory-motor repair

In session, I asked D to explore body tension. This was explored both through query, sensation tracking, and through educative touch. The major tension area that appeared was around the belly and navel. I invited D to push out through his navel area, and to touch my hand with his stomach. This allowed D to motor in his umbilical area, rather than simply receiving sensation. I suggested he look for sensation of healthy push and power that came with motoring and not orient toward the established pain pathway (see sensory-motor balance, Body Resources chapter). I also had him meet the energy of annihilation he felt and push it away.

Sometimes I treat in warm-water and use a 15 foot circular warm pool that is chest deep. This warm water work supports healing of attachment dynamics, ease of movement, and supports a return to a sense of early protective womb state. It is useful in repairing early impressions. Many of D's sessions were in the pool. I placed my hand on D's navel area and had D push me around the warm pool from his navel area. This led to D feeling his body energy going down into his legs. His joint pain began to decrease.

Ancestral history

Once D had a sensation of energy down his legs, he was able to reduce the fear. We then explored on land sessions the generational influence of disempowerment of his father. I was curious what was behind the emotional abuse.

D's family ancestral background included involvement in the holocaust. There was generational disempowerment of men due to this holocaust history, wherein many fathers were unable to protect their families from atrocity. I acknowledged the rage and wounding of the masculine and how this contributed in part to D's father's emotional abuse. Often when one experiences perpetration and is forced into a victim role, they also record the perpetrator energy. If this is not met and processed, it often becomes projected onto their spouses.

Naming ancestral history supported D to include another level of differentiation. He was able to let the past live more in the past and not pick up that vibrational field. We did many sessions related to the holocaust, and D later traveled to Auschwitz, and worked specifically with releasing and digesting the imprints of his past.

All this work contributed to a sense of empowerment. As D felt more empowered he could organize and differentiate sensation in his navel area. This blend of body work and cognitive, emotional processing allowed D to find new sensation of safety. His inflammation lessened and then completely vanished. D practiced pushing out from the navel area numerous times during sessions and was given homework to continue this practice. The inflammation never returned, which eased the projected neediness in sexual dynamics with his partner.

Case B

Background

J was an adult male, age 48, and father of two sons. He reported chronic digestive problems. J had difficulty with intimacy and resorted to criticism or was punitive and dramatic when relating to his wife. Through the course of many sessions, it became clear that J had never experienced his potency during birth. His mother was given anesthesia before the birth had even begun. This was routine in many hospitals during the 30s into the late 50s and interrupted mother/infant bonding and connection.

Anesthesia very much influences both digestion and the umbilical area. As treatment progressed, J reported feeling abandoned by his mother, invaded by the birth chemicals, and that he dissociated into the "fog" of impotence when his body was numb.

Treatment

J tended to brace his body under stress, which sent defensive energy to his brain and heightened his critical nature. This energy was channeled into quick-witted sarcasm. We used body methods to interrupt this dysfunctional behavior. J learned to inhibit this mental response, track sensation, and motor the energy of rage at invasion from the chemicals, plus the fear of abandonment underneath the rage. I used educative touch with J to help him experience other sensations in the umbilical area. Through these methods he was able to clear the umbilical affect of bracing at the navel.

I discovered that he did not have to take in energy that was toxic to him and developed a boundary of self-protection before he became overwhelmed. This led to greater ability to digest, and ultimately to a sense of trusting connection rather than bracing for the worst. J was able to increase his ability to stay present during conflict, to refrain from criticism, and to empathize with others experiences rather than dissociate into a sense of "powerless fogging out."

The umbilicus provides nourishment. Yet when there are chemicals, nourishment becomes paired with toxins and danger and creates confusion for an infant. They must ingest toxins in order to obtain nutrients. They allow toxicity to come too close and do not differentiate well when things appear threatening. The navel area is considered the movement or power center area of the third chakra in the Hindi chakra energy system. Clearing the umbilical area of imprints is essential to obtain full body connection and to have a sense of place and self in the world.

Clinical Themes

Self-esteem
Potency as safe
Survivor's guilt
Prenatal horror
Bonding through grief
Shame
Abandonment
Dealing with death

Overview

A number of emotional complications occur when a person loses a twin during the birth or during time *in utero*. A lost twin represents the most intimate relationship of a connected undifferentiated other. Post-birth time allows one to develop a separate self and separate personality. If birth is filled with the grief and shock of a dead twin, it is hard to complete the differentiation and sense of separate identity.

Both early vanishing twin and death of a twin can leave some confusion about who stayed and who went. In the case of twin death, it seems more that a part of the psyche of the living twin splits off and stays with the one who died. There can be ambivalence about arriving, guilt about surviving, and rage, shock, and grief about losing that special friend.

The shock in the birthing environment is intense. In utero death means doctors and nurses anticipate the birth of a stillborn. Mothers often have to birth the dead baby. This is a horrific shock of nature and the intensity of this shock affects the living twin and everyone in the delivery room. Mother must emotionally process death while greeting her new baby.

The confusion of feelings including joy, grief, and perhaps a body felt horror are likely present and create intense confusion for the living baby. The living twin may feel both relief and loss. No longer does it live in gestation proximity to the unresponsive dead body of its sibling. That could be a relief. Yet the birth is the final separation from that twin. I don't imagine most birthing attendants would hold the stillborn up for mother and new baby to say goodbye. Mothers may not want to see the dead twin or may not be allowed to see or say goodbye. One can imagine the confusion of this setting.

The new baby can internalize Mom's confusion as she welcomes the living twin. This baby can also internalize the shock of the delivery room attendants. It takes diligent work to help a person differentiate and integrate the horror of such experience.

Below are two examples of twin loss. The first occurred during the seventh month of pregnancy and the second occurred during the birth.

Twin Death *in Utero* at month 7

Background

K is a 31 year old single mother of two children. She came to therapy on the advice of a friend who knew about perinatal work. K's goals in therapy were to release an underlying sense of depression and to work with the intense anger that emerged in dealing with her children.

K's face had the look of being overly hesitant; she was present yet held back. Her face had a noticeable affect of reluctance. K tended to listen and nod a lot but not reciprocate in conversation unless asked a direct question. She had intense shame and berated herself with a consistent negative self-talk.

Treatment

Treatment consisted of body-centered work. We focused on releasing fear, awakening facial expression, tracking emotions as they emerged when K made direct eye contact, and helping K to feel her impulse to respond to others rather than hold back. We worked to help her identify inner support and follow it in order to reach for contact.

During treatment K realized that her twin had been on her left side. She had turned away from the dead sister and numbed out that left side tissue. Work with various movements, gestures, and expressions helped K rebalance and inhabit both sides of her body. Key support that shifted K's amygdala and hippocampus (survival and associative brain centers) was for her to identify and express many conflicting emotions. She felt rage at being left, the terror of relating to a live and then unresponsive dead sibling, and the horror of gestating with death present before she had even experienced birth. She also worked with the feelings that she had somehow been at fault.

In addition to expressive emotions, K worked with parasympathetic shock. She addressed the dissociation of staying slightly aloof (back in spirit). It allowed her to maintain contact with her twin. She had to navigate extreme resistance to releasing this tie and to arrive as a differentiated person. For two entire sessions, the consistent response was "I don't want to do this!" Identifying the cost of maintaining this tie while working with the sensations of resistance to letting go allowed K to finally yield to the body memory of this experience. Doing so allowed the deep grieving necessary so that K could release her loyalty to remaining in the spirit world to keep the bond with her dead sister. K was finally able to feel her desire to be fully connected with the world of the living.

Working with field dynamics

The emotional field was extremely complex during K's birth. Birth meant she lost contact with her twin. Mother's welcome was laced with confusion and grief, making it difficult to trust. K personalized the horror of simultaneous birth and stillborn loss and concluded that she was abhorrent. She was filled with shame and afraid of her own potency. K was reluctant to be visible and powerful as her potency experienced prenatally and at birth was coupled with her sister's death. K was reluctant to emerge and engage in life. We worked diligently to tease apart the confusion and name the double binds of identity that were layered into K's belief system.

Differentiation

The consistent support was to find differentiation at each layer of emotion. First from the horror present in the hospital staff that helped a mother birth a dead baby. K came to realize she was not horrific, and this awareness supported her to release her intense shame. Once she released shame, confusion could emerge. "Did Mom want me or not? If so, why was she so sad?"

K differentiated Mother's mixed feelings about her dead sister and those that were about her. She interrupted her self-attack once she realized that this internal berating voice was an attempt to have a locus of control in an untenable situation. She began to treat herself with respect and care.

Emotional reckoning and reorganizing required many months of sessions in order to dispel fears and integrate new behavioral choices. K felt she had finally gotten to the crux of her self-esteem issues and was able to heal them by revealing the complexity of her birth and taking time to process the emotions.

Twin death during birth

Background

C was born with a living twin throughout gestation who then died in the birth process. C believed her power hurt others. She was confused whether she was to blame for her twin's death and was enraged at being abandoned by her sibling. Such complexity of identity beliefs created difficulty in friendships. C was afraid of loss and so behaved in ways that minimized her needs. C speaks about this in her own words in the text that follows.

Dealing with death and birth at the same time is shocking to all who are present in the birthing environment

Cynthia A wrote the following story. I include it unedited so the reader can grasp the felt-sense of Cynthia A's experiences. She writes of how her life was impacted by the death of her twin that occurred during birth and her journey to heal this deep and confusing beginning.

Writing by Cynthia A

"My twin brother died during the birth process. I was born first, and my sense is that he died as I was being born. Neither of my parents understood their own grief over this loss, and definitely did not understand how their newborn daughter might have big feelings about this as well. I was initially a "fussy baby", and difficult to nurse, so after a week my mother began bottle feeding me. She believed in regular nap and bedtimes, and I was allowed to cry myself to sleep. I was my mother's third child, and she had 2 toddlers to take care of as well as me. Consequently, I learned quickly to be a quiet, easy baby, although I was sick often as a young child and into my teens, mostly throat and respiratory

ailments. I was very shy and compliant as a child, prone to melancholy, and also prone to startle easily. Eventually, there were 7 children in my family; we were well cared for physically, but there was little emotional expression in the home. I had this sense from an early age that my life had to have some big meaning, that I had to justify my right to live, although I was easily discouraged when I would begin to bump into difficulties in some new endeavor. As a teenager I began to have boyfriends, and I tended through my teens, twenties and thirties to chose boys, and later men, who somehow were not really available emotionally, as well as men who could not seem to get their own life together. I would usually end these relationships with a great deal of relief, but also of guilt and sadness. I carried a constant layer of tension in my neck and shoulders and jaw, and was a severe teeth-grinder.

It has taken me several years of focused perinatal therapy to work through some of the layers of my birth experience. One of the first layers to emerge was a sense of hopelessness, intertwined with a foggy place that I associate with the anesthesia that my Mom was given. I had to struggle to find any potency in my body, and when I started to contact any energy, it would quickly shift to tearful sobbing, or to shaking and trembling. I had to learn to separate out all the shock and grief that I was carrying – to get a felt-sense of what was my own shock, and my own grief, and what really belonged to other people at that time.

Eventually I was able to access a place of deep rage – at the birth room medical staff, at my parents, and eventually at my twin brother for leaving me, and rage at myself for choosing life over going into death with him. I have had to really work out what it means to have healthy boundaries, especially with men – that it is okay for me to have my own opinion and to actually disagree.

I have finally come to the realization that there will always be a place in me that feels a sense of "incompleteness" over the loss of my twin: a depth of grief that I don't have to keep trying to fix. This has allowed me to open myself to joy in a much fuller way in my life – that it is okay to tenderly contain that early grief- place, AND to still invite in joy and creativity and connection. I can still have a tendency in any creative endeavor to go into a hyper-aroused, "this is life or death" place if things are not going well; I am able to recognize it sooner, and shift the energy with more compassion. I have noticed a much easier time forming healthy intimate connections since doing this work, and as well a clearer access to my own sense of choice – discovering that it is okay for me to have my own voice.

Author's note

Cynthia A shared with us common conditions relating to death of a twin. These conditions include: physical numbness due to the intensity of emotions, resorting to a "life or death" reactivity under difficulty, the fear of displeasing men in her life related to a dead male twin, and the fear of her own potency. Releasing these impressions allows room for a good enough life and sustained emotional well-being. It is a courageous and rewarding task to address these issues at a body-mind level.

Clinical Themes

Body awareness and freeze response

Confusion and disorientation

Sensitivity when in crowds of people

Sperm energy issues

This case study involves a 30-year-old women who had a deep seated freeze response. She came to treatment to sort through an advanced ambivalence about whether to attend graduate school. The course of treatment was one and a half years on average of weekly sessions.

Identifying the freeze response

R had two sisters, and all children were conceived via sperm donor. Parents remain happily married. There is a high value placed on education on both ancestral sides. As R confronted her decision about graduate school, she froze in her torso and facial expression in an unusually dissociative manner. I was interested in the quality of this freeze response and curious about associative preconception memory, which can surface in perinatal work. I wondered aloud if she knew that sperm were exposed to centrifuging and then rapidly frozen for sperm banks. Due to R's overall emotional health and healthy family background, I was drawn to explore with her the earliest of imprints.

Treatment started in the circular warm pool I use to treat early attachment issues. Water provides a greater range of movement options. Being floated through water provided a gradual thawing of R's freeze response. From there we added splashing, kicking, and moving both physical and emotional energy. This accessed a needed vitality to work with in contrast to freeze. As R found new options, she began to notice and track her tendency to freeze and found ways to return to a sensory motor balance in her tissue.

Releasing core freezing

Many sessions included Body-Mind Centering with both hands on and movement work. We used primitive reflexes as well as BMC vertebral patterns adapted for water work. (See from Conception to Crawling, by this author). Hands on work included BMC and Biodynamic Cranio-Sacral sessions. Touch and movement were an important component that allowed R to mobilize rather than freeze. Mobility produced a general sense of well being that led to an ability to stay present and identify her discomfort with internal freezing rather than simply disappear beneath it. Use of subtle micro movements in tissue supported new neural pathway choices to emerge and influence thought patterns and behavior.

Releasing the confusion of this type of conception

Sperm donor conception means the conceptus does not experience the natural pleasure and movement of orgasmic energy. The sperm experiences a technological energy in the field, and a number of people are involved between ejaculation and the act of conception. Navigating all this complexity and the fogginess that occurred with the freeze was key in R having relief from her difficulty with decision-making. She unwound several double binds around choice to arrive and have an energetic desire and follow through to completion.

Note that the normal startle energy that precedes a freeze response was not present with ART. What presented most was a blissful numbing and a disengaged attitude. Imagine the contrast in consciousness of a frozen donor sperm to that of an ejaculated sperm vitally engaged in choosing which Fallopian tube and finding the egg. Such frozen sperm could be dissociative and not oriented to following the energy of a life imperative mission. Making major life decisions could easily activate confusion.

Releasing magical thinking and the lack of orientation

Naming the complexity of donor issues and working physically produced the best results. We worked with the disinterest that was deeply engaged in R's nervous system using the "Satisfaction Cycle." This is movement that sequences to resolution based on BMC developmental actions from yield to push, reach, take hold, pull, and back to yield. Finding satisfaction brought on more vitality and interest.

We allowed necessary slow time to warm the repetitive deep chills that R experienced in treatment. This engaged her interest and supported her to track sensation and make meaning of this early imprint. Parasympathetic overwhelm was prevalent and the subsequent Magical thinking when death feels near. Focused work identified this felt- sense and R learned to seek alternative body-felt sensations. She began to engage with decisions and enjoy the ability to choose.

Her first decision was really to arrive within the conception experience that occurred without natural male ejaculation energy that carries sperm toward the egg.

Name the egg experience of waiting

R found that she could wait and wait for decisions. We related that to the need for the sperm to "thaw" and for the egg to patiently wait. When R added a body-felt sense of thawing and sequenced that to potency her decisions became easier and more enjoyable.

R was able to move through her confusion and successfully navigate her educational and career choices. Her experience of ART is an invaluable aid to people working with behavior. ART is a growing fertility method used in Western pregnancies. Understanding its impact and listening for its expression is a necessary skill set for clinicians.

I asked R if she would be willing to write about her experience. The following is her report of progress during treatment.

R's report of her sense of progress from treatment

1. Freezing

I have a much more in depth awareness about the ways in which my life force can freeze. Often times this freezing can take on a quality of feeling like I am not totally "here" or that I have actually journeyed somewhere near the bottom of the ocean. I have gained specific awareness about how circumstances that feel pressure-filled, intense or contain a lot of energy can exacerbate my freeze response and make it really hard for me to locate my potency, power, and true sense of self.

2. Disorientation

Along with freezing, I have become very familiar with and more capable of relating to my experience of disorientation. The phrases "I don't know who I am" and "I don't know where I am" and "I don't know where I'm going" are very habitual thoughts for me. Throughout my work with Annie I have done a lot of work on being able to more skillfully locate the mid-line of my being. Using breath, movement, imagery, sand trays and much, much more I have learned many skills for finding my way back to an "orientation." This doesn't mean that I don't continue to get disoriented easily, but rather that I can more readily identify when I am having trouble locating myself, slow down, find support and re-locate myself.

3. Masculine and feminine principles

We've worked a lot with the egg and sperm journeys of my particular conception story. My bodily understanding of what the sperm went through has provided so much context for me in relationship to my freezing and to the masculine in general. Realizing that the sperm was literally flash frozen and was forced to be dormant without knowing whether or not it would ever taste life again has been so important for me in working with my relationship to death and therefore how I live my life. I definitely possess a strong masculine force in my life and I often have the experience of pushing and exerting very hard in a worldly sense. Sometimes after a huge push, however, there is a quality of collapse and a feeling of "death" --- as if the exertion of energy were too much for me to handle and I don't know how to remain buoyant or resilient. At times I have also experienced a profound longing to only exist in the being and feeling realms (typically associated with the feminine). There has been tremendous grief at having to leave the state of vast, juicy, open space and this has been something we have worked on as well. There is SO much to say about the journey of the masculine and feminine~but this is definitely a highlight for me from exploring my conception story.

4. Depth of soul

Another big recognition that has come out of my exploration into my conception is about the depth that I carry in my soul ---something that at times has felt very isolating and like a burden. This feels connected to my understanding of and relationship to death. The states of catatonia that I can journey to especially when experiencing a freeze are totally extreme. I feel as if I am floating in a dark, vast space where no one can reach me. The continuous work to not get stuck there and to identify the imprint before it gets so extreme has been paramount in my life. This part of the exploration has also given me great appreciation for my soul, what it has been through and what it understands about such watery, ambiguous, bardo type places/states. I really trust that this knowing is also a gift that I can share (in its health) with others.

5. Intimacy

All of the insights, realizations and knowings that have arisen out of our work together have contributed to deep transformation in all areas of my life. Particularly in my primary relationship with my partner, I feel infinitely more capable of navigating painful and difficult territory together now that I have such greater understanding of where my consciousness goes under pressure and feelings of threat. I am SO much more capable of tracking sensation in my body as well as perceiving and tracking energy in his body so that we can more often than not arrive back into places of connection.

Conclusion of case study chapter

This chapter offered case studies to show perinatal treatment in action. All names of clients were changed, and many other stories could have been offered. For further information on this topic, purchase *Birth's Hidden Legacy: Volume Two.*

I am grateful to all the adults, families, couples, and children who have let me learn and grow as we worked together to unravel these pre-cognitive memories. They have shown me, through their courage, tenacity, and intelligence, the amazing ability of the human bodymindspirit to reorganize and to thrive. I am blessed to have known these people and appreciate the gift of experiences they bring to the reader. Perhaps all our healing and sharing can bring a greater aware intelligence to those who support practices of birth, post-birth, and prenatal care.

- Annie Brook

Chapter 6: Conclusion and Resources

Further explorations of this material support a deeper understanding of how birth influences behavior. See Volume Two for in-depth clinical information and interventions. This next chapter concludes Volume One and lists many skilled colleagues as resources for further support and interest.

Conclusion of Volume One

Clinical sessions have shown that 0-18 months in an infants lifetime are highly precious in forming identity beliefs and behavior responses. Any nervous system overwhelm that occurred during that time creates brain states and body-centered imprints that govern emotions and behaviors under stress. Knowing this can help one understand and offer support at a more effective level. Listening for and understanding how these early imprints influence behavior helps treatment address the earliest of perceptions and behavior response patterns. Getting to the roots of inaccurate identity beliefs and meaning making constructs supports true change and self-care.

Parents and clinicians who wish for behavior change can help clients and children to identify and discharge imprint-based energy blocks. These residual shock imprints hide overwhelming moments that may have formed life-long protective habits and contain latent misconceptions about self and world. Resolution of such early cellular imprints can repair intimacy issues in infants through adults.

Adults who recognize how birth imprints influence their behavior are more effective as therapists, parents, and teachers; they recognize and name early themes and integrate experience into a coherent narrative. Knowing "the story" and putting it to rest results in more trust and resiliency in social settings. One has less need to be "in control" and transitions become easier. Later difficult events are not as devastating.

Identifying the strengths developed during early times of stress helps reduces re-orient; there is not a sense of being a victim or self-deprecating thoughts. Imprints become normalized and no longer hijack emotions. Defensive energy is freed to be available for creativity and accomplishment.

Thanks to the reader for exploring this provocative and sensitive material. I hope these case studies and theories of pre-and perinatal psychology can help you to better understand your children, yourself, your clients, and the complexity of human experience related to early times.

I'm continually grateful to all the teachers and teachings that helped me to formulate these understandings and also to all the clients who taught and trained me how to listen for the early stories beneath difficult behaviors. They have gifted me with their courage in this in-depth learning and discovery of how to repair the nervous system and inaccurate identity beliefs.

May the sharings in this book be a resource and benefit to people interested in uncovering behavioral difficulties and finding ease.

Please refer to Volume Two for further information and skills. The sidebar gives a brief content description. Birth, as the "Crashing of Mountains" is a natural and impactful experience that is part of ones identity. Support that experience to become integrated in the deep brain stem and relieved of associative trauma and responses. Clearing Perinatal imprints and shock clears energy. One can highlight the resilience of having survived and enjoy the gift of life with the fullness of emotions, ease in the body, and creative pleasure we are designed to enjoy. This work has been a gift to my own unfolding and I hope it provides some missing answers for you in understanding "the Hidden Stories" related to birth and how they influence the nervous system and behavior.

Birth's Hidden Legacy: Volume Two

For further learning, please read Volume Two. It contains the following:

1.**Psychotherapuetic theory:** on early attachment dynamics, body character style influences, a Jungian perspective on early development, and IBP (Integrated Body Psychotherapy) views, plus David Sawyer's excellent map for perinatal treatment protocol.

2. **Tips for Therapists**: props, interventions, and treatment protocols.

3.**Body-based Interventions and theory** for re-patterning shock and trauma: Body-Mind Centering perspectives on overwhelm of the nervous system and Sensory-Motor development, and guided re-patterning somatizations.

4. **Summary Charts** for quick organization and treatment protocol

Important Voices and Useful Contacts

BodyMind Somaunatics & Somatic Attachment Training. http://www.bodymindsomanautics.com

Colorado Therapies, LLC: Individual and family treatment for functional adults and families, and special needs children.
http://www.coloradotherapies.com

David Sawyer, founder of the Prenatal Journey: d.saywer@comcast.net

John & Anna Chitty: BioDynamic Craniol-Sacral Training: http://www.energyschool.com

Melissa Michaels: Golden Bridge Program: http://www.goldenbridge.org

Karen Strange: Neonatal Resuscitation and Midwife Educator: http://www.newbornbreath.com

Michael Trout: Infant Parent Institute: http://www.infant-parent.com

Myrna Martin: www.myrnamartin.net

Dr. Nils Bergman: Kangaroo Care: http://www.kangaroomothercare.com

Pam England: http://www.birthingfromwithing.com

Ray Castellino: Building and Enhancing Bonding and Attachment: www.beba.org

Sarah Buckley http://http://www.orgasmicbirth.com/what-is-orgasmic-birth

Stephanie Johnson MA, R-DMT, LPC: http://www.sageeducationcenter.com

Susan Aposhyan: BodyMind Psychotherapy training: http://www.bodymindpsychotherapy.com

Wendy Anne McCarty: http://www.wondrousbeginnings.com

European Sources

Ludwig Juhanus Lujanus@aol.com

Michele Odent: http://www.primalhealthresearch.com

Terence Dowling: http://www.primalhealth.org

Dr. Rupert Linder: post@dr-linder.de

Training Progams

BodyMind Somaunatics & Somatic Attachment Training. http://www.bodymindsomanautics.com

Colorado Therapies, LLC: Individual and family treatment for functional adults and families, and special needs children. http://www.coloradotherapies.com

Center for Somatic Psychology, LLC: http://www.somaticpsychotherapycenter.org,

John & Anna Chitty: BioDynamic Cranio-Sacral Training: http://www.energyschool.com

Dr. William Emerson: http://www.emersonbirthrx.com

Myrna Martin: http://www.myrnamartin.com

Degree Programs University of Integrated Learning: (UIL) www.aiwp.org [degrees in pre- and perinatal education in conjunction with Bodymind Somanuatics.]

Bibliography

Aposhyan, S. (6). *Natural Intelligence: Body-Mind Integration and Human Development.* Baltimore, MD: Williams and Wilkins.

Aposhyan, S. (2004). *Body-Mind Psychotherapy: Principles, Techniques, and Practical Applications*, New York, NY: W.W. Norton & Company.

Bainbridge Cohen, B. (3). *Sensing, Feeling, and Action.* North Hampton, MA: Contact Editions.

Berry Brazelton, T. and Cramer, B. (1). *Earliest Relationship: Parents, Infants, and the Drama of Early Attachment.* New York, NY: Perseus Books Group.

Brennan, B (8). *Hands of Light*, (Chapter 12, 13)., (3). *Light Emerging*, (Chapter 15). New York, NY: Random House Publishing.

Brook, A. (2001). *From Conception to Crawling.* Boulder, CO: Smart Body Books.

Elliott, D. (2000). *Cellular Echoes: Environmental Influences in the Journey from the Womb to the World.*

Faber, A. and Mazlish, E. (9). *How to Talk So Kids Will Listen & Listen so Kids Will Talk.* New York, NY: Avon Books, Inc.

Forbes, H. and Post, B. (2006). *Beyond Consequences, Logic, and Control.* Boulder, CO: Beyond Consequences Institute, LLC.

Johnson, S. (7). *Humanizing the Narcissistic Style*, and (4). *Character Styles.* New York, NY: W. W. Norton & Company.

Mahler, Pine, and Bergman (1975) *The Psychological Birth of the Human Infant.* Harper and Collins, USA.

Odent, M. (2001). *The Scientification of Love.* Free Association Books.

Pearce, Joseph Chilton, *The Biology of Transcendence*, (2004) and *Magical Child* (2).

Pollack, Miriam. (June 27, 2011). *Tikun Magazine*, Article: Circumcision, Identity and Power. Boulder, CO.

Sawyer, D. (9). *Birthing the Self: Water Based Approaches to Treating Prenatal and Birth Trauma.* Boulder, CO: Self Published.

Schore, A. (4). *Affect Regulation and the Origin of the Self.* Hillside, NJ: Lawrence Erlbaum Associates.

Siegel, D. (9). *The Developing Mind: How Relationships and the Brain Interact to Shape Who We Are.* New York, NY: Guilford Press.

Siegel, D. (2007). *The Mindful Brain: Reflection and Attunement in the Cultivation of Well-Being.* New York, NY: W.W. Norton.

Siegel, D. and Solomon, M., editors. (2003). *Healing Trauma: attachment, mind, body and brain.* New York, NY: Norton Publishing.

Stern, D. (5). *The Interpersonal World of the Infant: A View of Psychoanalysis & Developmental Psychology.* New York, NY: Basic Books.

Wolf, J. (2009) *Deliver Me From Pain.* Balitmore, MD: The Johns Hopkins University Press.

On birth pain

(excepted from Deliver Me From Pain by J. Wolf)

(pg 7) One retired obstetrician recalled that as a first-year resident in 1951, his training included sitting with women for lengthy periods while they labored. Again and again, he would find a woman screaming in agony and fear, sit next to her bed, take her hand, talk to her quietly, and find that the distraught woman calmed down and remained in control as long as he remained by her bedside. These experiences taught him a valuable lesson: The doctor in the room... {is] worth 100 milligrams of Demerol."

Many mothers charged in the 1950s that callous treatment by nurses and doctors in maternity wards worsened the mothers painful ordeals. The cavalier treatment also likely made women more amenable to receiving drugs during labor;

How a sufferer anticipates pain often dictates the amount and type of medication required to subdue the pain. The vast obstetric anesthesia arsenal for the mid twentieth century could have been a self-fulfilling prophecy of sorts;

(pg 5) Witnesses to labor have traditionally misinterpreted women's experience. Although transition causes the vast majority of women by far the most discomfort, second-stage labor looks and sounds to observers like the most painful portion. Watching women strain with the force of their uterine muscles as she pushes the fetus out of the womb is a powerfully disquieting sight. Yet the sight is deceptive. One physician and mother of four, who was a lay midwife for ten years before starting medical school in 6, described second-stage labor in the same ways so many other women do; as painless, or more accurately as better than painless. She explained, "It actually feels good to push." She admitted, though, that unschooled observers often think they are witnessing indescribable agony as women push, she recalled, "we midwives used to call it "animaling out." The unsettling sights and sounds of second-stage labor are likely why doctors, beginning with the introduction of anesthesia in the mid-nineteenth century and continuing well into the 1960s customarily administered general or regional anesthesia only at the end of second-stage labor, as the baby's head crowned. In other words, women often weathered the first stage, transition, and most of the second stage without any anesthesia, only to be rendered unconscious as their babies were born. The experience of the physician-witness trumped the experience of the patient, highlighting the importance of 'physicians--as opposed to patients'-perceptions when formulating medical treatment. The traditional timing of the administration of obstetric anesthesia is a classic example of medical authority usurping patient needs when defining "necessary" medical protocol.

Obstetrician's medical writings in the 19th and early 20th century were ... subjective ... James Young Simpson said of second-stage labor: "the extremity of suffering seems to be beyond endurance." Joseph DeLee, in his 1925 edition of The Theory and Practice of Obstetrics, explained that a woman feels "the greatest anguish" as her baby's head emerges from her body—"as if she were torn open." He warned ominously, "the pain may be so great that the patient faints or is temporarily insane."

He contended that the severity of labor pain depended on a woman's race and class. Women of "uncivilized races" had easy labors, whereas "highly cultured women" had "hard, painful labors." DeLee also argued that women's personality quirks shaped their labors; women of "quiet even temperament" weather labor easily, whereas nervous, hysterical women tend to turn an otherwise normal labor into a pathological trend.

... Physicians strip pain of personal significance and transform it into a meaningless, if troublesome, sensation, of interest only because of the clinical messages it conveys to the physician. Culture and experience dictate how pain should be expressed, and that expression-stoic silence, occasional wincing, low moaning, constant complaining or uncontrolled hysterics... can further shape the nature of that physical feeling...where the custom is to remain silent, women experience the sensation of labor differently than in cultures where screaming is the expected reaction.

Terrible torture or the nicest sensation I ever had...

of all the bitterly contested obstetric treatment of the past 160 years, the administration of anesthesia for labor pain has prompted the longest-lasting disagreement. William TB Morton inadvertently sparked this discussion when he demonstrated the miraculous use of ether during surgery before an enthralled audience at MA General Hospital in Boston in 1846. Within a year, James Young Simpson exhibited the anesthetic properties of chloroform to similarly enthusiastic colleagues in Edinburgh, Scotland. In the wake to these two exciting discoveries, doctors almost immediately began using ether and chloroform during childbirth as well as surgery. Controversy generated by that move has been a hallmark of obstetrics ever since.

Timing of administering anesthesia

(pg 4) ... the vast majority of women report that transition is the most painful part of labor ... the cervix dilates rapidly (in 10-20 minutes) from about 8 to 10 centimeters. Contractions intensify at this time, coming one after another ... Whereas hard-to-handle pain is the salient characteristic of transition, the urge to push is the salient characteristic of second-stage labor ... women describe early first-stage labor as "easily handled." Some women have described second-stage labor as "the fun part" of birth ... not one woman in Bradleys survey chose early first-stage labor, any portion of second-stage labor, or the moment of birth for this imaginary respite (pg 14). Commissioner of Health in New York, Cyrus Edson, likened.

the suffering of laboring women to the agony of martyrs tortured during the middle ages. He contended that giving birth transformed vulnerable women into lifelong invalids and blamed girls increased access to formal education for the tragedy. "Sitting in a classroom during puberty ... drained girls strength, leaving little in reserve for childbirth in coming years."

By the mid 19th century being a woman and being weak seemed to go hand in hand ... Physicians identified new diseases that affected mostly women. Neuranesthesia (exhaustion due to irritability, fear of responsibility, exhaustion after defecation and urination, dry hair, and sensitivity to weather changes. Genteel urban women ... lived artificial lives. The unnaturalness of cities had turned them into "hot-house products unable to withstand the rigors of "natural" activities such as birth.

Books/DVDs/Audio CDs

- Book: *Contact Improvisation and Body-Mind Centering*, a manual for teaching and learning movement
- Book: *From Conception to Crawling*, a foundation for Developmental Movement
- Book: German Translation: *From Conception to Crawling*, a foundation for Developmental Movement
- DVD: *From Conception to Crawling*, a 3 disc set
- Audio CD: *The Hidden Stories Behind Difficult Behaviors*, an interview with Dr. Annie Brook
- Various talks as lecture series

Articles

Free articles available on AnnieBrook.com. Check the website for topics to download.

Articles for purchase on the subjects of:

- shock and trauma
- performance art
- movement integration
- couples practices

On-Line Course

Applied Neuroplasticity

eBooks

- *Couples* (free)
- *Couples Communion*

See AnnieBrook.com to order articles, online courses, and media products.
For international book purchases, order through Amazon.com.